What People Are Saying About
The TRUTH, TEETH, AND TRAVEL Series

Lively, real, informational, and relatable, the Truth, Teeth, and Travel series will not only wrap around your heart with Dr. Bob and Diane Meyer's powerful stories, but **will inspire you to discover and follow your own unique calling to wisely make a difference in the world.**

> RAMONA CRAMER TUCKER, Former Editor, *Today's Christian Woman* and Executive Editor, *Virtue* (Christianity Today, International), Former Senior Editor, Tyndale House Publishers

A heart-warming—and at times, heart-wrenching—story that spotlights the joys, the love, and sometimes the challenges and friction of mission trips. Readers, particularly those who share the passion of giving their time and skills to the less fortunate, will enjoy reading this genuine recollection. It's perfect for people with time constraints, who want to read one adventure at a time, and for those who will devour it in its entirety since they can't put it down.

> SHARYN MARKUS, MA, MLS, Executive Director, Colorado Springs Dental Society

An honest, unique, easily readable book of short stories that **merges exotic cultures and people who have a passionate desire to both heal physical pain and bring spiritual healing to the world** through dentistry. *Truth, Teeth, and Travel* is a must-read for dental professionals and others considering dental mission work. But through Bob and Diane's struggles, as well as their victories, they encourage all of us going through hard times to persevere and allow God to grow us in our faith.

> DR. RANDY SANDERS, Past president and board member of the Christian Dental Society

Truth, Teeth, and Travel, Volumes I and II, are **vividly written, helping readers feel as if they were really there.** Bob and Diane tell the good, the bad, and the difficulties one faces while trying to be a servant to others.

> DR. RON LAMB, Founder and president of World Dental Relief, past president and board member of the Christian Dental Society, and recipient of the American Dental Association Humanitarian Award in 2012

Our trip to Africa was **life-changing** and definitely in the top ten experiences of my life (even when counting the births of four babies!). On the trip, Jesus was our Shepherd, and Bob and Diane were the team's caring sheep dogs.

MRS. SUE POREMBA, A team dentist assistant and a descendant of six generations of dentists

TRUTH TEETH & TRAVEL

vol 2

Dear Shari, Joey, Bryce,
Aubrey, Shayla & Gia!
Words cannot express how
much we love you & how
proud we are of all of you!

Heartwarming, adventurous journeys into fascinating, exotic cultures

Dr. Bob and Diane Meyer

Dr. Bob & Diane
(Dad,   (Mom)
Grandpa)   Grandma)

OAKTARA
www.oaktara.com

Truth, Teeth, and Travel
Vol. II

OakTara
www.oaktara.com

Published in the U.S. by:
OakTara Publishers
www.oaktara.com

Cover design by Yvonne Parks at www.pearcreative.ca
Cover images © shutterstock.com: people holding hands around globe/Basheera Designs, 61529197; tooth/Yoko Design, 121995553
Interior photos © Bob and Diane Meyer

Copyright © 2013 by Bob and Diane Meyer. All rights reserved.

Cover and interior design © 2013, OakTara Publishers. All rights reserved. No part of this publication may be reproduced, stored in a retrieval system, or transmitted in any form or by any means without the prior written permission of the publisher. The only exception is brief quotations in professional reviews.

Unless otherwise noted, all Scripture quotations are taken from the *Life Application ® Bible,* New International Version®, NIV®, is published jointly by Tyndale House Publishers, Inc., and Zondervan. *Life Application Bible* copyright © 1988, 1989, 1990, 1991, by Tyndale House Publishers, Inc., Wheaton, IL 60189. All rights reserved. Bible text copyright © 1973, 1978, 1984, by Biblica, Inc.™ Used by permission. All rights reserved worldwide.

ISBN-13: 978-1-60290-384-5
ISBN-10: 1-60290-384-0

The perspective, opinions, and worldview represented by this book are those of the author and are not intended to be a reflection or endorsement of the publisher's views.

Printed in the U.S.A.

* * *

Lovingly dedicated to
our faithful parents,
DR. JOSEPH AND ORA MAE MEYER
REV. WES AND VIOLA TUCKER

You inspired us with spiritual and educational values,
and the desire to serve our world using our God-given gifts,
while spreading the Good News of Christ.

* * *

All proceeds from the sale of this book and any donations to
Dr. Bob and Diane's dental ministry
will go directly to the CHRISTIAN DENTAL SOCIETY
for the purpose of encouraging, assisting, and equipping dental
personnel to use their gifts to further His kingdom.

For more info on this wonderful organization:
www.christiandental.org

Contents

* * *

Note from the Heart

* * *

WHILE VISITING A MUSLIM VILLAGE IN EGYPT with a Habitat for Humanity team, we'd taken our portable dental equipment along with hopes of relieving pain and reflecting God's light to those we met. The local officials formally ushered us into a meeting room upon our arrival. They served tea, but we felt like the ones in hot water as they interrogated us concerning our motives. Our Egyptian friend translated, gently stressing our calling to reflect God's light by helping others, regardless of beliefs.

As we left the village, one tall, daunting leader said, "At first I hated you, because you are American Christians. But since we've worked and talked together, I feel differently. We would now die for you!" This sentiment of loyalty showed a committed friendship they would defend to the death. We'd met our goal of dispelling misunderstanding, building relationships, and presenting our Christian worldview through kindness.

We—Bob, an ex-Army commander and dentist, and I, a nurse and educator—believe wholeheartedly in using our talents to find significance in giving, while encouraging members on varied teams to use their diverse and unique gifts. We wish to "finish well" before the watchful eyes of the upcoming generations in our family and communities.

Our journeys have yielded enlightenment and satisfaction as we've discovered wonderment and joy in fascinating cultural diversity. We hope to amaze, invigorate, and entertain you with our experiences. Perhaps some of you, too, will catch the "travel bug" and decide to launch your own "adventures with a purpose" across the globe. For those of you who can't travel, why not participate in service organizations in local neighborhoods, or through donating resources or prayer support to humanitarian efforts anywhere?

Not only will others be blessed by your efforts, but you will feel that ultimate reward of hearing God say, "Well done, good and faithful servant!" (Matthew 25:21).

BOB AND DIANE

EGYPT
Bob helps build
a Muslim Habitat for Humanity house.

Egypt

Building Bridges and Homes
with Habitat for Humanity

* * *

LEAVING THE EGYPTIAN MUSLIM VILLAGE AFTER TWO DAYS was tougher than we'd thought, as we now clasped hands in friendship.

Bob and I had arrived in trepidation and fear on our first foray into the Islamist arena as we once again traveled to spread our faith-based truth, while lending credibility to Christian organizations through our gift of dentistry. The leaders had intensely interrogated us as to our mission over tea. We were the first American Christians they had met.

But when the tall, intimidating leader who had organized the interrogation confessed as we departed the village, "You are the first American Christians I had met. You have become part of us. We would now die for you!" we were amazed.

Loyalty had been built in the Muslim world. Once Islamists have committed to friendship, many will fight to the death to defend their allies. We'd become comrades in their eyes. We were humbled as we pondered the difference several days of caring and conversation can make in changing the distrust and bias of others. How little it takes to bring affirming, positive progress on both sides of a seemingly wide cultural abyss!

As we said good-bye to the Muslim villagers, they honestly seemed sad to see us go. In that short time, we'd all been impacted deeply through working for a common cause in friendship.

Anyone who is fascinated by history dreams of visiting Egypt. Our church team of eleven included two singles in their early thirties, two men in their seventies, and seven of us within the forty-to fifty-year range. Our leader, Mustafah—currently a physical therapist in America—had been raised and educated as a physician in Egypt. Because his family claimed Christianity, they had emigrated to American at the loss of much of their land and assets, taken from them and nationalized by Nassar's administration. Mustafah's network of connections with relatives and friends in Egypt gave us a slight measure of comfort. Mustafah, a jolly and likable man, kept us laughing throughout the trip. It didn't take Bob long to discover that Mustafah responded happily to teasing and tickles.

With various team goals for the trip, we wondered if it would all mesh— our purpose, of course, being dentistry. Our team's assignment involved continuing the twelve-year involvement our American church had with a "Cairo Connection" established years before. We planned to see Egyptian friends and ministry partners associated with our church and to help in two Habitat for Humanity endeavors. The "Connection" occurred due to a three-pronged vision of outreach: 1. Cairo was the center of the Muslim world; 2. Cairo was a relatively safe, stable city; and 3. The city's administration seemed at least tolerant of Christians, if not somewhat open.

The last two statements would change significantly after the revolution of 2011.

Mustafah briefed us, saying, "Habitat for Humanity is a powerful, non-profit, ecumenical Christian housing ministry that seeks to eliminate poverty, inadequate housing, and homelessness from the world. I personally know the leader of the Egyptian chapter of Habitat for Humanity, founded in 1989." The construction team's overriding purpose entailed bearing the monetary gift to make it all happen.

"Tell us about the costs," we beseeched Mustafah at the first meeting.

"The houses Habitat constructs in Egypt are simple, affordable, and durable. They measure about 800-square feet and cost around $1,200 (all money in this book is quoted in American dollars) each to build. With cement or tiled floors, plastered or limestone brick walls, and secure wooden, flat roofs, they must have enough rooms to separate parents from children, boys from girls, and families from livestock. The access to clean water and sanitation systems, segregation from animals, and good ventilation all serve to improve the health of families and their communities. We equip each house with electricity and water, and several homes often share a septic tank. All new homeowners must repay the loan so that funds will be available to construct additional houses."

"So, the Egyptian families will be sweating with us?" we asked, "and they could be Muslim or Christian, or a mix of both? They actually work together?"

"Muslim or Christian, or a mix of both?
They actually work together?"

4

"That's right." Mustafah smiled, telling us facts from a brochure he held. "Habitat invites people of all backgrounds, races, and religions to build houses together in partnership with families in need. Often Muslims help Christians and vice versa. Isn't that wonderful? Around the world to date, 400,000 acceptable, affordable houses have been completed, with two million people served. In Egypt, about 12,000 homes have been constructed or renovated in twenty-five communities."

We scheduled our trip for February, the middle of the winter in Egypt, when high temperatures lingered around seventy and lows stayed in the fifties. Flying into the country in the evening highlighted the dryness of the land, which looked brown and dusty as far as we could see, with the exception of a narrow green strip of irrigated land along the Nile. Nervous about getting the dental equipment into the country (as usual), we hoped and prayed. The customs people opened up one bag that held some syringes, but Mustafah explained (and slipped some money into some hands), and we passed through without further incident. However, this would not be the case on our third trip in several years.

*

For the first two days, we recovered from jet lag, resting well in a comfortable hotel, about the ranking of a three-star hotel in America. Since we'd skipped over nine time zones, our bodies demanded sleep by 3:00 p.m.

Through the slits of sleepy eyes we visited some thrilling sights of Cairo. The immense Mohamed Ali Mosque, built in the first half of the nineteenth century, is the most visible mosque in Cairo. It took twenty-seven years to construct under the rule of Mohamed Ali Pasha, considered the founder of modern Egypt due to the dramatic reforms he instituted. The dynasty he established ruled Egypt and Sudan until the Egyptian revolution of 1952 overthrew King Farouk, the great-great grandson of Mohammed Ali. The lavish lifestyle of the nineteenth- and twentieth-century Egyptian royalty awed us. King Farouk lived in the Manial Palace, built by Prince Ali Tewfik (his uncle), that incorporated many traditional European and Islamic architectural styles. Farouk, even during the hardships of World War II—with heavy fighting in Egypt's western desert—continued to fill his hunting museum located at the palace with taxidermic animal trophies that loomed above us as we witnessed his life of splendor.

"It looks so peaceful up here on this hill, and the Al Ahazar Park is just stunning, Mustafah," I said.

We stood on the sun-drenched lawn, which carried panoramic overviews of Cairo in all directions.

"Although we feel so far above the city, the racket is unbelievable," I added, "Of course, it's Friday, the weekly holy day. I read Cairo has the greatest concentration of mosques in the world."

Even at this distance above the city, we heard loud sermons and blaring music from the various mosque minarets visible at frequent, strategic intervals throughout the city. From them came the call for the prayers required of Muslims five times each day—at dawn, noon, afternoon, evening, and nightfall. "Tell us more about these prayer rituals of the Muslims," Bob and I requested.

"It's amazing how the prayers often bring the city to a virtual halt. A crier, or muezzin, announces prayer time from the minarets (the mosque towers), and Muslims ceremonially must wash their face, hands, and feet prior to prayer. On Friday, Muslims expect to attend noon prayers at a mosque, preceded by a sermon. The prayer leader faces Mecca. The men stand behind him. And the women know their place in the back or often out of sight. Prayers consist of reciting passages from the Koran and other phrases of praise to God. They include such movements as bowing from the hips and kneeling with faces to the ground."

"The prayers often bring the city to a virtual halt."

"Yeah, I've noticed quite a few men with big red or brown bumps on their foreheads."

Mustafah nodded. "I know. It seems to be spiritual pride to show how faithful individuals are to their prayer life by the way they've worn their head."

A modern, air-conditioned tour bus picked us up, with a likable young Muslim guide named Iman, who remained talkative and friendly. While we ate lunch he ducked out to attend prayer at his mosque as we discussed expectantly our tour of the world-renowned Egyptian Museum. The enormity was impressive, but inside it was disappointingly disorganized and filthy. Many items stood open and unprotected from the hordes of people who milled about. I could hardly stay awake, since our bodies screamed for sleep in the heat and the overwhelming crowds. At the museum little English could be seen, heard, or understood.

Still, Bob tried to lighten things up by being funny. "I want my mummy," he quipped, as we toured the world-famous King Tut exhibit with the world's finest mummies. "Look! Most of the ancient Egyptian mummies show severe dental problems consisting of decayed, abscessed, or missing teeth and advanced periodontal disease (bone loss). Some things never change!"

"Most of the ancient Egyptian mummies show severe dental problems. Some things never change!"

The small Arabic and English display cards described the medical history of the mummies, often noting that the person showed signs of dental discomfort. It reinforced our conclusion that most of the world—past and present—suffered and suffers from the pain of dental disease.

At a papyrus store, attractive girls demonstrated how this five-to-nine-foot green, stalk plant can be pounded, rolled, pressed, and dried to make a strong, parchment-like paper. Because of the arid climate of Egypt, papyrus stayed a very stable writing material, being rot resistant due to the cellulose substance of the plants. Originally written and preserved on papyrus, over 120 papyri of the Bible have been found. They're considered the earliest and best witnesses to the reliability of the Scripture's original texts. Papyrus materials were also used to construct functional items, including boats, mattresses, mats, rope, sandals, and baskets. The creative artwork, maps, and detailed pictures beautifully painted on papyrus at the gift shop enticed everyone in our group to make purchases.

*

The next day we toured an outdoor museum in the town of Memphis that had a 3,200-year-old, 91-ton statue of Ramses the Second, housed in a gigantic, rectangular building. Often regarded as the most celebrated and powerful pharaoh of the ancient Egyptian empire, Ramses the Second reigned in the 1200s B.C. He ruled for over sixty-six years, and records show that he suffered severe dental problems through observations of his mummy.

We lunched at Barry's Oriental Restaurant, which had an open view to the Giza Pyramids, the oldest of the ancient wonders of the world, built around 2500 BC. To date, 138 pyramids have been discovered, built as tombs for the Pharaohs and their queens. Several members of our group came back unimpressed with the creepy and stale interior of the Khafre pyramid, which consisted of a straight shaft sloping downward into the bedrock, a leveled-off area, and then a short climb to the burial chamber, which contained only the sarcophagus.

The Sun Boat Museum held the large Khufu ship found sealed into a pit in the Giza pyramid complex. As the world's oldest intact ship, it functioned as a ritual vessel thought to carry the resurrected king across the heavens. We also saw the humongous 5,000-year-old Sphinx nearby, the oldest monumental sculpture known on earth. It represents a mythical creature with the body of a lion and the head of a man. Without an associated inscription, no one knows why it exists.

We also had our pictures taken on a camel, though we did not ride them until a later trip.

While I looked in the market, Bob—ever the non-shopper—talked to our guide, Iman.

"Egyptians often feel offended with how Americans view and treat us," Iman admitted, then paused.

"You know," Bob said softly, "we travel often to meet people from other places and religions, and we realize that misunderstanding and poor communication often occur between our country and yours. But we come because we want to develop friendships and help others understand Americans and Christians, as well."

"Egyptians often feel offended with how Americans view and treat us."

Now that honesty and openness seemed safe, Iman started asking Bob about American politics and the distrust the United States has of the Muslim world. The candor exchanged between two men from very different lands and opposing views opened unexpected dialogue.

"I'd just like to apologize to you for our government's frequent distrust and poor reaction to you, our brothers and sisters in Egypt," Bob suddenly felt led to say. "We as a nation must continue to acknowledge your feelings and to show respect for you in our common humanity."

"Thank you so much for understanding." Iman seemed to be fighting back tears, feeling the warmth, acknowledgment, and respect from Bob, whom he knew to be part of the American military.

The encounter provided a bond and true connection for the rest of our time together. Mustafah said Iman asked many questions about Christianity after that. Since we discovered that Iman would soon become a father, I quilted a baby blanket for Iman's family when we returned home. Mustafah took the quilt when visiting Egypt about six months later, reporting that it thrilled Iman to receive it and that he continued to ask deeper questions about the Christian faith. It brought us joy to see the true exchange of friendship between people of differing cultural and spiritual traditions.

Our team met with some of our ministry partners, and on Sunday we attended a cathedral that kept ties with our church at home. It is also the congregation Mustafah's family worshipped with for generations when they lived in Cairo.

> It brought us joy to see the true exchange of friendship between people of differing cultural and spiritual traditions.

"Wow, this church is as large and nice as ours in Colorado," we marveled, "and in a wealthy part of town, too."

The congregation, well-dressed in western attire, impressed us with their friendly and hospitable demeanors. The meeting included some familiar hymn tunes, with the Arabic language use as the only perceptible difference from many American church services.

With a police escort leading the way, we left that afternoon on a five-hour bus ride to El Minya. An armed security guard had accompanied us on our tour bus since we'd arrived. The expectation in the country is for a guard to protect visitors from harm. Egyptian leaders know violence would devastate the tourist industry so vital to their economy.

As evening prayer time approached, we stopped at a rest area along the way. "Couldn't get near the sink," Bob commented. "A long line of men washing their feet in the basins in the restroom held us up. They must've been getting ready for prayers."

We arrived at the old and battered Cleopatra Hotel about 9:00 p.m. and found it set on a very busy and noisy street corner, with honking at all hours. Ear plugs provided our only hope of sleep.

About one half of Egypt's population lives in rural areas. In the country Egyptians generally live in houses consisting of three small rooms and a courtyard, which they share with their animals. The men wear pants and a full, shirt-like garment called a *galabiyah*. Women wear long burkas, frequently in dark colors completely covering themselves, except for their faces. Western dress can be seen, as well. The first Habitat work site, located in a Christian village about a two-hour drive from the hotel, had been the site of Jimmy Carter's work project in 2002. The Egyptian Habitat engineer responsible for the construction, Sherif, split the group into teams.

A little room on the top floor of the church became our dental clinic, and a local dentist arrived to spend the first morning with us. His much-appreciated stay stretched to two days. The Egyptian dentist, sharply dressed with an impressively bright mind, loved the professional interaction. He translated and watched Bob's procedures closely.

"I think he's bringing me all of his difficult patients, and he wants me to work on him as well," Bob whispered to me. "It seems he doesn't trust anyone here since no one sterilizes their instruments."

"What?! Unbelievable! They don't sterilize?" It shocked me.

"No, they usually only wash the instruments and at best use disinfectants, but it's not sufficient to kill all the bad bugs. Spread of infectious disease is common in developing countries that can't afford expensive autoclaves. They haven't seen any alternatives, but we can show them our simple, effective method."

"Teaching dentistry is what you do best, but our most valuable contribution could be our sterilization information. Who would imagine that?"

*

The next day, I thrilled to the opportunity of training the Egyptian dentist's office assistant, who came along hesitantly. I attempted to reassure her. "It's almost like doing dishes! We have this four-quart pressure pot, and we heat it on this simple electric hot plate, with a cup of water poured in to provide steam. It's virtually a steam autoclave. With this specially made, two-inch round weight, we can bring the steam pressure up to 25 psi."

"P.S. why?" She laughed as she understood very little English. Her dentist tried to translate.

"P.S.I." I repeated. "It stands for pounds per square inch. It just means that all the bugs are blasted away, completely sterilizing the instruments. This procedure kills all micro-organisms, including bacteria, viruses, and yeasts that cause diseases such as HIV, hepatitis, and tuberculosis."

"Yes?" The Egyptian assistant's voice shook slightly.

"Don't worry," I encouraged. "You can do this! Put on gloves. Just take the dirty instruments and place them into this basin of soapy water and scrub them with these brushes until the blood is off and rinse in this basin of clear water. Put them in the pot with a little water and when it all starts chugging, set this timer for ten minutes. When the timer sounds, take the cooker off the heating element and release the pressure by removing the weight on top of the lid. Open the lid, pour out the excess water, then dump the hot instruments out onto this tray and they'll dry instantly—perfectly sterilized."

I spent the day providing the young lady hands-on training in using the pressure pot for sterilization. Hopefully, the ripple effect of these two sharing techniques with others might make an impact on the safety of dental care in the country.

The other volunteers on the trip took turns working on roofs by nailing thin strips of wood on top of horizontal cross beams. Later a sheet of plastic and a layer of concrete would cover the roof. Others plastered interior walls, which required more skill than the Americans possessed, and the Egyptian workers soon lost patience with our team. They could obviously work more rapidly than the Americans, who didn't claim to be builders by trade. The Egyptians insisted they would do the plastering and sent the Americans outside to "screen sand." The sand for the plaster is imported from various locations in Egypt, since desert sand is salty and is too rounded in shape.

When Sherif arrived and asked the Americans why they seemed to be basically playing in the sand (our take), he ordered, "Let's go back inside. There's still plenty of work to do here." Everyone tried his or her hands at plastering as Sherif expected the inexperienced Americans to do the work. Our church provided the funds to pay for the construction. More important than efficiency was the interaction and the side-by-side involvement with the nationals.

Timeouts for tea came frequently (we called tea our "break fluid") with little cups too hot to handle. Sherif told us that holding our earlobes would cool our fingers. It actually worked! When the Habitat supervisors weren't around, the Egyptian workers often asked our team members for money. Bartering, bribes, and begging occurs everywhere, although possibly in more sophisticated ways in developed countries.

> Sherif told us that holding our earlobes would cool our fingers. It actually worked!

After work, we threw Frisbees with kids. One sixteen-year-old boy with a cross tattoo on his wrist told us, "America good, Bush (the current President) good!" He wanted some of the team members to visit his house, but the guards wouldn't allow it.

The omnipresent government security men also wanted to join the Frisbee games. It must get boring watching over foreigners all day. One of our team members carried a Polaroid camera, which created enormous interest, and the children flocked around her continually. Finally, she was out of self-developing film. When she hid out in the Habitat office, groups came and cried out her name incessantly and she was forced to admit she had no more film, much to their disappointment.

The villages and the roads often looked like scenes out of the Bible. The people wore long, full clothes with turbans or head coverings, and they rode donkeys or carried items on their heads. As an agrarian society, they worked in fields with ancient tools. Their homes consisted of simple, brick rectangular structures similar to housing 2,000 years ago. It felt like a time tunnel into an antiquated world. We rode some of the donkeys that stood everywhere, and the villagers howled at our excitement.

> Their homes consisted of simple, brick rectangular structures
> similar to housing 2,000 years ago.
> It felt like a time tunnel into an antiquated world.

Many years prior, a team members' aunt had helped found a mission school for girls in Khartoum, Sudan. We met a staff member of the local Egypt Habitat establishment who'd attended that very school. God uses people in the past to influence later generations. We thought, *What legacy are we leaving?*

For dinner at the Cleopatra Hotel some ordered "scallops," thinking it was seafood, but it appeared as chicken-fried steak. We were also offered "kentacky fried chicken" and "bear" (beer) to drink. Alcoholism is a huge problem in many cultures (although alcohol consumption is not allowed by Muslims). We refuse alcoholic beverages as we try to stay culturally sensitive everywhere. This causes friction with some of our American team members who enjoy drinking alcohol, but we require abstention on our trips. It seems that every trip has several teammates we call "caffiends"—those who can't live without their coffee-fix, often exhibited with tea and soda habits, as well. Caffeine, a strong stimulant, often turns into a necessity. Many volunteers are happy to drink water (using bottled drinks in foreign lands) and to save their money.

*

After two days in the Christian village, we braved a Muslim village, Bani Mohamed. Upon arrival, the local officials ushered us into a meeting room, which seemed formal and intimidating. The village council members, threatening and touchy, questioned our motives as this proved their first encounter with Habitat for Humanity. They asked pointed questions.

"If there is poverty in America, why don't you help there instead of coming here? What do you think of our right to believe in Islam?"

Mustafah translated our answers and told us later that he'd "fixed" what we'd said so that it wouldn't be offensive. He'd steered clear of pushing our Christian beliefs, stressing in a gentle way our desire to help others around the world, regardless of beliefs.

We can't argue, or sometimes even discuss, Christianity with those opposed and truly win with words. The people on the disputing side seem to become more entrenched in what they insist upon, even if deep down they're not sure that they totally understand what they believe. It becomes a matter of "saving face" or staying within cultural expectations before their family unit and peers, something extremely important in most cultures.

> We can't argue, or sometimes even discuss, Christianity with those opposed and truly win with words.

One compelling aspect that is unique to Christian beliefs, however, is God's unconditional love. Many religions point to miraculous signs, good works, high-sounding doctrines, or honorable actions, but none show the unending compassion that we see in the sacrifices Jesus gave in reflecting God's heart. Jesus came to earth to die and to save us from the penalty of sin that we deserve. We are recipients of God's transforming love ourselves and wish to show God's care by accepting and nurturing others.

Since the village leaders did not feel comfortable with allowing dentistry that first day, we hauled blocks with the team, and Bob built foundations and walls. My tasks involved screening sand and carrying blocks and mortar into the house, right through the room where the family cooked their next meal. Most house expansions involved building "up"—second-story rooms—as land rarely is available for new structures. By hand we mixed cement on the ground while local workers used the one motorized cement mixer.

*

On the second day in the Muslim village, the team worked only a few hours since a flat tire delayed our arrival. The Muslim community leaders met us at the bus and asked if we would bring in our dental equipment. We set up in a tiny room, with low benches on which to place the instruments and the sterilization set up. We treated a few community dignitaries, but soon the American construction team finished for the day. Instructed at noon to pack up (we'd just gotten started), the leaders announced we'd have a felluca (the traditional wooden sailing boat) ride on the Nile River for lunch. Without enough wind to sail, a large man from the shore pulled the boat along. As this proved difficult, the ride didn't take long.

With so many dental patients to see, we couldn't have hoped to even scratch the surface, anyway. In that village of 12,000 people, 5,000 were children under the age of twelve. Egypt's demand for housing is due to a population explosion occurring everywhere in the country (with many refugees flooding in from surrounding countries). Although land availability remains the same, the number of people is growing exponentially.

Afterwards, we departed to Cairo, again with a police escort of four men in the car ahead of us. It hadn't played out as we'd wished, and we felt the day wasted for us dentally. We'd hoped to serve and to interact with the Muslims. We often say that "being flexible" is the main mantra on mission trips. However, we were frustrated that every day we'd been forced to stop our dentistry after a few hours. The team worked for three to four hours each day, and—just when we got our operation flowing smoothly—the team wanted to leave. They seemed irritated when waiting for us. This became an issue and provided another example of the difficulty of attaching ourselves to a multi-task group. Seeing a pattern led to our decision in several years to venture on "dental-specific" missions.

One man on the team kept a journal. He gave copies to the team members after we returned home. In it we read this comment:

> Each day while we waited for Bob and Diane to pack up the dental equipment, kids gathered to watch us. Occasionally, men would yell fiercely at the children and they scattered, returning in a few minutes. At one point a man came along on a bicycle and ran over a little girl who got in his way. He just got back on his bike and continued along.

We felt sad when we read that, as if there'd been a connection between us holding the team up and the girl getting hit. I'm sure he didn't mean it, but we often felt a negative attitude toward our work.

We ended up in bed early, as the dentistry always tires us out, and perpetual jet lag contributes to exhaustion. Often other team members' tasks aren't as fatiguing, and they go out long hours into the night, eating, socializing, or even shopping, as many markets in developing countries stay open into the early morning hours. Due to cooler temperatures, night life is exciting in hotter climates. We can't stay up late if we expect to work productively during the days.

Next, our team visited the Evangelical Theological Seminary of Cairo, one of the few theological training centers for Protestant Christians in Egypt. Founded by missionaries around 1855, the seminary gradually built a strong reputation along the Nile. They offer both undergraduate and graduate theological programs with a present enrollment of 240 students. The current president said the seminary could not admit anyone Muslim or people even bearing a Muslim name.

A student from Iraq said, "Christians endure intense persecution in Iraq. Would there be anyone in your group who might have a heart for the Church in Iraq and could help in some way?" His plea seemed extremely complicated, although we sympathized with his plight.

One of the professors told us, "I'm not opposed to American involvement in Iraq, but I wish your President Bush would've waited to get more support from the Arab states before invading. I also hope America will not withdraw too quickly, because the Christians will be killed."

His main disagreement with America involved our policies toward Israel and the Palestinians, a similar conversation we've had with many Egyptians, even Christians, who are usually raised with a deep resentment toward Jews.

The professor also thought Iran would be a more serious problem for America than Iraq. It surprised us that he'd answer our questions about politics. When we apologized, he said, "That's fine. Egyptians love to discuss politics and religion." When one of our team members remarked that the two dangerous subjects should possibly be avoided, he replied, "Not if you approach them correctly."

> "Egyptians love to discuss
> politics and religion."

We assembled our dental clinic in an office in the seminary but had no interpreter. Mustafah, our Egyptian leader on the trip, said, "I can interpret, but I don't like blood. I hope I can handle watching."

This seemed odd, since as an Egyptian-educated physician, he now ran a physical therapy clinic in Colorado Springs. Finally, it made sense to us why he never visited the dental clinic for long. Many of the patients tried to manipulate us to see family or friends not on our list. Although we felt sorry for their need, we didn't quite understand their desperation. With sufficient monetary resources, anyone can buy whatever is needed in Cairo—even acceptable dentistry generally through Western-trained dentists.

Mustafah explained, "The problem in Egypt, as in most developing countries, is that 90 percent of the people live a subsistence existence, and wealth and privileges go only to the top 10 percent of the population who can access the large population centers. Outside the major cities and to those who remain perpetually poor, good dentistry is unavailable. Any Egyptian would be fortunate to get an extraction with the benefit of anesthesia or proper sterilization."

> "Ninety percent of the people live a subsistence existence."

Our bus driver mentioned his toothaches at intervals all week when we'd been inundated with villagers. We scheduled him on the last day at the seminary, but when Bob saw the difficulty and knew it would compromise his ability to drive us home and around Cairo that evening (as he'd been contracted to do), Bob felt it best not to incapacitate him to that extent. It saddened us, and we received pressure from our team. The journal-writing man commented on it negatively in an entry we read after we returned home. For once the team acted willing to wait for us, though time was not the issue.

The traffic, always horrendous in the city, seemed impossible that Friday night. "Why is it called rush hour when nothing is moving?" We've asked that often.

As the driver finally got rolling in the midst of close-and-fast traffic, we suddenly saw a gigantic truck careening toward us. We watched in terror from the front seat as the bus driver pounded fiercely on the brakes, coming within inches and milliseconds of what almost became a horrible collision. It frightened everyone to think how close to a tragic accident we had come.

Bob leaned over and whispered to me, "If I'd taken his teeth out, our driver wouldn't have kept the reaction skills he'd needed there, and who knows if we'd all be alive. I think blood froze in my bones right then."

We had made the right decision in not treating our bus driver that afternoon.

*

With two days left in Cairo before we flew back, we felt disappointed that we hadn't provided more dentistry overall. Since we couldn't be autonomous and keep our unity with the larger group, we knew we had compromised our abilities. They'd done little construction work, but we realized we'd accomplished the overall mission goal of assisting Habitat for Humanity and visiting our various ministry partners. The team leader prioritized those objectives and also showed the team many of Egypt's sights.

"When we join a mixed-purpose team, we must not expect to accomplish as much dentistry as we'd like," Bob reflected to me on the last day. "Many of these trips emphasize relationship-building and demonstrating our Christian message of love to all, including toward our team members."

I nodded. "You're right, and we'll have to stop trying to bother other team members to carry our dental supplies, too."

> "Many of these trips emphasize relationship-building and demonstrating our Christian message of love to all."

That was another lesson we'd learned. We wanted to bring scads of supplies but found no one taking any real interest. They felt we were intruding on the private space owed them in their luggage, especially that holding room for buying items to bring back to families and friends. Since then, we've learned how to pack a complete dental clinic in our four allowed, fifty-pound checked bags and to use our carry-on, small bags for our personal items.

Driving the last two days, we especially embraced the history and the sights around Cairo including the famous "Hanging Church" and the Coptic Museum, where seminary faculty knowledgeably toured us around. The Gayer-Anderson house was owned by a British general in the early 1900s when Egypt existed as a British protectorate. At several mosques, I donned the scarf I'd brought. All women covered their heads and followed restrictions that forced them into special areas for women only. Our Muslim guide repeatedly emphasized the importance of religion to Egyptians. Over 85 percent of the population of Egypt is Muslim. The three main Christian religions in Egypt are Orthodox (13 percent), Protestant (.85 percent), and Catholic (0.32 percent).

"The Coptic Orthodox Church of Alexandria (referred to as Copts or Coptics) is, according to tradition, the church apostle Mark established around 42 A.D." Bob presented this topic to the team in a pre-trip meeting. "The belief that God chose Egypt as a safe place for His infant son to hide from Herod brings a great source of pride to the Egyptian Christians. It's surprising to learn that the Catholic Pope in Rome, who succeeds from the apostle Peter, is not the only Christian pope today. There is also an uninterrupted succession of popes of the Coptic Church. The current one, Shenouda III, is the 117th successor to Saint Mark, showing the endurance of the Coptic Church."

"Didn't Christians predominate until the Muslim conquest of Egypt?" I asked.

"Right," Bob concurred. "The Muslims took over in 639 A.D., which at that time was 95 percent Christian. At first Muslim overlords tolerated the Coptic Christians, because they, like the Jews, were considered 'People of the Book.' Gradually, Muslims began to tax the Christians more heavily and serious persecution began. In the eighth century they burned identifying marks on the hands of Christians to identify and control them. Forced in the ninth century to wear five-pound crosses around their necks, Copts watched while their churches burned, and public worship became restricted. The population of the Copts decreased from nine million at the time of the Muslim conquest to about 700,000 in the early 1900s."

"Tell us more of what you learned," Mustafah encouraged.

> "Forced in the ninth century to wear five-pound crosses around their necks, Copts watched while their churches burned."

"Most of the early Muslim rulers needed the knowledge of the Copts to govern the country and to collect taxes. The history shows a vicious cycle in which the Muslim leaders hired Copts for their abilities, skill, and honesty to administer the government's affairs. When the Copts did well and prospered, the Muslim rulers expelled them from government jobs and confiscated their property, often jailing and killing them."

Mustafah told how adverse political changes affected his family. "Nassar became Egypt's ruler after an Army coup in 1952, with many of his protégés espousing the more fundamentalist Islamic teachings. The Nassar government followed a socialist regime and nationalized most of the private enterprises, which hit us—the Copts—hard, as we depended on private businesses for our livelihood. The economic pressures and religious discrimination caused Copts to start immigrating to democratic countries such as America. My family moved to California."

In cities, the majority of Egyptians live in apartments due to the scarcity of land. We visited a middle-class, three-bedroom apartment (not different from those in America), the home of the leader of a talented group of Christians devoted to spreading the message of the Bible with technologically sophisticated methods. Through the production of satellite television programming, audio and video production, and live concert appearances, they reach out to people throughout Egypt and the Middle East. As extremely attractive young adults with appealing star power, they target all age groups with a message of love, renewal, and hope. Even in the poorest sections of the world, air waves remain open, and almost everyone has access to radio or television, making it an excellent medium for dispersing Christian beliefs.

When we arrived at the hotel that night, we stepped into a sumptuous wedding reception that resembled one in America. Although the deafening music chased some of us past the celebrants who spilled into the street, our youngest male team member snapped pictures, and the family invited him to dance. With his fanciest footwork, he brought howls of appreciation from the wedding guests. He'd become our most audacious, bold, and enterprising member, receiving the reputation as the renegade of our group—there seems to be one on each trip. He tried unconventional food (pigeon) and smoked the shishah (water pipe) with a tobacco mixed with molasses. He commented on its distinctive taste, aroma, and supposed buzz. The water pipe seemed inseparable from Egyptian café society.

*

On Sunday, our last day in Cairo, we again attended the Evangelical Church. The guest speaker from Switzerland spoke in French with an Arabic interpreter. Our team sat in the balcony and met the leader of the International Bible Society, who interpreted the sermon into English. The Bible Society of Egypt exists to make Scriptures available and accessible to all, at an affordable price and in the language of the people.

The Bible Society executive's wife humbly bears the affectionate name, "Mother Theresa of Cairo," given by recipients of her care. Through spiritual, education, and medical interventions, she assists the poverty-stricken in areas all over the city. She invited us to one of her target neighborhoods that afternoon, explaining, "The 'garbage city' is where poor Christians live and sort trash that is delivered from all over Cairo. Pigs feed off the refuse, making this off limits for Muslims, who have religious restrictions on pork."

> "The 'garbage city' is where poor Christians live and sort trash that is delivered from all over Cairo."

The unhygienic and horribly filthy slums sobered us immediately. Our "Mother Theresa" also ran a Sudanese refugee school, which we would visit on our next trip to Egypt. Located beyond that community existed the Cave Churches, where oppressed Christians hid during various persecutions.

There we heard about a miracle where the God of the Bible literally moved a mountain to show His power to Muslims. In various places around Cairo, artwork and mosaics related the story from 979 A.D. The event involved a Muslim leader who heard someone ask the Coptic Pope, a believer in the Bible, about Matthew 17:20, where Jesus says, "If you have faith as small as a mustard seed, you can say to the mountain, 'Move from here to there,' and it will move." The Muslim leader demanded that the Coptic (Christian) Pope cause this to happen or he'd have the Copts killed.

Given three days, the Copts prayed and fasted, involving the Orthodox Saint Simon. The Copts stood by Mokattam Mountain in Cairo, and, as the people praised the Lord, a great earthquake swept over the area. Beautifully pictured in Egyptian art, the mountain rose up, and the sun could be seen shining through underneath. Records document that the Muslim leader said to the Pope, "I recognize the correctness of thy faith." There is no proof that the Muslim leader converted to Christianity, but he did welcome the beloved Pope warmly thereafter. In commemoration of this miracle, the Coptic Orthodox Church observes three extra days of fasting at the beginning of Advent each year. This miracle, confirmed in many old writings, is now documented on the Internet (under *Simon the Tanner* at wikipedia.com).

> The Muslim leader said to the Pope,
> "I recognize the correctness of thy faith."

On the way back to the hotel we stopped at the Anwar Sadat memorial, commemorating the third president of Egypt who served from 1970 until his assassination by a fundamentalist army officer in 1981. Although the impressive memorial included ceremonial guards in full uniform, along with a few workers cleaning the large expanse of stone, we saw no Egyptian visitors—possibly reflecting the unpopularity of Sadat in recent years. The guards seemed lonely and friendly, suggesting they would pose with us for pictures.

*

As we flew out at 3:45 a.m. the next morning, we reflected on our time in Egypt, where working in the villages remained the highlight. Not thrilled with crowded and polluted Cairo, we preferred not to experience that large city again. I suffered from the pollution, having allergy-like symptoms with the loss of my voice for several days.

We'd been impressed with the Habitat for Humanity organization and thought the Habitat staff well-organized and sociable. The houses built by the Christians and the Muslims working peacefully together had demonstrated an inspiring example of solidarity and cooperation within those communities. A young female team member planned to return to work in their Egyptian office. Later we learned it had been difficult for her to assimilate the foreign culture, and she'd come home disillusioned.

Mustafah left us several times to visit areas where he runs an organization called the Touch of Love. He explained, "I have a network of people in small villages throughout Egypt that provide revolving micro-loans that enable poor families to increase their incomes and to improve their standard of living. When they become self-sufficient, they pay back the loans and funnel funds to others who need help." Loans granted by his local committees have supported projects such as chicken farming, camel breeding, feed stores, general merchandise shops, an electronics repair outlet, and a variety of other ventures. As the community witnesses these abundant results, hope and motivation inspires change.

Embedded in an immensely strong fusion within the family, politics, and the social network, Islam makes it unthinkable for most to follow another religion. Iman, our guide, and others emphasized that, to understand Egypt, one must realize that Egyptians commit to be religious people. We firmly relate! It seems to be the nature of humankind to aspire to an understanding of creation and an intelligent designer. We hope that the Habitat home building and the caring dental work made an opportune start toward establishing good will and a positive consideration of Christians' and Americans' motives. So much harmful and untrue propaganda circulates through the Middle East, causing them to hate the West, including our culture and beliefs.

> To understand Egypt, one must realize that Egyptians
> commit to be religious people.

I mused later, "There is always a lot to admire about other cultures, and I come away wishing we could incorporate some features into our lifestyle. I especially enjoyed the feeling of social connectedness we observed in Egypt, notably expressed in the closeness of intergenerational and extended families."

Bob agreed. "Yes, it's quite a bit different from many Americans who are often isolated in their homes with high-tech entertainment."

"I like how people frequent the bazaars and outdoor markets to shop and to visit with family and friends. They commune at coffeehouses, where lively discussion supersedes all other entertainment," I added. "Those we visited with seemed to have a fine sense of humor and gracious manner."

"One thing that is shockingly different in Egypt, though, is that a Muslim man may have up to four wives, provided he can look after them and treat them fairly and well. However, what man can hope to accomplish that?" Bob laughed.

The cultural exchange we'd experienced in Egypt had been both rewarding and intensely challenging. But on our next trip to Africa, the most challenging team to date awaited us.

SENEGAL, SOUTH AFRICA, AND MADAGASCAR

Fascinating Humans
and Wild Animals

* * *

"THIS TRIP IS SHAPING UP TO BE FAIRLY FORMIDABLE, and I'm not sure it'll be comfortable for us," I expressed, wary of the combination of personalities enrolling for our summer trip to Madagascar via Senegal. "It sounds a little like cuddling a litter of tigers, but we'll hope for the best."

Sir led the team again and brought his fifty-year-old son. For many years Sir had cajoled his dentist, Dr. Jerome, to accompany him to Madagascar. Dr. Jerome fended Sir off while generously donating toothbrushes and toothpaste. Dr. Jerome, a gentle, dignified man who hails from Midwest farming roots, stayed gripped in the throes of his private practice, the main hurdle that keeps most dentists from traveling on missions.

"We're lucky we finally got Dr. Jerome to go with us," Bob told me. "It's very difficult for dentists to leave their work, especially solo practitioners. We must support Dr. Jerome in his brave decision. It's the same conflict I hear from dentists all the time. The cost of the trip is not the major factor, but more serious is that the loss of income and that the office overhead costs continue in their absence. They must provide for their staff members who usually rely on the weekly income. Dentists also feel a responsibility to their patients who might need them—and who may find another dentist in their absence…"

"And his wife isn't able to come due to health issues. Did you hear he's been asking around for someone to come and assist him?" I asked.

"That's another serious snag," Bob explained. "If the dentist's spouse can't support the endeavor, that's usually a show stopper. The best-case scenario is if the spouse will come to help or, at least, will agree to the dentist's trip. Dentists work diligently every clinical day at their own office, and so—during their breaks or vacations—they'd obviously prefer a rest from dentistry. It's truly a sacrifice to go on a difficult assignment full of unknowns, where they don't even have the comforts of their own office. This becomes quite understandable, so we have to realize it takes a very special dentist who can overcome these obstacles. I'm so lucky to have your sweet support, ya know…"

"Aww…" I nudged him. "I couldn't do it without you. Granted, it *was* my idea, first. I'm the one who always wanted to travel and do missionary work." I grinned. "We're quite the unusual team."

Dr. Jerome expressed yet another problem at our first meeting. "My son is married to a Dutch woman whose family runs a mission in Dakar, Senegal. I'm not sure I can go to any other location until I assist my relatives first, as they've also requested for years that I visit them with dentistry." This factor was a real issue that had bothered Dr. Jerome for years.

Bob shrugged, "Why don't we go to Senegal for a week and then on to Madagascar?"

It was a done deal when Dr. Jerome found a lovely eighteen-year-old patient, Pam, who wanted to volunteer as his assistant.

Some acquaintances from a humanitarian dental team in our hometown also expressed interest in the trip. We often shared equipment, but we had never traveled together. With much experience, Dr. Braden led motivated teams to many places around the world. He emphasized hard work and revelry, where adventures, fine food, and brews lured members to his teams. Dr. Braden, a high-octane guy in his sixties, brought his youngish wife, who seemed fun and easygoing. Dr. Braden could be charming or pesky with his quirky jokes and roguish grin. Two currently single, fiftyish women with colorful personalities followed him faithfully as his seasoned travel buddies, self-described as his "harem."

The team also included the dental hygienist, Michelle, who'd traveled with us before to Ukraine, and I'd struggled with her hyper-professionalism. Processing the relationship after the last trip, I decided that, in her case, often a bit of bluster indicates insecurity. It had been an uncertain trip for us all. I hoped I could cope better now that I realized Michelle conscientiously tried to do her best.

Often a bit of bluster indicates insecurity.

We had admired our own daughter, Shari, who was now a wonderful dental hygienist. She had made Bob exceedingly happy when she started working with him at the dental office in Colorado Springs. If it wasn't so important to her to have children, we may have nabbed her for our trips. We know there is a season for everything, as we didn't travel to developing countries for years while our children were young.

Meshing everyone on this next trip was beginning to sound complicated. As we analyzed the team makeup, it promised some yet-unknown mixture of the best and the beasts! We'd probably struck a rich vein of crazy, where the extent of insaneness remained unknown as of yet.

> As we analyzed the team makeup, it promised some yet-unknown mixture of the best and the beasts! We'd probably struck a rich vein of crazy.

Already faced with many possible stressors going into a trip, I quoted my family's pithy sayings that I'd heard for years while growing up. With every change or new adventure, someone in my family always piped up to say, "All beginnings are hard." This phrase hopefully reassured the family member, who would soon overcome the challenging, steep learning curve of whatever fresh situation he or she encountered. My family also coached each other to do one's "*reasonable* best." Balance is important, and one couldn't be best at everything.

Another family saying was created when my sister had several ticks on her neck after a picnic in the woods. Dad and Mom, concerned about the spread of disease through tick bites, told a doctor of their fears. He reassured them. "Not to worry, if symptoms develop, *we'll treat it.*" Those three words represented how we'd handle the unknown perils we might encounter, reminding us not to worry until the problem develops (which it didn't in my sister's case). We hoped we'd not have to treat too many difficulties on this trip.

"Tell me what you know about Senegal," I queried Bob on the plane from New York.

"Okay, Dr. Jerome just gave me this travel guide I'm lookin' over. Senegal is slightly smaller than South Dakota but has a population of eleven million. It's on the west side of Africa, bordering the Atlantic. As a colony of France for years, French is still the main language, with literacy around 40 percent. The fertility rate is at almost five babies to each woman. The median age of the population is eighteen, with life expectancy to the mid-fifties. Currently, unemployment is 45 percent, with over 50 percent of the population below the poverty line. Most of the working people follow agricultural occupations. The main products are peanuts, millet, corn, sorghum, rice, cotton, tomatoes, green vegetables, cattle, poultry, pigs, and fish. France continues as one of Senegal's main export and import partners."

"What religion prevails—French Catholic?"

"Nope. Ninety-four percent are Muslim, with Catholicism at 5 percent and others at 1 percent. We're 'others' since we've come to help the Dutch Reformed Protestant Mission—truly a minority."

*

Senegal

Greatly exhausted, we arrived in Dakar, Senegal, early on a Saturday morning. Picked up by extremely dark-faced locals in a van with faded scenes and rainbow colors painted on each side, the vehicle projected an antique-plush, yet tired, look. Stowing the luggage on top and inside seemed a burden almost too much for the chugging van. As we took off, one suitcase fell off the top, and the driver pulled over as his assistant chased it down.

Bob cringed. "Hope that one doesn't hold fragile dental equipment!"

> As we took off, one suitcase fell off the top,
> and the driver pulled over as his assistant chased it down.

The erratic traffic proved a crowded conglomeration of honking and diesel pollution. Built on a sandbar, the city boasted little vegetation. Garbage lay everywhere with no bushes to hide the litter. Sand and squalor defined Dakar.

Our hosting compound opened to a large front yard behind a colossal gated and walled enclosure.

Annie—the mother of Dr. Jerome's daughter-in-law—was a gritty missionary with an indomitable spirit. She'd established the ministry on that site over twenty years ago. As a striking, blond woman in her fifties, Annie remained statuesque, athletic, and tanned. She'd accompanied her husband, a Bible translator for the Wycliffe Bible Organization, who'd labored over a Bible translation into the Wolof dialect, spoken by over 40 percent of the Senegalese people. He'd died of malaria five years prior to our arrival, and Annie stayed on in loyalty to the calling they had shared.

On property with a sandy base, gangly plants and bushes grew around the perimeter. Annie lived in the front house that held several living areas, four bedrooms, three bathrooms and a ten-by-twenty-foot kitchen—not unlike a fair-sized American home. Dr. Jerome, the most favored member due to his "family" status, and some single volunteers, stayed in the house with Annie.

Annie's thirty-year-old son, Jimmy (her "crown prince," we discovered) also lived there between trips home to see his wife and several small children in Colorado. In Dakar, he ministered to searching, thinking young men who were assimilating their values and worldview in a community of Christian love. Jimmy taught these local lads occupational skills—drum making, wood working, and hands-on skills—as income insurance in the likelihood they'll be disowned by their families if they spurn their Muslim upbringing by accepting Christ. Jimmy developed a small business where the young men welded heavy-duty bumpers on cars to protect the front and the back of vehicles from accidents on the treacherous roads.

Jimmy had built a lovely home for his wife at the back of the property since he'd hoped to interest her in residing permanently in Senegal,. It was not to be, as she could not tolerate the life there. Half the team stayed in Jimmy's home, a very large, modern, and comfortable single-level dwelling with commodious bathrooms and thick walls for natural insulation. The home sat only steps away from the enticing new and well-maintained swimming pool and bathhouse that a supportive church in Holland gifted to the mission, making the compound more livable.

The two couples—Dr. Braden and his wife, and us—stayed in separate small huts inside the compound's back fence. Each round structure contained

four twin beds around the perimeter of the ten-foot circumference set on a cement floor. Topped with a thatched roof, a bare light bulb hung for illumination, and the soft beds seemed comfortable enough, if one didn't mind sharing with bugs. Bob, as usual, attracted more bites than me. As I like to say, "You get more nibbles probably due to your sweetness, Bob!"

"They're more like Texas bee stingers than nibblers," Bob groused.

We enjoyed the privacy and the uniqueness of the arrangement, but the hut stayed stuffy, as the outside temperature hovered in the nineties. The blaring of the mosque minaret located just over the wall was a huge drawback to our setting.

In all seriousness, Dr. Braden asked Annie if we could stop at the closest Walmart to buy shampoo, as they'd run out of time while packing at home. It turned out to be a joke, as we never saw anything resembling an all-purpose store, and they never found any shampoo while in the country. We all shared what we could with them.

The meals, prepared by women Annie hired, simmered in the front yard in gigantic pots over open fires. One enormous kettle of rice warmed as an ever-present staple, and a stew-like concoction of chicken or fish bubbled in another pot. At serving time, the cooks piled rice in the middle of a flat dish the size of a jumbo pizza pan, with the stew drizzled on top. Everyone grabbed a spoon and sat on a grass woven mat while the pan was placed on a plastic tablecloth. Legs tucked behind, six people gathered around each pan to eat together. The delectable food seemed quite nutritious, if one didn't mind stray sand in the mix and each spoon clanking against those of others.

Senegal

We ate family-style off a common plate.

"What are they doing?" we asked after a meal one day as we observed locals sucking on twigs. Certain trees in the yard produced small branches that—with the bark easily peeled off—made bristly little brushes of inner green cellulose. These performed well as soft and sanitary toothbrushes, keeping mouth hygiene fresh and fun. We all joined in to support the excellent, although unconventional, regional tooth-brushing technique.

Jimmy's nice house provided a wonderful clinic location, where the three dentists and the hygienist each claimed one of the four corners of the main living room. Another Dutch widow who had accompanied her husband to Senegal forty years earlier became our translator. We valued her meticulous knowledge of the language and sweet spirit as we'd treasure a precious jewel.

The assistant from Dr. Braden's harem despised emptying the collection bottle out of the operative machine that contained suction fluids—usually some shade of unappealing red. Since she refused to mess with it, I tried to help, between assisting Bob and being distracted with other people and duties around the clinic.

"Oh, no!" I gasped on the second day. As I'd hurried to dump the jar for the other assistant, I'd dropped it, the contents flowing over a large part of the clinic floor, splashing on my scrubs as well. I hastened to mop it up with used patient bibs from the trash, wishing I'd be swallowed by the floor in one gulp, as everyone stared, revolted, at the spreading gross, blood-stained liquid. When done mopping as best I could, I raced for the shower. While wearing gloves, I rinsed out my uniform bottoms and changed in our little hut.

After that, Bob ended my helpfulness, insisting that if the assistant couldn't handle the full container, the dentist could empty it himself. I never noticed who dispensed the distasteful task thereafter. But I do know that I left those pants hanging on the clothesline as a gift to whoever claimed them as I was definitely finished with them! The HIV/AIDS rate of Senegal seemed to be reported skeptically low at less than 1 percent, but I wasn't taking any chances.

Senegal

Dental clinic for three dentists and a hygienist.

Dr. Jerome, always wanting to smooth things over, reassured me when I returned. "The nice thing about being imperfect is the joy it brings to others. Thanks for helping!"

That night some well-traveled members of the team discussed laundry. One woman suggested a "laundry stomping method" that we've adopted on subsequent trips. All that is required is a cement base in the shower stall. This method involves taking the dirty laundry of each day to one's shower at night. (Usually with the hot, steamy weather most people rinse off after a day's work, even if they also showered in the morning.) We "stomp" on our dirty clothes while the shampoo, soap, and water run off our bodies in the shower. Gently agitating the clothes with one's feet for several minutes as one washes hair and body, the suds also clean the clothes. When finished, the clothes can be rinsed, squeezed, and hung to air dry. The lightweight cotton clothes dry quickly, sometimes ready for use the next day. It's helpful to take several clothespins and a small laundry rope along that can be strung in temporary bedrooms.

The attractive Senegalese impressed us with their dark skin, strong physiques, and graceful, swaying movements.

"Will you look at that?" Bob whispered upon examining one of the earlier patients, pointing to her black gums, and looking inquisitively at our interpreter. "I thought gums came only in pink!"

Many of the patients tattooed their gums. With such dark skin, it made sense that they didn't like the look of pink gums shining out of their otherwise black faces.

"I thought gums came only in pink!"

"Did you know that God has a tattoo?" Dr. Jerome appeared serious.

Dr. Braden rose to the bait. "Go ahead and lay it on me."

"You can find it in Jeremiah, which says, "I have written your name on my hand."

Everyone laughed.

Dr. Braden mumbled, "I guess I'll have to read my Bible more closely."

Several people had missing front teeth, which we always enjoy fixing. Patients can't believe their appearance improves so dramatically after the space is filled with a partial, or the black holes filled with composite. Missing her four front teeth from an accident, one sixteen-year-old girl came in very nicely groomed with striking sapphire-blue clothes and matching jewelry. When Bob filled her space with the partial, she glowed radiantly. One can only suppose it made a positive difference in her future love life. The women of our group bantered that men, in any country, seem to *see* better than they *think*, making beauty, unfortunately, the most sought-after courtship attribute in almost any culture.

"Whatever happened to Proverbs 31:30, which says, 'Beauty is fleeting, but a woman who fears the Lord is to be praised'?" asked our seasoned translator, smiling at the women in the room unoffensively. "Or, in 1 Peter 3, where it says the inner beauty of a gentle, quiet, and obedient spirit is preferable to outward adornment?"

We all appreciated the point she made.

We diligently try to invite only patients whom we know we'll have time to treat, emphasizing that to our hosts wherever we go. No one absorbed that message at this location, although Bob stressed it repeatedly. We issued tickets, but people still showed up with additional family members and friends in tow. Aggression and strong negative responses resulted from those attempting to manipulate the system. We also felt a lack of appreciation from most patients as they bulldozed their way in, claiming their right to be seen. Their verbal and nonverbal responses made us feel we couldn't do enough to please them.

"I guess we're accustomed to being at least somewhat acknowledged for our services in a seminary, an orphanage, or church groups," Bob reflected. "It's a struggle to understand these neighborhood people who obtain a ticket but remain unhappy."

Aware of the possibility that our mission and goals weren't clearly defined on this leg of the trip—other than to "help" Dr. Jerome's relatives— Bob continued to advise caution to Annie about publicizing our presence.

While clutching only one ticket, a hefty mother arrived with her small child. By then we'd been forced to watch more carefully as many people sneaked in. The mother plopped in the dental chair as the little girl began crying over her own toothache. Demanding considerably more treatment than we had time to give, the mother became belligerent. Bob, upset at the mother's dominating, hostile, and self-serving attitude, treated the child, too, even though she didn't have a ticket.

After the mother flounced out in anger, I told Bob, "I feel sorry for the children and the victims of a society that fosters such ungrateful self-centeredness." It made me thankful that in most places we've been, the locals seem aware of our limitations and express gratitude for what they receive.

> In most places we've been, the locals seem aware of our limitations and express gratitude for what they receive.

*

By the last clinic day, Annie still refused to set limits, and the neighborhood became extremely unruly. Word had gotten out on the streets that dentists were at the compound, and a riot almost ensued at the front gate. The strong, local men inside rushed out to contain the problem. We were sad to hear that, as we always desire only goodwill as a result of our efforts.

"Here we are, sitting around until 9:00 a.m. again," Bob complained.

We'd asked to begin earlier so we could see more patients. In America, Bob seats his first patient at 7:00 a.m., but our schedules must change to match the culture. Our last patients left by 6:00 p.m. in Senegal and, due to the heat and trials of the day, we would have preferred to eat an immediate dinner and wind down toward bed. Instead, we waited hours for our evening meal, since the normal dinner time was about 10:00 p.m.

We'd written abstention from alcohol into our team policy, which Sir adamantly enforced in Madagascar the following week.

But Annie actually encouraged wine for dinner, stating, "You can't survive a day in Senegal if you don't drink." Sir, his son, and we didn't, but everyone else drank plenty. Imbibing occurred exclusively with the team present. We were relieved that anyone who might be influenced adversely wasn't witnessing the drinking. We get uneasy if the locals observe alcohol consumption, as it can give the wrong impression about Christians and Americans, especially in cultures where alcoholism is forbidden (Muslim countries) or places where alcoholism remains a devastating curse to many.

> Alcohol consumption can give the wrong impression about Christians and Americans, especially in cultures where alcoholism is forbidden.

After work, our evenings in Dakar started with drinks and salty, sandy peanuts (a leading export of the country). We slouched on the sofas as Michelle started "The Question of the Night Activity." She provided a topic that everyone took his or her turn to answer.

What is the favorite place you've lived?

Tell something unusual that has happened to you.

The booze and the babbling got everyone through until dinner finally materialized three to four hours later. Annie tried to do some of the cooking and drafted team members to help. The team was given instructions on the correct way to cut mangos. The sometimes questionable meals seemed hardly worth waiting for when one's head slumped on the table.

One day Jimmy and some of his young men went deep-sea fishing and flaunted their capture of a six-foot-long marlin, which was unremarkable and bland.

Another night the sewage backed up in the main house, and Bob spent most of the evening up to his shoulders in oozy debris as he unplugged the system. Human waste became very personal to us there, as the neighbors on the other side of the fence just disposed of theirs by throwing it on our side. Annie ranted about that disgusting method for years.

Annie's friend, an intriguing, single, neighborhood German woman, invited us for tea one day. Taking her small subsistence check from Germany, Frau moved to Senegal, originally following a lover who failed her. Frau managed to build a walled compound, complete with a three-bedroom house, a garden, and a small animal shelter. She grew food and flowers, cooked, played a lovely piano she'd acquired, and hired men for any task, including one to guard the place. Her motto of simplicity showcased her home's usefulness, beauty, and joy. Frau lacked only an engulfing faith to complete her philosophy of life, something Annie discussed with her frequently. Her little German retirement check seemed adequate to provide a genteel lifestyle for her, and she fascinated us with her courage, spunk, and slight eccentricity.

*

"Oh, this little African church fits right in with the visualizations I've had all my life!" I gushed as we sauntered there on Sunday.

It resembled the round, thatched hut we slept in, except for its open sides. We stepped over a foot-high wall that kept out the snakes and the critters. About twenty nationals walked in from the surrounding area, and several groups stood under peripheral trees to allow seating for our team. The sweet, soulful African songs carried to the surrounding hills. Although we didn't understand the language, it was apparent that the few, colorfully dressed followers of Christ cherished their beliefs.

> The sweet, soulful African songs carried to the surrounding hills.

"You know, I used to feel cheated over the years when I'd make the effort to attend church and came away with little inspiration. I do feel it's necessary to attend church at least weekly, as the worship, mingling with other Christians, and being open to hearing something that God impresses on me is all important. It happens with our trips, too. I can't get much out of church due to language barriers," I told some of the team as we walked back. "Then I heard something that's helped me. When it comes right down to it—comparing spiritual food to physical food—only babies and old people get hand fed. Healthy adults feed themselves. So I've learned that it's my own responsibility to study the Bible or other spiritual readings, if I am going to maintain my Christian life. It makes me aware of being answerable for my own personal growth."

The young men whom Jimmy worked with organized a soccer team—a boisterous, backyard brood without uniforms. Some boys had shoes, but many remained barefoot. Since Dr. Jerome knew of them previously, he'd purchased soccer outfits which we'd wedged into our various bags. When presented with the gift, the stunned team donned them immediately, swaggering and strutting in their new duds. We watched the first game with great interest, as their matching red shirts, shorts, and socks without a doubt added to their decisive win. Now a proud and mighty force in their glorious garb, we heard they performed with distinction after our departure.

*

We'd planned a sightseeing tour as we completed our clinic week. We were ready and eager to leave at 9:00 a.m., but our zest dispersed after several hours of waiting for the driver. Annie seemed unconcerned, and we'd now accepted that African time did not resemble American time in the least. Finally, our groggy chauffeur showed up, and Annie teased him about sleeping in.

"If we'd realized he'd been only next door, we might've awakened him with thrown rocks at the window," we whispered to each other.

> African time did not resemble American time in the least.

Our driver shrugged as if to say that anything worth doing is worth doing later, but he completely started on poor footing with our team. Due to oppressive heat, we'd opened the bus wide for ventilation by then. (There is little air conditioning in developing countries, and we'd seen none here.)

We drove for a half hour before I looked back from our seat near the front of the bus to notice that Dr. Jerome's face reflected several shades of pea green. Making a pathetic face, he feebly motioned to his stomach. Immediately I changed seats with him, which seemed to help momentarily.

Luckily, it wasn't long before we stopped at a market. Annie and some of the team suddenly disappeared, leaving the rest of us to wander in bewilderment within sight of the bus for an hour. When Annie returned with several who'd shopped (we all wished we'd been included), she asked if we'd like to take the elevator to a top-floor restaurant nearby that boasted a panoramic view of the city.

Identifying it to be like a short Eiffel Tower, I crowed, "Seems like another erector set that's made good."

Without thinking, I hopped onto the crowded elevator. My claustrophobia flooded over me with instant regret as the conveyor lurched to a halt and remained closed. Fighting back a scream by pressing my lips together, I sweated out several minutes until the door flew open. Pushing to the front and out, I fled, glad to take the many steps down to the street. Although some of the team made it to the top and raved about the view, I sighed, satisfied to have survived.

> My claustrophobia flooded over me with instant regret as the conveyor lurched to a halt and remained closed.

Through the afternoon with some sorrow, we explored Goree Island, which is famous as a destination for tourists interested in the Atlantic African slave trade. The island held a depressing museum, with original rooms where captors had kept chained slaves imprisoned awaiting the next ship. At the harrowing and tragic place, one could almost hear the songs of bitterness echoing faintly from the fort's formidable walls.

Later, when we went downtown, Dr. Braden asked Annie if she knew where he could get his camera fixed, and she immediately hailed a taxi, taking off with Dr. and Mrs. Braden. We (including Annie's beloved family member, Dr. Jerome) were once again abandoned on a busy street corner where the bus parked. Unbearable heat in the bus forced us outside, where putrid diesel smoke stung our eyes and nauseated our systems. Soon our water bottles registered empty, but we didn't feel we could leave. We only guessed when they might return.

After several hours our frayed nerves had utterly unwound. Annie and the Bradens finally appeared, happily smiling over the purchase of a new camera and the detour they'd taken to Annie's dentist, whose office occupied vaguely the same neighborhood. Somehow the three didn't think about the other two dentists, who would've been interested in the tour, as well. We've often laughed over the saying: "When you find yourself convinced that the world is moving too fast, all that is needed is to find a bank or a supermarket line" (or a street corner in Senegal, we always add).

Annie remained impulsive during our visit, and we finally just shrugged, saying, "She's been Africanized," meaning that time is not as important and that someone's immediate needs can supersede the welfare of the group. This is often the case in a developing country, as people seem oriented to do what suits them at the time, oblivious to the big picture. Dr. and Mrs. Braden couldn't understand why we seemed peevish, until we explained to them later that we'd been left to wait for them in a very uncomfortable site. Then they apologized. But in the midst of the fracas, we all grew to love Annie for her good intentions and spontaneity, as she tried to help anyone in whatever way she could.

We'd been invited to have dinner on the far side of the city with the Wycliffe Bible Translators at their work offices and neighborhood. A collection of foreigners (some from Europe, but also the brother of a famous author from Colorado Springs) resided there. The missionary sibling exuded intelligence, creativity, and character through the dedication of his life's work in the small, dusty office in Senegal, translating the Bible into a dialect spoken only by a few thousand locals. Blessed with a committed and devoted family, we admired greatly their courage and faithfulness and hoped his acclaimed brother also felt as fulfilled.

"Senegal has twenty official languages and over sixty others spoken throughout the country," the translators told us. "Of the 6,912 languages in the world, 4,845 possess no portion of the Bible published in their language, but most people can access the Bible in some language known to them, however, as many around the world speak several languages."

"Is accessibility a problem, though?" we asked.

"Yes, 85 percent of all Bibles printed today are in English for the 9 percent of the world who read English. Eighty percent of the world's people have never owned a Bible, while Americans keep an average of four in every household." The great need sobered us as the translators shared their hearts.

> "Eighty percent of the world's people have never owned a Bible, while Americans keep an average of four in every household."

We couldn't wait to move on after our week in Senegal, already somewhat sensitized to the different personalities on our team. I also still felt uneasy around Michelle, our hygienist, especially when she frequently showed her personal photo album to any national person, regardless of socio-economic status. Her album displayed her nice house in Michigan, the condominium she snow-birded to in Arizona, her striking church, and other pictures that showed an abundant life in America. Should we be showing the luxuries we have, when by choice or chance others don't or can't pursue it for themselves? I wondered. Bob and I found it embarrassing, and it helped us weigh the necessity of all our "necessities."

> Should we be showing the luxuries we have,
> when by choice or chance others don't or can't pursue it for themselves?

Also, Michelle—who'd probably insist that Mona Lisa needs eye shadow—taught our sweet, naive Pam how to apply makeup, which didn't seem appropriate in this setting. Pam had come along as Dr. Jerome's assistant and became Annie's disciple, our intrepid lead missionary. Ready to start college, home-schooled Pam displayed a conscientious and innocent nature. She worked diligently, helping our hygienist in the clinic and then becoming Annie's right-hand "daughter." Her unabashed curiosity and lack of experience caused her to adore everything about Senegal—although the rest of us who had traveled more widely found the country to be one of the most trying we'd experienced.

*

South Africa

After Senegal, we flew to South Africa, where we'd planned a short safari, after which we'd fly to Madagascar to continue the mission. From America, Dr. and Mrs. Braden and his "harem" had booked an upscale safari separate from the rest of the team. They probably wanted to make merry beyond what they thought Sir would allow. Not that it mattered any more since most of them ignored our agreements in Senegal.

The rest of us went to a cozy little area of Kruger National Park, where we delighted in a night ride and a day trip viewing hippos, rhinos, zebras, wallabies, water buffalos, giraffes, monkeys, alligators, and lions galore. One of our team members kept rising to take pictures, which we'd been warned not to do. As long as we stayed quiet and still—and the lions remained well fed—we'd been assured the animals wouldn't leap into the vehicles.

"Sit," I hissed at him. "They might make cherry cobbler of you any second. Down now!"

"Life can be the messy pits," he retorted but settled slowly.

"I can hear them cracking the bones with their teeth," Bob exclaimed as our Land Rover rolled unobtrusively within ten feet of a pride of lions and their fresh kill of a baby giraffe. The lions feasted and farted obliviously, much to our delight and disgust. They made soggy mincemeat of their prey in moments. The mother giraffe watched from the perimeter, and we whispered that she looked helpless and distraught, although maybe we projected our own parenting sympathies into her expression.

I sighed. "Think about the deepest longings we feel on earth as parents for our children's safety. These yearnings must be mere glimmers of the coveting ache God feels for us if we become lost to Him."

*

Madagascar

After our break, we felt refreshed as we flew to Madagascar via Johannesburg. It had been three years since we'd been in Madagascar when my father had passed away. The New Street Youth Center, completed by the combined efforts of a local construction team, was supported financially by churches in America and a succession of short-term Work and Witness construction teams spaced throughout the years.

Madagascar

Old Street
Youth Center

We stayed in a lovely guest area on the third floor, right above a large, clean meeting room that we turned into a dental clinic. The construction showcased American standards, demonstrated by the spacious apartments, bathrooms, kitchens, and conference areas—all with wonderfully large windows.

Our clinic days progressed smoothly as we cranked out dentistry, seeing most of the 350 students who attended school at the center. The new, winsome Malagasy female physician loved the children and, although willing to watch us extract teeth, showed little eagerness to learn as Dr. Selam had on our previous visit.

Dr. Selam and his family came to see us at the center in a snub-nosed, used car new to them, but decrepit and patched. The clunker required jump-starting, which could be only accomplished backwards down a car-lined, narrow, one-way street with oncoming traffic. They assigned this feat to Bob since Dr. Selam appeared to be a novice driver. Bob grinned and waved as they roared off after the challenging rescue. We still continue our friendship through an exchange of emails.

Madagascar

New Street
Youth Center

A few irritations soon developed at the clinic. One of the dentists wanted to compete by announcing the numbers of patients he'd treated. If one dentist is bent on productivity as the main consideration, this attitude becomes uncomfortable and competitive for others. This didn't mesh with Bob's philosophy of providing the best care for the most people possible, without stress or pressure for everyone involved. Also, our sterilization lady shouted "Fire in the Hole!" every time she released the pressure on the sterilizing pot. It was entertaining until the piercing whistle of steam and her shrill announcement occurred in the middle of a dental procedure.

After an intense week of dentistry, the team drove the four hours to the Lemur Park, where we'd mulled the death of my father on our last trip. Although a quiet retreat before, this time an abundance of locals and foreigners infringed on the peace we remembered. The group's alcohol imbibers continued with their bottles, although drinking in public had been listed as taboo in the trip's contract. Sir directed this portion of the trip. (We'd never figured out who'd presided in Senegal). Now Sir stepped up to reign in our group. He desired that our team who represented a Christian church give the best impression possible to any observers.

On the first night, Sir walked through the restaurant and saw Michelle sitting by herself, communing with spirits in a wine glass. Sir felt he should remind her of our agreement and faced her artful pout and unyielding pose.

The next day one of the local staff members from the Street Youth Center planned to head back that morning, a day early. Michelle decided she'd rather clean children's teeth in the clinic than stay with the group. It surprised us that Sir let her go, as we do not believe in splitting up a team if at all possible. No one else attempted to drink in public.

It was a lesson for us—to make sure that all team members consent to necessary restrictions of any trip, since we represent sponsors who have taken stands on issues. We decided that, in most cases, it's better to take team members who agree with the beliefs of the churches and the organizations we travel with. Several of the people on this trip had little religious leanings. That at least should have been discussed ahead.

*

Once again, back at the Street Youth Center, we worked with the missionary who had accused us of discrimination last time for saying that the blacks in Madagascar would present more difficult extractions than white people. We just couldn't win with him! He asked Bob to extract his partially impacted wisdom teeth. Although they hadn't been problematic, the missionary worried they'd act up sometime as he served overseas. He wondered if it might be advantageous to remove them during the dentists' visit.

"Since you return to America regularly," Bob counseled, "it would be best if you wait for your next trip home, where there would be less chance of complications and more thorough follow-up, if needed."

The next day, we glanced up and saw our statistic-keeping dentist seating the missionary in his chair to remove the controversial wisdom teeth, with the hygienist standing by. Enlisting Michelle's support, the missionary hadn't dropped the issue. We'll never know if he had manipulated the other two dental professionals or whether the dentist or the hygienist had known of Bob's decision.

"It appears he went right around our advice," Bob whispered to me, shaking his head. "If Mom says 'no,' go ask Dad…or something like that."

We didn't hear how the missionary healed after the hour-long, difficult procedure, but we all left the next day. His recovery couldn't have been easy.

Sir's married daughter and husband from Canada met us in Madagascar, much to our delight, as her husband worked as a renowned chef. They stayed in our apartment at the Street Youth Center, and we enjoyed the luscious meals they concocted.

While there, Sir celebrated his seventy-fifth birthday at a party arranged for him, complete with four hundred cupcakes and everyone in attendance from the Street Youth Center. Since he'd partnered with the school for many years, everyone adored him. We thought it special to be there on his big day, and it turned out to be the largest birthday party we had ever attended!

*

South Africa

On the way back from Madagascar, coordinating flights required a day's layover in Johannesburg, South Africa, one of the forty largest metropolitan areas in the world. The modern city, with a population over three million, also claimed surrounding suburbs of another eight million people. Although most of the team shopped, the historical significance of the area intrigued us.

Experiencing Soweto, a township established by the apartheid government for migrant workers (a type of shanty town), struck us as sobering. Its presence represented many who'd been banned there under racial discrimination policies. Surprised to be there on the annual holiday commemorating the racial struggles, we attended a museum with pictures and words describing the hostilities and the conflicts so many endured for racial equality. We mingled with many African young people and families. Since Johannesburg was a British colony in the recent past, the signs and the billboards were printed in English. On our tour of Nelson Mandela's home, the placards that related his life story were in English.

The flight back was the longest we'd taken anywhere. I gritted my teeth as we sat on one plane for nineteen hours. The flight stopped in Dakar, Senegal, for refueling for an hour, but passengers couldn't deplane—not that we hankered to after our mission there a week earlier!

"Although this group had its idiosyncrasies, I'm thrilled we served so many," Bob celebrated.

"Yeah, the petty hardships of any trip quickly fade as we realize that every team member did the best they could within their own contexts," I admitted. "We are all odd characters in our own ways, and we know that you and I also probably bug others without being aware of it. I guess there will always be personality and ideological differences, but we can't let those disturb us too much. Making small differences in lives—even in the lives of our team members—is our goal. I stretched some, too."

Michelle surprised me on the last day of the trip, by pulling me aside to say, "Of all the women on this trip, I would like most to emulate your servant's heart and attitude. I trust God will continue to help me grow."

I luxuriated in a little moment of thankfulness to the Lord for giving me the peace and the patience to see this trip through and for allowing this snatch of affirmation. We know the trip is never about us, and we must leave the results with God.

Feeling like salty vagabonds, with a lifetime supply of frequent flyer miles and thick passports, we'd learned to keep our mission bags packed—with duplicates of essentials and clothes always ready to go. We'd heard somewhere that travel is 90 percent anticipation and 10 percent recollection, so we always liked to have a trip dangling out there to dream about.

Travel is 90 percent anticipation and 10 percent recollection.

After the recent outlandish, often taxing, cultures of Mongolia, Egypt, Senegal, and Madagascar, we craved some good ol' Latino lovin'…but didn't know that I'd be tested by events that involved my two worst fears.

ECUADOR

Wonders on the Equator

* * *

ECUADOR REIGNED NEAR THE TOP OF OUR TRAVEL WISH LIST, declaring premier bio-diversity status, due to its popularity as a birder's paradise that included the famed Galapagos Islands.

"You bet we'll come," our dear dental friends, Dr. Frank and Shelly, enthused delightedly when approached.

Since I was teaching again, Bob and I had slowed our travel down some. We squeezed our mission trips in during school breaks, including this week-long spring break opportunity. Dr. Frank and Shelly, our previous partners to Argentina and Guatemala, loved going South, as Shelly liked speaking Spanish. The four of us banded together to form a fierce little traveler team. We found the saying true: "We cherish our friends not by their ability to amuse us, but by ours to amuse them." People who are comfortably easy to be with and who will indulge us by laughing at our silly jokes are adored. Our congenial chemistry came from small-town mentalities and down-home, wacky humor.

"Look," Bob reported, checking statistics, "Ecuador is about the same size as Colorado but has fourteen million people compared to Colorado's three million. The country is a natural paradise, with over nine living species per square kilometer. First place in the world regarding species per area, it's one of the smallest countries of South America."

"We'll be in the Andes Mountains," I said. "I saw that Quito is more than 9,000 feet above sea level on a plateau, so it should be quite temperate, if not cool. What do we know about the people?"

"The country is 95 percent Catholic with a democratic government. The official language is Spanish, but the indigenous population speaks Quichua or one of eighteen different languages among native communities."

Ecuador, a mission location for the same wonderful ministry group that had sponsored us in Peru, Acapulco, and Belize, felt right. We liked the in-country staff immediately when we met at the Quito airport late on a Saturday night. They dropped us at a lovely guest house operated by the first Christian missionary radio station in the world; a network that provides daily programming in Ecuador and throughout South America. "This is one of the most beautiful places we've stayed during a mission," Bob marveled.

It was complete with "house parents" from America who ran it. They provided a luscious breakfast, including a thought-out Bible reading. The radio ministry supported an impressive, modern hospital close by, which we toured. National staffers now manage the well-run facility.

*

That first Sunday morning we attended an exuberant local church service and then spent our five clinic days at five different churches in the area. Our missionary hostess seemed squeamish about helping us interpret, but after she realized we wouldn't hurt the patients, she jumped in and quickly became a favorite nurturer and translator.

Each morning we arrived at a new place (wherever they took us), set up, and started seeing patients until lunch. Church women provided yummy, local Hispanic fare, which included rice, beans, and usually chicken or beef seasoned with authentic flair. We ate copious amounts of the hot, fortifying food, much to the pleasure of our hosts. We laughingly realized, however, that these three square meals a day would soon yield very round people (not to mention the effects of the beans that Dr. Frank, who is from Texas, called "whistle berries").

> Church women provided yummy, local Hispanic fare, which included rice, beans, and usually chicken or beef seasoned with authentic flair.

"I'm getting *thick* and tired of all this food," I joked. "I'm going to have to move my belt over two decimal points at least! But I hope they don't stop outdoing themselves."

"Let's just eat, drink, and be merry, and tomorrow we'll diet," Bob advised on our last day.

We worked each day, with most of our patients being church members or staff, although we did reach out to the local areas to draw attention to the church's presence in the neighborhood.

"The best thing about these clinics is that they've arranged for a local pastor to present Bible lessons through chalk drawings to the families waiting," I told Bob who'd been "down in the mouth" doing dentistry for hours. "You've got to come see his enthusiastic illustrations of spiritual and biblical truths through his powerful chalk illustrations! Some people ask faith questions and are gaining new insights and answers to their life issues. This is great stuff!"

Even though weary at night, we dined at local staff homes (usually indigenous people, but sometimes American homes of full-time staff in the country). Local families cooked and ate with us, following safety guidelines, and our trip fees covered the cost of the food for everyone present. This proved less expensive and safer than eating at restaurants. We also heard awe-inspiring stories of God's impact on their lives.

Through an interpreter one beautiful, dark-haired lady told us over dinner, "I got 'lost' from my family when I was four, and no one could ever tell me what happened. I've always wondered if my kin intentionally abandoned me. I've been told authorities found me wandering alone. I remember only successive foster homes until I turned sixteen, where I experienced abuse and overwork without knowing anything about my roots."

We couldn't comprehend that rejection and grieved for her lack of loved ones who'd advocate for her. This striking lady became a true servant of God, ministering to the poor and the spiritually lost, with a compassion that reflected her own past. Situated at the end of an airport runway, her small apartment had barely escaped destruction weeks prior when a plane ran off the airstrip, stopping just short of her dwelling.

> "I remember only successive foster homes until I turned sixteen, where I experienced abuse and overwork without knowing anything about my roots."

Each day we carried all our dental equipment, which included seven large suitcases weighing fifty pounds each. Every night we stowed them in our safely gated guest house area. But when we arrived at the airport apartment, we had to park on the street. Once again we unloaded the luggage to store in our host's hallway, since it wasn't considered safe outside. We'd been cautioned that the car would quite possibly be broken into as thieves looked for valuables. It was challenging to hoist those bags in and out of places two to four times each day.

The two things I had most feared happened on this trip, and I survived! I hoped I'd never get stuck by a needle, but it happened. At times we've taught a local person to do sterilization, which is especially helpful when we have more than one efficient dentist contributing dirty instruments. Since an outgoing, local teenager at one of the churches desired to help, I taught her some basics of sterilizing but soon found she wasn't mature enough to really grasp it. She wasn't instinctually wary of the sharp instruments, and at one point, she left an uncapped needle on a tray with many other items. As I went to grab it, the girl moved abruptly, and the used needle punctured my finger.

The two things I had most feared happened on this trip, and I survived!

Knowing a "needle-stick" is always a dreaded event, I was irritated I hadn't seen it coming. We hoped we had traced the needle to a patient who didn't seem high risk, but we weren't entirely sure. A negative HIV test some time later relieved us. The lesson we learned is not to trust just anyone to work with the sharp, and often dangerous, instruments. It requires someone with basic medical training, who understands the perils of contaminated items and discernment of sterile and non-sterile articles. We are careful to distinguish abilities before accepting help, no matter how enthusiastic or willing—for their own safety and the protection of all. From then on, we allowed only dentists to handle the needles, placing them into a used, plastic water bottle kept at each dental station as a "sharps container," which burned intact when full. Therefore, it removes the dangers for inexperienced assistants, interpreters, or sterilization people.

The second undesirable event happened when an American missionary surgeon came in to observe Bob, and I again encountered my nemesis—the distraction test. The whistling sterilizer pot required removal from the hot plate, but I hadn't heard the timer ring above the confusion in the clinic. Preoccupied with assisting Bob and talking with the surgeon, I suddenly realized that all the water had evaporated from the smoking pot, causing the rubber seal to melt and rendering the pot unusable. Bob warns sterilizing personnel each trip about the importance of the water in the pot. Humiliated at the smoky smells and black mess, I also realized the immensity of the problem.

Shazzam! For the first time, Bob had included an extra rubber seal ring, which made the sterilizing pot once again intact. "You saved the day, Bobby!" I crooned in gratitude.

My ongoing challenge is to stay focused on a task—a precarious feat, at least for me, since I like to multi-task in everyone else's business. "It's inherent for a teacher to be aware of all that's going on," I explained to Bob. "The only way to escape unwanted incidents is to do nothing, to be nothing, and to say nothing. I'd have to be a robot at your side. A mistake is at least proof that I'm trying to accomplish something!"

When out of our comfort zones, one of the most important lessons is to be kind and charitable to ourselves, as so many varied factors make life complicated at each new place on a busy trip.

> "A mistake is at least proof
> that I'm trying to accomplish something!"

We gained some great advice from William James, the American psychologist and philosopher: "Three things in human life are important. The first is to be kind. The second is to be kind. And the third is to be kind." Judith Martin, "Miss Manners" says, "If you can't be kind, at least be vague." That is why we give everyone at least three "freebies" on our trips. Freebies are chances to do something utterly stupid and not get scolded for it. We laugh that they are "get out of jail free" cards. After all, we truly are only human!

*

We spent one overnight at Otavalo, a small town northeast of Quito, known for its large market where indigenous people sell handicrafts to tourists. Since it was spring break, we ran into vacationing American groups of students on sight-seeing tours, missions, or college-course studies. We worked in a church member's house out in a pastoral area and adored the pleasing temperatures and fresh mountain air. The locals served lunch in their kitchen that overlooked a stunning, mountainous vista.

I effusively extolled the wondrous, magical energy of it all. "I could live here forever!" I exclaimed. "Everywhere I turn is a screen-saver scene! I'll have to take pictures to rotate on my computer at home."

The local people stopped their Spanish conversation, catching my excitement but unable to decipher my words. As the translation became clear, their faces beamed in pleasure to realize the foreigners fancied their native land.

While Dr. Frank and his staff were at lunch, his camera disappeared from the bedroom their "dental office" occupied. They'd left several windows open that a passerby could easily access. This reminded us that luxury items are never secure anywhere and must be kept close. The likelihood of theft is high everywhere, even in America, where we once had a camera stolen from our hotel room in New York. We recommend the smallest of digital cameras that

48

can be carried in pockets, so that it's also readily available for those photo opportunities that wait only seconds before being lost forever.

*

On the way back to Quito, we visited the Cuicocha Lake, clear and unspoiled as it lay in the crater of a volcanic mountain. During a small boat tour, we explored the eco-reserve and pristine surroundings, worshipping in what seemed a scenic, natural shrine. We wanted to stay in the moment as long as possible, embracing the sensations and the beauty that overpowered our senses.

The towns all contained local character and charm, something we're losing in communities in America that have become homogenized with formula restaurants and look-alike exits off tedious and tiresome freeways. We feasted on excellent food, including prawns, shrimp, and tasty plantain and peanut-based dishes. Succulent fruits included sweet bananas, tree grapes, passion fruit, and peach palms.

> The towns all contained local character and charm, something we're losing in communities in America that have become homogenized.

As items seemed delightfully different, we acquired more in the markets of Ecuador than usual. The fine quality and excellent prices of woven tablecloths, alpaca (an animal related to a llama) fur jackets, and wool sweaters for our children and grandchildren packed easily, along with many tiny dolls for gifts. Dr. Frank wanted a "Panama" hat—an Ecuadorean invention—known as a "Jipijapa" there, after the town that claims its origin.

On the Saturday afternoon before we left, we showed up at the headgear factory, disappointed to find it closed. Dr. Frank found a jaunty Panama hat in a nearby, upscale shop, but he probably paid premium price.

I couldn't resist a silly joke. "So, what was the dentist doing in Panama? Looking for a root canal! Bad, huh?"

Everyone groaned.

While we thought the alpaca jackets were outstanding, we overheard our son-in-law whisper to our daughter that he'd wished he'd had it for the "ugly sweater" day they held at work. We hoped he was teasing, and later our daughter told us they'd seen that very jacket in an upscale catalog for 100 dollars. Relieved we'd only invested fifteen dollars to buy a jacket for each of our children and their spouses, we've learned that clothing purchases rarely please others.

"Can you believe we stood on the equator?" I asked. "I knew it crossed the country—that's what gives it the name *Ecuador,* the Spanish word for 'equator.'"

"Ecuador hasn't much variation in daylight hours during the course of a year, either," Bob noted. "Except for a few minutes resulting from a slight wobble in the earth as it rotates, sunrise and sunset are always at 6:00 a.m. and 6:00 p.m."

"This is funny, though," Dr. Frank said. "Look, there are two different tourist locations, a mile from each other. Each boasts that the equator passes through their area, but they both can't be right!" Our hosts took us to the one thought to be the accurate equator line by GPS, and it provided a fascinating tour. Various stations showed phenomenon that can be experienced only on the equator. A sink demonstrated how the water flows straight down at the equator. When the sink is moved only a short distance on either side of the equator, water swirls clockwise in the southern hemisphere and counter-clockwise in the northern hemisphere in response to the spinning earth. We experienced it all three ways.

An egg will stand on the head of a nail and balance due to the forces at the equator. Bob accepted a challenge to succeed at this still-difficult feat, and he accomplished it with his steady dental hands. Receiving a signed certificate to document it, this encounter scored high on his thrill-ometer. A small museum displayed diversely monstrous, deceased bugs and shrunken heads that extinct tribes fashioned from their enemies' skulls. Blow-gun demonstrations with available ancient weapons attracted our men, who blew feathered darts out of the six-foot-long tubes, hitting targets quite adeptly.

> An egg will stand on the head of a nail and balance
> due to the forces at the equator.

The trip, full of serendipitous surprises as they all seem to be, prompted Dr. Frank and Shelly to rave that it'd been their best foray to date, even when pitted against previous vacations they'd shared in glamorous parts of the world. We agreed.

*

I missed returning to school the Monday after spring break due to the flight schedule but returned on Tuesday animated over the success of the project. We had succeeded in showing the love of God through the relief of dental pain.

However, my colleagues, especially the director who'd covered my class for the one-day absence, wanted to hear nothing of it. She had rearranged the classroom, discarded some essential supplies, and made major changes to my functional structure. This difference of opinion, along with other leadership offenses, finally resulted in my resignation at the end of the year.

I realized firsthand through this experience that our true friends are those great people who make us feel that what we're doing counts for something. We avoid the small people who belittle our ambitions and dreams.

I then accepted a substitute position with the largest school district in the city. With forty elementary schools, I could work whenever I desired. That better employment position gave us the freedom to travel anytime during the school year for missions.

An even better reason to leave my preschool job was that we now had four grandchildren (two more would follow), and we were passionately committed to being attentive, affirming influences. Our love for these little creations of God is so strong that we agree with the Welsh proverb, which says, "Grandchildren bring a perfect and pure love that may not be obtainable in any other way." What a difference when we can have a carefree, fun-filled time with our grandchildren, giving our children their turn at gripping the armrests and wondering what to do at the crib sides.

But we're gratified to see that our kids are conscientious parents. On our part, Bob and I do try to follow the guidelines our young adults have set for their children, realizing that the humorous joke of loading the grandchildren with sugar before sending them home is irresponsible behavior. We treasure the fact that all of our children are involved in churches and are bringing our grandchildren to faith at young ages. One four-year-old granddaughter was dancing intently one day and glowing radiantly. When we asked what she was doing, she pronounced, "I'm praising God!"

An important quote by Chuck Colson, in a grandparent forum, cautioned, "Too many culture-weary Christians have retreated to the pews. We have not fulfilled our responsibility to be salt and light in the world, and to do so in a winsome way. It's one reason many of our grandchildren have turned away from the faith."

> "Too many culture-weary Christians have retreated to the pews. We have not fulfilled our responsibility to be salt and light in the world."
> CHUCK COLSON

We are so fortunate to have one grandson and three granddaughters born to our daughter, Shari, living within a mile of our home. I thrill to watch them at intervals each week. Their parents do work at jobs with hours conducive to family life.

Our other two granddaughters, belonging to our son, Dan, live five hours away, but we still see them often. We chuckled when one of those girls said, "We'd move by you, Grandma and Grandpa, but our house is too heavy!" We feel encouraged by our children to continue with missions, and hope for the day when they may join us again along with the grandchildren.

A missionary friend found us at church after we got back from Ecuador. "We need a dentist to go on a medical exchange to Cuba in several months, and Diane is welcome, due to her nursing license. Only medical people are eligible for entrance to Cuba right now. Interested?"

"We'd love to," we responded immediately.

However, I didn't dare ask for more time off after the recent response at school from the difficult director. Bob decided to go with what became an all-male, medical team of five. I was disgruntled when, shortly after Bob's team left for Cuba, my school director allowed another teacher to go on a month's trip to Korea to visit her family. But I laughed to myself when the director restructured that woman's room, as well.

So, Bob went to Cuba without me and came back saying he never wanted to do that again—along with other interesting pronouncements!

CUBA

Dreams of a Better Life

* * *

ALTHOUGH CUBA PROVED A FASCINATING PLACE for Bob to visit, it wielded its intimidations. Politically, in 2008, the United States held an isolation policy against Cuba with hopes that Communism would fail. Gaining access into the country required special governmental permission. Approval only came through extensive application paperwork and justifications of the trip as a "medical exchange of information."

"We especially need you, Bob," pitched the representative of the Christian-sponsoring agency. "Since the head of the Christian Medical and Dental association in Cuba is a dentist, we encourage you to support and to interact with him."

"Okay, but I'm not sure I get the politics," Bob replied.

"The sponsoring agency brings Christianity into politically problematic parts of the world, places like Vietnam and Cuba. Focusing on medical education and training to facilitate relationships with the medical leadership in Cuba, we hope to introduce Christianity into a society that appears to be opening to faith."

"What is the relationship between the medical profession and the current leadership?" Bob asked the team leader, still confused.

"Historically, authority in Cuba comes from the most educated professionals, such as physicians and dentists. By reaching them for Christianity, we strategize that as Cuba undergoes major leadership changes in the future, there will be Christian medical and dental personnel available to fill directive roles. You're the first dentist we've taken into the country to assess how dentistry can be used in Cuba and to support this dentist who is the current head of the Christian and Medical society in Cuba."

"I'll do what I can," Bob promised.

Introduced to the medical staff in the main hospital in Havana, Bob spent his first day with the chief oral surgeon there. Dismayed by the run-down facilities and the lack of medical instruments and supplies, Bob found that only one functioning handpiece equipped the operating suite. When Bob observed the extraction of a third molar, he noted the clinic didn't possess a "301 elevator" tool, a basic surgical instrument for removing teeth. The barest minimal cache of instruments and supplies pained Bob's heart.

"Cuba lost most of our economic support after the fall of the Soviet Union in 1990," the oral surgeon told Bob. "Together with the embargo imposed by the United States, Communism isn't working well."

"What does that mean for your lifestyle?" Bob asked.

"Well, the majority of available cars are still from the 1950s and '60s, prior to the revolution. After 1990, the possibility of new houses or apartments disappeared, and there's no money for paint or repairs on current houses. When people marry, they have no choice but to live with parents or in-laws, so multi-generations occupy all households."

"Wow, so many of the freedoms we take for granted are unavailable in Cuba because the State owns everything," Bob exclaimed, seeing the dentist's sad nod. Required to pay for an appointed Cuban tour guide (political advisor), Bob and the medical team endured constant chaperoning.

"You have to be careful around him," the team leader advised Bob, who sometimes questioned the official about sensitive issues. "You shouldn't ask him about Castro, life in Cuba, the government, and what he would like to know about America…"

"But he's just a normal person, tasked to do a job, and open to discussion on a variety of topics. It appears he wants things to be different in his country but feels his limited opportunities. He's trying to function within the system, and I like to interact with him," Bob countered.

"Well, puhlease be cautious," the leader warned.

Bob's team soon discovered that two monetary systems existed within the country—one for the Cubans and another for tourists. This scheme made it possible to gouge those visiting Cuba by charging in excess, while controlling the nationals on their low wages. Cubans were not allowed to eat or to stay in the tourist hotels, and few Cubans could have afforded it, anyway. The attractive tourist areas, regulated and supervised by the government, catered mainly to Canadians and Europeans, since the United States embargo kept American vacationers away. In conversation with the pastor who sponsored the group, Bob said, "I haven't seen one boat on this beautiful island."

Two monetary systems existed within the country—
one for the Cubans and another for tourists.

"There's an easy explanation. If a Cuban can set foot on American soil—a short ninety miles away—they're granted instant asylum, given financial support, English classes, housing, and employment by the American government."

"So the most sought-after possession is a boat."

"Exactly! My father owned a boat and kept it locked up. The boat, stolen by a group of escapees to America, was soon identified when they were caught. They—and my father—received prison sentences. My father had committed the crime of allowing his boat to be stolen! After he'd served his time, he sold his boat since it seemed impossible to keep it safe in a country where so many people desperately wished to flee the island. We later heard the boat had been burglarized from the new owners, and the thieves successfully made it to America. I'm sure the new owners paid dearly!"

> "My father had committed the crime
> of allowing his boat to be stolen!"

When Bob visited Miami, he toured one of the centers that adopted the Cuban "boat people." Whether in Miami or on the island, Bob communicated with Cubans who all loved America and desired to live and to prosper in the United States.

*

On the second day, the chief oral surgeon took Bob to the dental school in Havana in his "very old, beat-up piece of junk" (as the surgeon described it). As one of the privileged few in the country who owned a car, the surgeon push-started it for every outing. Although the driver's door didn't open, the auto delivered them to the dental school. Another requirement in Cuba is that those with cars must stop to pick up others who desire a ride until the car is full. Though an admirable idea in the purest sense of ecology, efficiency, and altruism, the government regulations easily embittered the populace.

The associate dean at the dental school toured Bob around, demonstrating the almost-nonfunctional, forty-year-old equipment. Most dental chairs, although available, had lost their height-adjusting ability many years ago. Necessities absent in most treatment areas included suction, air and water syringes, overhead lights, sinks, air-conditioning, and instruments.

One clinic area where Bob couldn't visit supposedly contained a show place that included a leading-edge dental facility reserved for the privileged few. Dentists told Bob that locations remained direly deficient in the outlying areas also.

"Cuban dentists and doctors do well to exist with few educational materials, supplies, and equipment," his host commented. "Only the top 5 percent of students qualify for dental studies, with about 90 percent female. The quality of dental students and instructors in Cuba is remarkable. English becomes a mandatory course of study for all dental and medical students as most of the professional medical literature is printed in English. Textbooks and journals are too expensive, so the Internet becomes an invaluable resource. We have many teaching programs and commendable students and instructors but have not been equipped properly or supplied since the fall of the Soviet Union."

"Are there any private dentists?" Bob asked.

"Absolutely not! The expectation is that all dentists will work for the government—with a universal payment of about thirty dollars a month—little more than a regular laborer earns. We're forced to endorse communism, after all. Cuba prides itself on medical and dental care for everyone, but in reality many don't get it for a variety of reasons. Most of the dentists find a way to do some moonlighting—working after hours for a fee—and capitalism is tolerated to a degree, if you pay the right people. Don't tell anyone I said that!"

"The expectation is that all dentists will work for the government— with a universal payment of about thirty dollars a month."

"What a shame for the professionals." Bob could clearly see their predicament.

"Cuba exports medical and dental professionals to underdeveloped countries in exchange for oil, money, and supplies. A major problem they've encountered is that once these medical personnel are out of Cuba, they try to find a way to seek asylum in another country. They don't want to come back to a system that makes them unhappy. Cuba limits those they send out of the country to people who have much to lose if they don't return. The loved ones left behind might be abused or jailed if the loaned worker doesn't return."

"Hmm, that's control!" Bob felt for the oppressed and dispirited people.

*

After a few days of interacting with the dental and the medical personnel in Havana, the team left the city to join a Christian gathering of religious leaders on a mini-retreat. The warm, spiritual dentist who headed the Christian Medical and Dental Society in Cuba was doing his utmost to be a witness for Christ.

"Supplies and equipment in Cuba are in such short supply that patients often try to get dental amalgam, composites, and anesthesia from relatives in America or on the black market before they go for dental treatment," one Cuban dentist told Bob. "I'm not proud of this, but I often don't have dental anesthesia. When I'm in short supply, I tell my patients: 'I will use this precious amount of anesthesia to numb your tooth before we extract it if you will read this Bible tract. Otherwise I will have to use it on the next patient.'"

Bob donated a curing light for setting dental fillings (costing about $1,000 in America), given by World Dental Relief. When presented from Christian dentists in America, the Cuban shed tears, as he could never hope to have one and needed it to treat his patients. Bob's impact on the trip resulted in relationships with Cuban Christian and non-Christian dentists through friendly support and goodwill.

"There's not a place for dentists from America to do dentistry in Cuba, for there are local dentists wanting to take care of their people," Bob reported to the sponsoring mission group. "No dentist can take dental equipment into Cuba, as weight is restricted by America's embargo to forty pounds per traveler, including carry-on luggage. Shipping containers remain expensive and difficult. Even if supplies make it into Cuba, the government would probably confiscate them and distribute to their own credit. I saw that done with another Christian medical organization while there."

After Bob's description, I speculated, "Sounds like Cuba endures as a fascinating place with great potential to be an island paradise."

"Absolutely," Bob concurred. "The people persevered with hospitality, intelligence, and hard work. Many show strong Christian beliefs, and the country is granting more religious freedoms as leaders discover faith provides hope and stability to the people. Most Cubans feel oppressed by the governmental system they forcibly serve, knowing their standard of living lingers at a low level. They envision this will soon change and look forward to seeing Cuba as a great nation in the near future."

> "Most Cubans feel oppressed by the governmental system they forcibly serve."

Bob's interesting interlude on this communistic island contrasted with our previous perceptions of post-communistic communities through our trips to Ukraine and Mongolia. Those countries had both struggled down a weary road to overcome deprivations imposed upon them by communism.

*

About this time we became aware of a great American movement that helped the neediest receive dental relief. This emerging concept has stirred nationwide attention as volunteers contribute dental care to the underserved and the indigent in many states at no charge to the patients. This non-profit, nonsectarian organization is funded totally by donations and seeks "to restore dignity to the sick, poor, and homeless by healing through love."

Our own involvement began when the Colorado Dental Association started this annual event in 2007. Each year 150-200 Colorado dentists and 300 dental personnel, including hygienists, assistants, and laboratory techs, as well as about 700 other volunteers, help about 1,500 suffering patients in a weekend extravaganza. Valued at over a million dollars annually, this dental care is provided during a two-day clinic at different sites across Colorado. Other states that have instituted their own dental weekends include Virginia, Kansas, North Carolina, Nebraska, Arkansas, Connecticut, and Iowa, with more coming on board each year.

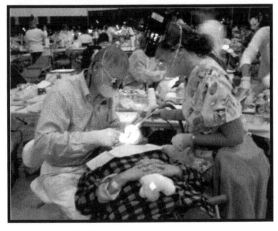

A warehouse and a national office in Kansas presently house a semi-truck and portable equipment to operate a portable dental clinic of 120 chairs that can be transported to the various state locations for these clinics.

So far we have worked at five of the clinics that have been held in different parts of the state: Alamosa (SE), Loveland (North Central), Brighton (north of Denver), Colorado Springs, and Pueblo. Bob has managed the restorative dentistry section in later years, supervising around sixty dentists and their assistants. So many indigent patients have been treated, and we received hugs and genuine thanks for the impact this weekend clinic has on those served. Several patients told us that they were job hunting and that their interviews would be enhanced with an improved smile. Others talked about living with dental pain that was now relieved.

One young man seemed especially inspired by the volunteers' giving and wanted to pay it back personally by doing something for us. The Colorado Springs clinic gave patients a list of organizations who needed volunteers so that they could "pay it forward," and other states have adopted this practice of encouraging patients to help in other community service projects. One man who received free care in the first clinic in Alamosa now returns to help in the clinics around Colorado each year. We receive pleasure in serving the needy in our own country, as well as internationally.

Our next overseas trip would take us to the poorest, post-communistic country in Eastern Europe—Moldova—bringing unexpected tragedy that kindled our compassion.

MOLDOVA

Where in the World Is That?

* * *

"DID YOU SMUGGLE BIBLES behind the Iron Curtain into Eastern Europe in the 1960s?" we asked the tall Dutchman and his spunky, blonde wife at the church social.

"Precisely. We attempted to strengthen and to support the underground Christian Church until the revolution began around 1989. The law actually forbids mention of God in communistic countries, and even 'best friends' or neighbors might spy and report on each other for the police. The communist state believed and taught that God didn't exist. The state was god."

I shivered. "Must've been dangerous."

"Exactly. We had some brushes with the government in unexpected inspections and such," they acknowledged. "But we stayed safe and have established a ministry now due to the connections we made in those years."

Today, more than 100 million people under the age of twenty-five live in Eastern Europe, with less than 1 percent of them embracing evangelical Christianity. After decades of hopelessness, freedom swept across the post-Soviet countries in the early 1990s, and Bible believers requested our friends provide training to local leaders who could reach children, youth, and families.

"We'd like to go to serve some of your people with short-term dentistry," we offered.

"Well, the poorest and neediest of all live in Moldova, with a population of around four million. The nation is east of Romania, although at one time they were joined."

Moldova, incorporated into the Soviet Union at the close of World War II, became independent in 1991, although Russian forces remained. The country depended on Soviet energy until 2005, when they banned Moldovan agricultural products, coupled with a decision to double the price Moldova paid for Russian natural gas. With the resulting economic quagmire, more than 20 percent of young workers immediately left for employment abroad.

"Wow!" I exclaimed. "Sounds like a desperate place. We'd be honored to go."

We always want to support underdogs. Bob especially enjoys assisting the unlikely winner. When neighborhood kids played team games with our children, Bob would ask, "Which side is losing?" Then he'd help them catch up.

Miskah, the Moldovan national leader for our friend's organization, is a passionate follower of God. His neighbor had told Miskah about Jesus when Miskah was a teenager. Under the pretext of going to the outhouse, Miskah often jumped the fence to visit next door, unbeknownst to his parents, who remained Soviet loyalists. Miskah's parents, convinced in their youth that the communistic lifestyle would bring a "paradise on earth" for its followers, never saw the dream realized.

"There certainly was trouble in paradise," Bob said. "What a staggering demise when communism dissolved. In fact, we have a piece of the Berlin Wall."

"Just so," the Dutchman agreed. "Miskah's father prized his position as a Russian military officer, and his mother worked in a weapons factory. The communistic political system fell apart about the time Miskah felt his unfulfilled spiritual need, connecting him to his neighbor and to the underground Protestant church."

"So, happy ending?" we hoped, guessing differently.

"Hardly! When it came to light that fifteen-year-old Miskah embraced belief in God, his parents severely beat him and banished him from the home. As he struggled to survive, Miskah worked diligently at a secular job, while studying the Bible with the help of other Christians during his off hours. He married and started working with our organization to reach youth and orphans around the country."

> "When it came to light that fifteen-year-old Miskah embraced belief in God, his parents severely beat him and banished him from the home."

Most young people in Moldova come from a background lacking any spiritual, let alone biblical, foundation. Therefore Miskah built a new worldview into his own thinking and that of those he mentors. His yearly goal includes a yearly summer camp for 900 youths, the provision of six national training conferences for church workers, and the enablement of staff in fifty youth clubs and public schools across the country. Miskah also labors to bring Christian teaching into the orphanages of Moldova, reaching those most vulnerable to drugs and gangs.

Into this climate the two of us ventured alone, arriving on a plane and hoping to recognize Miskah from pictures. As we transferred planes in Frankfurt, we finally found the obscure ticket counter to inquire about Moldova's gate location.

The ticket agents seemed baffled as they looked at us, convinced two nicely dressed Americans must have it wrong. "Surely you aren't going to Moldova—you must be confusing it with somewhere else." They hesitated.

"It's true," we asserted, displaying our itinerary papers. When we insisted, they still seemed skeptical, though they finally found the gate number. Arriving at the exit portal, we instantly felt conspicuous next to the predominately dark-haired, poorly dressed, expressionless clientele awaiting the plane. An air of quiet resignation resonated down the line. When we smiled at some, they looked away—shyly or suspiciously? We couldn't tell for sure.

> When we smiled at some, they looked away—
> shyly or suspiciously?

Riding the bus that would deliver us to the plane, we drove miles from the terminal, finally reaching the last grouping of planes, and boarded the farthest plane possible.

As we flew into the country, it looked untidily agricultural but sunny with fields of undeveloped, attractive land. Recognizing Miskah's youthful face, we found him to be the only English speaker as we met his sweet wife and two children.

Driving to the countryside, we picked up two young ladies accompanying us to our first assignment in a small village, our first clue to our destination and tasks. We'd paid Miskah to hire one lady as a translator, while the other woman spoke the local language and came to serve at the church. The golden sun descended, sending shining rays over the fluttering fields.

After dropping off his family near their apartment, Miskah drove the van fast and hard for three hours, passing somewhat recklessly according to us. Each country carries conventional rules of the road, so we don't watch too closely and trust.

Finally, the van slowed onto a slender street and halted in front of a dilapidated Soviet apartment building, with no lights to help our ascent up the grubby, crumbling stairs to a small, three-bedroom apartment. Miskah introduced us to a young pastor, with a wife who appeared about eighteen years old with two daughters in tow. Only the pastor spoke English.

Miskah soon left to return to his family, although we worried about the distance he'd travel at this late hour. Feeling jittery and unsettled, we wanted to call after him, "Really, you're just dumping us off and leaving so soon?"

We grabbed each other's hands, grateful to be allies after hours and orbits from anything familiar. This odd little family—and the two young ladies we'd briefly met before they fell asleep in the van—were years younger and counter-culture to us.

After exchanging brief pleasantries, we excused ourselves to sleep, exhausted by jet lag and two days in airports. Our hosts showed us to a narrow, linoleum-floored room, where a single twin, iron-framed bed awaited. They beckoned to a bathroom down the hall to be shared by all.

"It's basically an outhouse in an apartment," I reported to Bob. "The bathtub consists of a drain and a large container of very cold water that I dipped out of a barrel with a handled pan, pouring the water over myself to rinse off."

"Well, I pulled the mattress and the covers off the bed," Bob said, "since the twin appears much too small to accommodate us. Let's sleep on the floor."

We collapsed, falling immediately into sound slumber.

*

Warm sunshine cascaded through a large window as we awoke. Curling wallpaper and damaged panels were visible. The view out the window was a fresh green, rural setting, with a narrow, potholed road running four stories below us. The people in our apartment spoke in guttural-sounding Russian and laughed loudly but quieted and smiled weakly as we arrived for breakfast, dressed in our scrubs. The small girls eased the tension, as they giggled when we winked at them, reaching out hesitantly for the small toys we held in our hands. Their whole faces lit up above their grins. We had sent money ahead to pay for our meals, so we appreciated a large breakfast of baked rolls, boiled eggs, rice, deli meats, and fruit juices.

"I have a struggling church," the young pastor said sincerely and brokenly. "There is much alcoholism here, even within my family, including my father and some brothers. The town has many young people who are barely making a living. Sad and lonely children stay, left with a grandparent or poor relatives, while parents must leave this poor, dead country to find work in Europe, Turkey, or other far-away places. It leaves many orphans and deserted young ones."

Although we sympathized with his sorrows, we also felt his strength and tenacity. One of our favorite sayings is from Helen Keller: "We would never learn to be brave and patient if there were only joy in the world."

A short distance away we viewed the small church we'd come to serve. A tiny, side room seemed best for the clinic, and the main room of the church appeared smaller than most living rooms in America.

> "We would never learn to be brave and patient
> if there were only joy in the world."
> HELEN KELLER

Our young translator did a fine job technically when asked but possessed a Teflon mind. Nothing seemed to stick. She never learned our routine, even though we repeated the same procedure with each patient. Each time we reminded her to ask about the patient's chief complaint, to help seat the client, and to be ready to translate whenever needed. She preferred to gaze out the window and maintained a cold, indifferent manner with the patients. "Stay focused," we felt like scolding. "This is not a spectator sport." We wondered if she had the philosophy: "Hard work never killed anyone, but why take the chance?" Since then, we've learned to seriously pray for a congenial, conscientious interpreter for each trip.

The pastor planned to have us work on children from a state-run orphanage connected to the church. For numerous political reasons we didn't fully understand, we weren't allowed to see the orphans, much to the disappointment of everyone. A ministry of the young pastor included a male and a female transition home for orphans. At that time, the government dismissed orphans from the state-run home at age thirteen, expecting them to fend for themselves without the skills to cope. Prostitution and crime often resulted. The local church had instituted halfway houses to teach skills that might steer the orphans to a better life. We visited the clean and commodious homes and were impressed by caring staffs.

For several days we worked on young people from the transitional homes, going back to the apartment for lunch and a brief rest. The pastor's young wife had a slew of cavities, and we spent hours with her. Tearfully grateful when we finished, she embraced us tightly. We also thrilled a fourteen-year-old boy with composite (white) fillings applied to black holes in several of his front teeth. He emerged quite handsome.

After several hours on the first day of our clinic, we asked a group of young men standing around outside the clinic to dump our waste water in the outhouse, showing pouring motions in hand signs, and pointing to the full, foot-long plastic containers. Time passed and they didn't return.

We finally asked the translator to investigate. "They've thrown the plastic boxes into the outhouse hole," she reported back.

We needed those holders for the remainder of our clinics, and we had no others. So Bob found wire and sticks and fished them out of the smelly holes, which was not an easy task. I labored to clean and to disinfect them, not a pleasant pursuit. Since then we've been more careful with our instructions!

*

On Saturday afternoon, as we worked intently on patients, the pastor and a few other young men practiced music together for the next day's services. Before our clinic that day, the pastor had proudly exhibited his office, which contained posters taped to the walls that listed his goals. A map of the area was marked with the families and communities he yearned to reach. Although a small man, the spare toughness of his build gave the illusion of strength, power, and height. His dark eyes shone, and his acne-pocked face radiated as he spoke of his dreams to help people out of depression, addictions, and broken lives.

"You know, unworthiness is a common thread through all addictions," Bob advised. "Only through the gospel can we show how God values everyone immeasurably." As we went back to work, we heard the rugged timbre of the men's voices as worshipful songs floated down the hall from the tiny church sanctuary: "…more love, more power, more of You (Christ) in my life…" We cherished their devoted and tender hearts as they sincerely, willingly, and humbly served God and others.

"Unworthiness is a common thread through all addictions."

Primarily young people attended the church, and we socialized with them on Saturday night. We met at a "city park," unkempt but pretty in an overgrown fashion. Bob played soccer with a competitive group of young men, and I attempted volleyball and cheered for the soccer game, holding my breath when Bob seemed overly rambunctious with the rough-necked youth.

Later, the group drove to another park with several old memorials to Russian wars, including some rusty Soviet tanks we could climb on.

Bob laughed. "At Fort Sill, Oklahoma—home of the Army's artillery—similar models of these sat out in the field for target practice. They represented the Soviet enemy in a polarized war between the East and the West, and now, ironically, here we are treating and loving our former enemies...those I trained to defend against!"

> "Ironically, here we are treating and loving our former enemies... those I trained to defend against!"

Life is surprising in its twists and turnabouts. War most often affects common people, and I've always believed most humans are not hostile. Rather, it's the leaders who often push for conquest, scarring the lives of so many.

*

We looked forward to a break from dentistry on Sunday, although Bob was slightly skittish to preach in an unfamiliar culture. Miskah had left us for three days, but we remarked at how well it had gone. Miskah planned to return on Sunday to bring a projector for Bob to transmit his power-point sermon onto the wall. We anxiously awaited his arrival after packing for our next clinic location, but Miskah kept us guessing until ten minutes before church started, a little unnervingly close for us. Bob's presentation on "Christian Hope" was well received, and we felt moved by an older couple in shabby clothes who came forward to pray at the end, kneeling and crying as if their hearts would break. Many of the church members moved close to encourage them.

Later Miskah told us, "That poor couple recently lost their home and child in a house fire and have naturally been so sad. The church tries to minister to them, and it is a beautiful thing to see. Even the hurting ones of the church reach out to them with whatever they can spare."

Bob had a faraway look in his eyes as we headed out with Miskah for our next assignment. "Let me tell you one of my fire stories. I fought forest fires as my summer job at age sixteen."

"Tell me," Miskah replied. "We've got all day in the van!"

"One summer day at two in the morning, I was called to fight a fire started by lightning on an isolated hill top in the forest not far from my home. My twenty-one-year-old ranger boss and I drove several hours up old logging roads until we could get no closer. Then we struck out on foot, guided by a helicopter to the top of a steep hill several miles up, where we encountered a huge, burning tree. The force of lightning had shattered a 120-foot pine, leaving twenty-foot-long splinters of wood and a fifty-foot burning stump that could easily start a forest fire. We each carried a trusty *pulaske,* a special tool combining an axe to cut wood on one side and a reinforced hoe to dig soil on the other side. We also hauled a chain saw, a gallon of water, and a heavy radio for communication (there were no portable cell phones in those days). On the steep slope, we worked furiously to build a fire break around where we thought the tree would fall eventually. We cut and cleared brush while digging a trench to catch hot coals from cascading down the hillside. The incendiary roaring covered any other sounds. Suddenly, I heard a voice. I glanced up and saw the huge tree falling toward me! Instinctively I dove, and the tree barely missed me."

"Whew!" Miskah exclaimed. "So you think God or an angel called out to you?"

"I'm sure! Also, we ran out of water halfway through the day. We barely got back to our vehicle for more water before I collapsed due to heat exhaustion. I couldn't keep anything down for hours as I'd become dangerously dehydrated and delusional. That was my second close call with death that one day! As a teenager, it excited me to be earning the $1.77 for what I thought reflected a real man's job! But that one day convinced me forever that I wasn't in control of my own life, that a guardian angel watched over me, and that God wanted me alive."

"That reminds me of the loss of your Army dental friend in Germany," I reflected. "Tell Miskah about that terrible thing."

> "That one day convinced me forever that I wasn't in control of my own life, that a guardian angel watched over me, and that God wanted me alive."

"Oh, yeah. The Army taught us that vigorous exercise and heat can rapidly dehydrate...so, as leaders, we push the intake of water on everyone. If a human gets too hot, one can rapidly reach heat stroke, and the body loses its ability to regulate its internal temperature."

"Yes, I understand," Miskah said, surprising us with his command of English.

Bob continued. "Earlier that year I'd completed a fifty-mile international military march through the Swiss Alps with my friend, Kevin, and knew he was in good shape. Kevin competed for the coveted German Armed Forces

Military Efficiency Badge in Gold, which I'd already earned, so I was not present. The medal required finishing many timed athletic events. The last day happened to be a warm, humid day. Kevin ran a three-mile race but then collapsed. By the time the race officials got him to the hospital, his core body temperature measured 109 degrees Fahrenheit, and he never regained consciousness. It was a sobering story, where mistakes left two small children fatherless. I would have recognized his problem due to my fire dehydration incident and so wished I could've been there to save him."

We all shook our heads, lost in our own thoughts for some time.

As we continued through the countryside, Miskah stopped at several historic churches and seminaries, one with a monastery and a gift shop on site. Ninety-five percent of Moldova's population is Eastern Orthodox, and the priests we encountered appeared quite proud of their advanced spirituality. When I tried to buy one of the crosses for my collection, they refused to sell it to us, saying we were not of their religion. They considered evangelical Christians to be inferior spiritually and didn't feel we truly followed God. Although disturbing and hurtful, we see religious biases everywhere and often search our own hearts for prejudicial or judgmental attitudes.

As we left, Miskah grinned. "Guess they don't know about your relationship to God and that angel after your fire."

> We see religious biases everywhere and often search our own hearts for prejudicial or judgmental attitudes.

Inspired by Miskah and the many burdens for others that he carried, we admired his skill set for the tasks God had given him. He took us to the other side of Moldova to stay in a pleasant country home with a lovely family who served as leaders in a small Protestant church. Raising animals and a huge garden, they produced delicious meals and a room for us with a bathroom that, to our delight, had a hot water system.

Again, only the pastor spoke broken English. We ate the first meal as Miskah talked animatedly with the family in the Moldovan language for a half hour. Astonished that they didn't try to include us, we felt uncomfortable without even a brief translation of what they discussed. It was a good reminder to always include others in some way whenever we converse around those of other languages.

Miskah dropped us off once again! After he left, the family seemed polite but reserved with us. Our popularity with them diminished when Bob performed dental exams on each of the four, beautiful, chubby young daughters, all of whom disclosed numerous cavities. They snacked all day on fruit and produce from their garden, unaware of the relationship between constant sugars in the mouth and considerable cavities. The idea crushed them when they understood that they'd have to change their lifestyle of food gratification if they wanted to control their weight and cavity formation.

*

"Hello, it's great to see someone from America," announced a young, blonde man who came in late that night to stay in the bedroom next to us. "I'm a twenty-two-year-old seminary student from New Orleans, and I've come to claim my bride."

His adorable Southern accent matched his ear-to-ear grin. It seems he'd met a young orphan woman on a previous mission trip and planned to take her home to America to marry when her visa cleared. She appeared very young to us, spoke little English, and seemed clingy in many ways, but he obviously loved her dearly and was bent on rescuing her. He worked in the clinic with us for several days, and we appreciated his caring help and contagious joy.

About six months after we'd returned home, we received pictures of their lovely wedding in New Orleans.

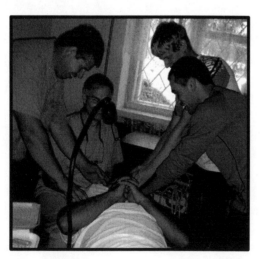

Moldova

Pastors pray for a fellow pastor.

We provided dentistry in two different orphanages that the local churches befriended. One administrator was a prototypic, atheistic Russian woman, cool and suspicious initially. She obviously had worked diligently on her appearance, since she wore a tub of makeup and was quite excited to tell me that she had Mary Kay cosmetics from a relative in America. By then I had given up trying to be well groomed with the warm, sticky weather, erratic restrooms, and work demands.

The administrator's attitude toward us changed as she saw the painless and attractive work we performed on many of her orphans. Soon she brought her seventeen-year-old son to us, and we fixed the black holes in his front teeth, solidifying our friendship with her forever. She presented us with small treasures and keepsake pictures the orphans had drawn.

Our new assistant intelligently and instantaneously picked up every routine following his first exposure, with excellent English skills. He was the most amazing translator we'd ever had, bar none. He seemed especially exceptional after the marginal interpreter in the previous village. He begged to give an injection, which he did well, and pulled several teeth, needing only minimal instruction. Vigilantly observing every movement Bob made, he could remarkably imitate many procedures. He nurtured the patients with the warmest chairside manner we've ever seen.

It broke our hearts to leave him in his impoverished state. We hope our encouragement led to opportunities within his world reality. He conscientiously worked a menial job to help support his mother and siblings. He also studied to be a pastor while saving money in hopes of marrying a sweet girl he lovingly introduced to us. We trust God can use his uncanny skills in appropriate avenues, as he revealed unschooled brilliance. Miskah said, "I have ideas for that one." And we have to believe God does, as well.

He nurtured the patients with
the warmest chairside manner we've ever seen.

"I know we'd planned to have a last day of sightseeing before you left Moldova," Miskah told us a little nervously when he came to collect us. "But, instead, would you be able to help a team of young people assist in the worst flood crisis in two hundred years in Moldova?"

"We heard about the deluge before we left America. What's happened?"

"There's been over ten billion dollars of water damage, with many homes destroyed and countless families' subsistence ruined. The high water has ruined agricultural products and preserved food, leaving many destitute for the coming winter. Would you have anything to contribute to this great need?"

We still held a significant amount in cash that we'd brought in case of a personal emergency, as we knew we'd be alone in a country far from home. We decided on the spot to give it to those in need, holding only a few dollars back to get us through the airports on our way home.

*

The next morning Miskah appeared with ten college-aged Christians. He'd packed his van full with bags of rice, beans, and other staples that'd been purchased with our dollars. Having little inspiration on how to get the supplies to the neediest, we headed far out to the country. We all prayed that God would lead us.

Miskah had called the local pastor of one of the hardest-hit communities and, although unable to reach him, we decided to go anyway. Seeing the vast area underwater from high on a viewpoint, we drove to a nearby town.

In the first intersection of the small farming village, Miskah called out a Moldovan greeting to a lone young man. The fellow standing there attended the church of the pastor we sought! Since we'd heard there were few Christian believers in town, this encounter seemed miraculous. Our new friend jumped into the van and directed us to the pastor's home, where the family spontaneously set up for lunch that we financed with our money that Miskah had set aside for the day's necessities.

Moldova

Students sort food
for flood relief.

The pastor and our newfound friend led us to the town's administrative headquarters, where they provided a list of the most indigent families in the community. A turnout in the road allowed us to package bags of food that would feed forty households for a month. Finding people with flooded homes, devastated gardens, and ruined lives, we spent the day distributing bags. It proved an incredibly heartbreaking task to absorb the victims' tales of their loss and hardship—an unbearable experience that drained us emotionally. Although the words didn't make sense to us, the angst and the bitter tears registered bleak reality. The anguish and the grief on the faces of these people reflected no savings, family help, resources, or government assistance to sustain them. So many countries hold no safety nets for their people.

"I can't get into my house," one lady explained. After the flood, the walls had settled around the entry door and could not be pried open. Since she slept on a borrowed mattress on the porch, the pastor promised he'd bring some men from his church to help her regain entry.

Another older lady, who was caring for several grandchildren, told us of her fight against breast cancer. She held no hope for medical care, which would be accessible in a developed country. The end of her life loomed, and there was little we could do other than offer her our prayers and some much-needed food. The memory of that conversation would jolt me like a lightning bolt in later years.

Tragically, one lady's husband left the farm to find other employment out of the country, as no local jobs materialized. Several years had passed without word from him, and she'd recently found out from others that he'd remarried in a far-off land.

One older man in a wheelchair lived by himself, while both his frostbitten legs had been amputated when he lost the resources to heat his house. The local pastor promised he'd be watching over these souls, caring for them through God's love. What relief to us! Many of the people unveiled a hunger for faith as well as food, and we left prayers, Christian literature, and our own testimonies. We felt humbled and honored that we could show caring and could give a token gift toward their survival.

> Both his frostbitten legs had been amputated when he lost the resources to heat his house.

Often people just need someone to walk with them, holding their hands, even for a memorable moment. Often no one comes to visit or to express care for the plight of the helpless. Everyone needs validation: "I see you...hear you…what you say matters to me." It is truly a privilege to find oneself in that position of empathy and to build one's own muscle for compassion. Listening is the best gift, and we learn immeasurably more when our lips aren't moving. We were humbled by the chance to give to others, realizing that we had resources only because we'd been blessed by God. In America, we often take for granted the opportunities given us through our education and our freedom.

> Everyone needs validation: "I see you…hear you… what you say matters to me."

"The government can be a huge hindrance to progress with the human greed and corruption it perpetuates," Miskah told us. "Listen to this example. An American with modern capitalistic idealism launched a pizza restaurant chain that became a successful franchise. The president's son of Moldova saw this as a chance to become rich. The political powers arranged for the owner of the successful pizza chain to be deported from the country, while the ruler's son took over the business, which soon failed due to the son's lack of ability. When our citizens see that, they realize they have no hope of prospering with a government ready to strip them of any achievement. The government controls most of the gas products, milk supply, and many other staples of life. Most of the youth of Moldova seek ways to depart this lovely country because there is no future for them at this point."

Since Miskah had no space in his two-room apartment to host us, we stayed several nights with his parents, who maintained minimal and cautious cooperation. As a short-term source of income for Miskah's parents, our trip resources allowed them to provide for our food and shelter. Miskah's parents had grudgingly accepted him back into their lives as their only child, although they still refused to consider faith in God. Miskah's father, the ex-Russian officer, now ran a small fruit stand on a corner near their Soviet-style, one-bedroom, disintegrating apartment. Miskah's mother continued to work in the same factory, which now produced appliances, not weapons.

The irony didn't escape us that we were staying with our previous enemies in the Cold War. Miskah's father settled on the couch and refused to sit at the table when we ate. The thought crossed our minds that maybe the food was poisoned.

We slept on a foldout couch in their tiny combination living and dining room, sharing their only bathroom. It resembled an airplane's restroom, with the addition of a miniscule shower. We recalled laughing when a flight attendant once said in her announcement, "Folks, make up your mind what you're going to do before entering the lavatory, because once you close the door, there's no turning around!"

As we went to sleep that night, we heard low murmurs from the old couple's bedroom, voices soft, yet strained. We couldn't fathom what apprehensions or sorrows spilled into those melancholy cadences. I felt somewhat claustrophobic in the fourth-floor, cinderblock, steel, and functionally basic apartment. Although we couldn't speak their language, we brought out pictures of our grandchildren, and Miskah's mother showed us old family momentos. Although somewhat uncomfortable, it represented a winning combination for both couples. We exchanged this reasonable and convenient cohabitation for almost-nonexistent hotels or restaurants.

"Folks, make up your mind what you're going to do before entering the lavatory, because once you close the door, there's no turning around!"

Miskah's mother shook her head quite vigorously in displeasure when I presented an apron I'd made and brought as a hospitality gift. Miskah's mother finally accepted it, although we couldn't tell if the gift offended her, or whether she thought she'd already received compensation for her efforts toward us. Maybe she felt concerned that she had nothing to reciprocate. We only could hope that our smiles and handshakes would move them closer to the true Creator God they'd been taught to reject. Each Christian touches lives in the hope of bringing people nearer to faith. Our responsibility is to expose the gospel to others, and the Holy Spirit reaps the results through His call to God's lost children. We attempt to plant faith seeds in hearts but are usually not there to harvest. We attempt to inspire the local Christians to follow up with those seeking faith and continue to pray for those we've touched with the Gospel.

We mourned for the godless, communistic culture that had promised its people a heaven on earth and left them with shattered dreams. Six months later we would be in another society that also existed in suspicion of American Christians. Meanwhile, we didn't desire to return to Egypt, but God had a different idea…and we dared not resist.

EGYPT

A Hospital in Need
on the Nile

* * *

ALTHOUGH WE'D GROWN THROUGH OUR FIRST FASCINATING DENTAL MISSION to Cairo working with Habitat for Humanity, the trip proved arduous, especially the pollution, the crowding, and the challenging Muslim culture. The earlier team's focus was on building relationships, which hadn't meshed with the longer hours of dentistry we'd desired. Also, we aimed to go somewhere different each time. "So many places to go, too little time!"

"Have I ever got a hospital that needs you!" Mustafah, our ticklish Egyptian friend said when he approached us at church. "Aswan, a beautiful paradise on the Nile, is about a two-hour plane flight south of Cairo." It sounded intriguing, and we've admitted that it's hard to say no to Mustafah's charm.

A significant purpose and dual incentive existed as the hospital staff begged us to leave a dental clinic on site and to train an Egyptian dentist in its use. Our own church in Colorado Springs expressed interest in allotting money from their missionary fund to help equip and set up a dental clinic that would service the hospital and two outlying clinics. Our portable clinic concept seemed perfect for the setting; and through the $5,000 gift from our church, we bought a portable chair, a dental operating unit, a dental light, sterilization equipment, supplies, and instruments. Bob received donations for many additional materials, generously given by individuals, including Bob's mother. Organizations involved included World Dental Relief, Project Cure, Henry Schein, Aseptico, GC America, Septodont, and Ultradent. As the only dental personnel on a team that included a physician (a diabetes specialist), Mustafah (a physical therapist), and four women who'd planned a retreat for the ladies in the Evangelical church Aswan, we hesitated to ask the group to carry equipment for us, but we had no choice with the clinic items we'd leave.

When we got to Cairo, most of our bunch wanted to sightsee at the pyramids and museum, but since we'd been there recently, we offered to go with Mustafah and a group from Texas he was sponsoring to help in a Sudanese refugee school. That team consisted of ten young women, three of whom were married, although none had children. Mustafah had come to Egypt two weeks ahead of us, and we chose to tag along as he closed out the Texas group's short-term trip.

"Tell us about the school," we inquired of the administrators as Mustafah translated.

"The refugee school, established over ten years ago, meets each weekday from 8:00 a.m. to 2:00 p.m., servicing 276 students divided between eighteen teachers. We use the public Sudanese school curriculum, since there is hope that many of the displaced children can go back to their own country to complete school at some point. Thirty percent of the students are Muslim, with the remainder Christian."

Each school room measured about twelve-foot square, with a dozen rooms lining the sides of a rectangular open-air concrete slab about the size of a gymnasium. Each room held up to twenty children, with forty children in grade one. Behind these rooms on most sides loomed tall, high-rise buildings, many partially built apartments of fifteen stories under hasty construction for occupation by refugees.

Egypt has over one million Sudanese refugees seeking new lives and opportunity, and people from several unstable countries also stream into Cairo seeking safety. It is a city of opportunity for many, but it is vastly overcrowded. The school desperately required relocation, as the ongoing construction all around it caused a danger to the children. Falling construction items often rained down on the school.

"They are a wild, chaotic mass of humanity," Bob whispered in my ear.

I felt hopeful. "These ten ladies from Texas seem valiantly prepared. They've brought songs, games, crafts, face-painting supplies, as well as skinny balloons and pumps to create balloon animals. That should last a little while anyway."

"They are a wild, chaotic mass of humanity."

Our eagerness to help diminished after time in the blazing sun, our jet-lagged condition, and a serious cold Bob had acquired along the way.

As Bob tried to blow up balloons, the kids fought fiercely over them. We insisted they form a line, but discipline remained elusive. These Sudanese refugee children were toughened by lives of survival honed in the midst of civil war and violence. Many had lost parents and all grieved loved ones.

Without this oasis of life and hope created by our "Mother Theresa of Egypt," these little ones would indeed be lost and forgotten.

"I'm getting beaten to death," Bob hissed when I came for a break from face painting.

"I know what you mean." I sighed. "These kids just push and shove—or worse."

I watched for a moment as hoards of children crowded around Bob, punching him as they vied for attention to obtain a balloon. Several times the smaller children inadvertently (?) smacked Bob's groin, doubling him over in pain. We asked a teacher to speak to the children and lodged ourselves in a corner by a doorway as the only way to stay safe. We pumped up hundreds of balloons, but they didn't last long in this frenzied place. A half hour after we finished handing out the balloons, nothing but shredded remains of multicolored pieces of rubber lay littered on the cement.

After several hours of ferocious "fun," an Egyptian, Christian high school group arrived to perform a music concert with skits, songs, and taped music. It provided a relief from the panicked pace thus far, and the children snuggled in relative calm, clinging to adults and each other. They yearned for attention and seemed starved for affection. Prayers and a talk about God and His caring generated some meaningful moments.

Afterwards, a bus arrived loaded with Christmas shoeboxes for the Sudan refugee students from America. "You know, we've packed these boxes, but they've gone out to the great abyss, and I've never visualized the receiving end. What pure joy to hand these boxes of love out to children in each classroom!" I told Bob later.

"Ditto. I just stood back beholding the wonder…so many cute gifts of toys, treats, small clothing items, and toiletries sent by caring American families," Bob agreed.

*

The next morning we flew to Aswan and found it to be a heavenly place, a tropical location on the Nile River, much quieter and cleaner than Cairo. Our hosts drove us immediately to the German church held in the hospital's chapel, which featured inspiring songs and a power-point sermon on perseverance.

We settled into the hotel next door, enthralled with our room's window that unveiled a picture-perfect view of the Nile right across the street. Lined along the banks were numerous river boats supporting a thriving Nile cruise tourist business. Large floating hotels lent a lively, festive atmosphere.

ASWAN, EGYPT
We viewed feluccas and Nile river boats from our hotel window.

"I've got a Nile joke," I quipped. "Why was Pharaoh's daughter a female financier?"

Bob rolled his eyes but beckoned for the answer.

"Because she went down to the banks of the Nile and drew out a little prophet!"

"I love you for your funnies, but in this case…get thou to a punnery." He laughed as he hugged me close.

That afternoon we rode on a felucca (sailboat) on the Nile with many of the friendly medical doctors and their families from the hospital. Splashes of glorious color captured our imagination as sunlight played off the sapphire water. With little wind that afternoon, another boat dragged us along the calm and peaceful river.

Afterwards, we all squeezed into a doctor's house in the hospital compound. As a charming anesthesiologist married to a nurturing pediatrician, they had quite the modest home for such successful professionals. We felt welcomed and appreciated as they graciously entertained us in the small, toasty apartment on the third floor that they shared with their two teenage children. Impressed with the commitment of the hospital staff, we saw they so willingly gave at the sacrifice of their own comfort and lifestyle. Without fanfare they served cake, chocolate, specialty nuts, and drinks to the capacity crowd.

> They so willingly gave at the sacrifice
> of their own comfort and lifestyle.

"Tell us about the hospital," we asked of the talkative, gregarious anesthesiologist, who spoke English fluently.

"The mission hospital, although founded in 1913 by Christians from Germany, is currently under Egyptian leadership, but we still receive support from Germany church groups with finances and staffing. As a charitable institution, its excellent reputation extends beyond the boundaries of Aswan. For almost 100 years, the hospital has been an important part of the non-governmental sector of health care in the region and is a Christian beacon of light." His face showed utter animation as he warmed to his passion.

"How is it connected to outlying clinics? We heard we will get to go to several."

"Yes, yes. The hospital's popular name, Al Germaniyya, is revered for its long-standing outlying clinic service to the Nubian people, which are an ethnic group originally from northern Sudan and southern Egypt. They were victimized and disregarded by many Egyptians and were displaced from their homes by the construction of the Aswan dam and the large body of water that became Lake Nassar. However, patients from all sectors and levels of society seek help, irrespective of their religious orientation or racial origin. Some of them travel as far as 200 miles for treatment. Our medical care is an unusually fine quality at rates that even the poorer section of society can afford. Each year more than 2,000 inpatients are cared for, and outpatient clinics treat over 20,000 clients each year in the fields of surgery, internal medicine, urology, pediatrics, ophthalmology, ear/nose/throat (ENT), tropical medicine, general practice, and anesthesiology. Two rural clinics care for an additional 5,000 patients each year. The hospital's medical team is comprised of Egyptian doctors, Egyptian and German nurses, visiting foreign consultants—like yourselves—as well as fifty Egyptian employees." Our anesthesiologist glowed when describing the hospital.

Walking through winding, darkened alleys and over rough, rocky streets to reach the simple structure, we attended the small, village Protestant church that night. A woman pastor from our team preached, and we shared "communion" with the believers, remembering times we've shared the cup and the bread with others around the world, embracing the "common union" that Jesus desires. We met the short, likeable female dentist, Dr. Deira, who desired further training in the clinic the following week. After inhaling a delicious German dinner at the guest house (home-cooked by visiting Deutsch helpers) at 9:30 p.m., we collapsed into bed.

*

Each day at the hospital started at 8:00 a.m. with devotional talks and singing at the chapel. By 9:00 a.m. the first morning, we set up in a small room with a sink. Dr. Deira translated, helped assist, and was mentored by Bob. Dr. Deira preferred this role and absorbed knowledge like a dehydrated plant soaks up water in a desert. We felt gratified to treat the hospital staff, since they faithfully give their best care to others, often neglecting or unable to seek healthcare themselves. Dental care in Aswan is almost nonexistent, and local dentists seldom utilized trustworthy sterilization practices.

Almost every medical provider in the hospital had infected teeth requiring extractions, while most of the spouses had teeth that could be restored. We couldn't really understand the correlation but joked that the women must take better care of their teeth than the men. Bob thought that if the conscientious medical staff showed these sorry mouths, the rest of Aswan was sure to be worse. No wonder the hospital made the establishment of a dental clinic a high priority.

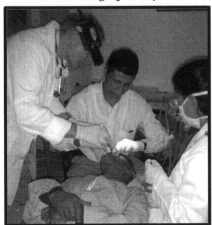

Dr. Kahn, the chief of the Family Practice Residency program, had an interest in learning how to extract teeth and we had the opportunity during the week to train him on dental anesthesia, and the extraction of simple teeth, leaving him with a set of basic oral surgical instruments.

"Dr. Deira told me she most wanted to learn filling procedures," Bob said. "She's skilled at extracting teeth, as that's her job every day at a government facility—although she claims they don't even have an operating handpiece at her hospital clinic. She pulls one tooth on each patient and charges a buck, providing for many patients in a day."

"I always thought buck teeth were a condition, not a price," I said and chuckled. "But, really, that's all she's allowed to do? How incredibly sad with her potential."

Several days later, Dr. Deira proudly showed us her private office, a small room on the second floor of a corner building in her village. Her antique equipment, although organized and clean, included a minimal number of instruments and limited supplies. To her credit, she did use an acceptable, although old-fashioned, sterilizing machine. After she completed her daily work for the government, she radiated caring and concern for the patients she saw on her own time.

We hoped to rest during the hot part of each afternoon, with the hospital staff's expectation that we'd hold a dental clinic from 6:00 to 9:00 p.m. each evening, after which dinner would be available in the guesthouse kitchen. Drained after our first, demandingly long day—we hadn't rested in the afternoon due to conversations with many from the hospital staff—we ate a late dinner. Although we didn't want to stuff ourselves right before bed, we couldn't resist the pickled cauliflower, lentil soup, lasagna-like casserole, and baklava, all cooked by the German volunteers.

> After she completed her daily work for the government, she radiated caring and concern for the patients she saw on her own time.

Our schedule while there seemed enormously different from our routine at home, and interactions over lunch seemed necessary and would be rude to ignore. As such, we never acquired rest in the afternoons. Each day was more grueling and lengthy, and we only hoped that our journey to the outlying clinics might somehow break the rigorous hospital schedule that threatened to engulf us in exhaustion.

With trepidation we left for the outlying clinics early one morning, as two accompanying security guards told us not to wear our lab coats as that might draw unnecessary attention. Were we in danger?

Relief filled the car as officials merely waved us through several checkpoints.

My world was momentarily shaken as I met the two women who manned the clinics. Initially I idealized their lives, which spoke to my childhood yearnings. Similar to me in age, they'd also trained as nurses. Both ran plantation-like compounds, where they served people from the surrounding villages, and I suddenly saw a rendition of my dream as a young girl. I'd often imagined myself as a nurse in some isolated corner of the planet, nurturing the needy locals and bringing them to faith in God. Reality shimmered as I told Bob, "This might have been me!"

"Well, let's analyze these scenarios up close," Bob suggested.

Our visit to Mindy's place revealed a large, walled compound on a lovely acreage with a huge house, an immaculate clinic, and a gigantic garden. Reflecting a beauty and grace as appealing as any bed and breakfast, we enjoyed staying overnight in the spacious home after a full day's clinic.

Mindy, a missionary nurse from Germany, bustled around the place like a queen managing her empire. Her quick wit, ready laugh, and enthusiastic curiosity about everything lent softness and vulnerability to the commanding words she addressed to all her worker bees. Her impeccable hospitality provided frequent breaks that lavished delectable treats upon us: herb tea, dates, cinnamon bread, cheese, and guava juice.

> Mindy, a missionary nurse from Germany, bustled around the place like a queen managing her empire.

We provided dentistry for pastors, the plantation workers, children, and villagers all day, while our dynamic Nurse Mindy orchestrated patient flow and efficiently fostered goodwill. For dinner, she previously had prepared an entire German meal for us: spaetzle (cheesy, homemade noodles with onions), a garden salad with pickled dressing, warm pita bread, beets, and a bitter orange drink. Admitting her frequent homesickness for Deutschland, Mindy spoke of her mother in Germany.

That evening we walked the short distance to the Nile, just as the sun cast ethereal silhouettes of the surrounding hills and sailboats. We rode in one of the three-wheeled, motorized, scooter-like taxis, and ended a perfect day by sleeping in a clean, soothing, green-and-white-themed, frilly bedroom in Mindy's lovely home. The only sour note was the Muslim mosque nearby that let rip raucous calls-to-prayer at 4:30 a.m.

*

At 7:00 a.m. we left for the hour's drive to the compound that Nurse Felicia from Finland administrated. It was a matched set to Mindy's place. They'd been best friends for the thirty-something years they labored at these assignments. There we chomped on a breakfast of cheese, three types of Egyptian breads, sweet spreads, fresh oranges (picked that morning off her trees), miniature bananas, tea, and more guava juice. Nurse Felicia initially desired to go to Ethiopia when she'd finished her Finland nursing school in the early 1970s, but she'd been diverted to Aswan, never to leave.

"How has it gone for you all these years?" we asked.

We appreciated Felicia's quiet, no-nonsense demeanor, a contrast to Mindy's equally appealing, emphatic affability.

"Hmm…the people here have become like family." She gazed out the window. "I've lost my parents and my brother while assigned in Egypt." She brightened. "The Finnish government supported this mission all these years, as they allocate funds for Finnish humanitarian staff around the world. I can't say it's been easy, but I've built a life—and I've always had my big dogs and this little turtle, Lucy." She stooped and picked up the turtle, a perfect size to cup in her hands.

Later, Felicia marched around her meticulous clinic with a purposeful tap of sensible shoes.

"The people here have become like family."

I couldn't help but compare lives and ended up realizing that these ladies, although giants in God's kingdom, had not savored the fullness of life that I possessed myself. They had never cherished a loving husband, children, and grandchildren, or traveled to many diverse countries in God's service. Both expressed regrets that they'd never married, had often missed their families back home, and felt saddened that so few people had accepted God on their watch.

We again visited the outlying clinics on our third trip to Egypt a year later, and sorely missed Nurse Mindy, who'd recently returned to Germany for treatment of depression and exhaustion. Nurse Felicia, although admitting to health problems, still served faithfully, but she planned to retire when a replacement could be found. I once again rejoiced in my own favored life.

The Nubian Muslim women who came to the clinics garbed in their dark burkas were covered from head to toe as modestly as we could imagine. They carefully removed their facial veils to reveal only the part of their face necessary for dental treatment. Even more fascinating to observe was the behavior of their husbands, who bustled nearby, demanding a sheet to cover their wives below the waist and over their feet even though their clothes already blocked any view of their bodies.

It also shocked us to learn that as high as 96 percent of women in this part of Egypt received genital mutilation as young girls, seemingly to mandate purity in women. This surgical procedure removes the clitoris, often resulting in painful intercourse and infections throughout the women's lives, sometimes even resulting in death. It seemed to be a cultural norm, rather than a religious rite, as the Christian community performed these procedures almost as regularly as the Muslims.

> As high as 96 percent of women in this part of Egypt received genital mutilation as young girls.

In Egypt's culture and in other countries where female circumcision is practiced, sex is primarily prescribed for procreation and not for pleasure, as this procedure makes intimacy for the female devoid of enjoyment and often infused with pain. Of course, our Christian worldview objects to the practice, as we believe these cultures have taken something God intended to be beautiful and turned mutilation into an evil that destroys the great joy and the intimacy that brings a special bond within marriage. Totally committing to one another in mutual fulfillment is a euphoric experience a circumcised female can't enjoy. We've seen male-dominated societies, where animals are often treated better than women. We feel the unity, the strength, and the stability of a marriage—and the community as a whole—is severely compromised in governments where female circumcision is practiced. Some of these countries have outlawed the procedure in legislation, but in Egypt and in other places, the ruling is not routinely enforced.

It saddened us to think of the many issues women have dealt with in that land, including the challenges of multi-wife relationships. When men in the Muslim world are allowed up to four wives, we couldn't help but think it must result in competitiveness, insecurity, resentment, and problems within the families. It does not seem fair, right, or in God's plan. It did remind us of when a Sunday school youngster ironically answered a question about King Solomon in the Bible who had 600 wives and 400 *porcupines* (instead of the correct answer—"concubines").

Our final days at the hospital brought us exposure to fascinating people. Pastor Victor, a colorful chaplain who greatly feared dental treatment due to multiple previously negative experiences, spoke with tears in his eyes. "That is the first time I visited the dentist and it didn't hurt. Everyone here is very thankful for you."

*

During an evening touring an outside rock sculpture garden, we enjoyed a couple destined to become our friends, visiting us at our home in Colorado a year later. Although raised in Egypt, Dr. Khan received his medical education in Oklahoma, where he married an American woman. His brother, also a doctor in Aswan, married a German who'd come to serve at the hospital after college. Close to our age, the couples had growing families and careers dedicated to giving to others, full of love for God and hurting people. We valued them highly, but they also had dental problems they'd put off because they didn't trust the dentistry in Egypt.

"How are your family's teeth?" Bob asked Dr. Kahn when they came to Colorado.

"I'd love for you to check out my family," he replied. "And…I've had this toothache for some time."

"Really?" Bob asked. "I'm surprised you haven't gotten it fixed in Egypt. You're the top there—surely you have the resources and the pull to find the best care possible!"

"Well, I'd rather lose this tooth than get hepatitis or AIDS. You know that few, if any, dentists seems to sterilize their equipment in Egypt."

I'd rather lose this tooth than get hepatitis or AIDS.

I still cringe over one incident that occurred when Dr. Kahn's family visited us that summer. Their oldest son, age twelve, seemed quite unimpressed with the scenic sights I showed them around Colorado Springs. He relished skateboarding, however, so I drove to a park that had ramps and half-pipes with many teens skateboarding at midday. This shy young man seemed taken with it, but he refused to participate. I half-jokingly said that if he got up early the next morning, I'd take him to the skateboarding area without the crowds. Somewhat surprised to see him at 6:00 a.m., I felt compelled to drive him there.

The deserted park glowed in the early sunlight. Our young friend grabbed his skateboard and wiped out with his first roll down a small half-pipe. He hit the pavement, landing on his back with a horrendous look of pain and shock, appearing unable to breathe. Although he'd probably just knocked the wind out of his lungs, I panicked and called 9-1-1—the first time in my life I'd ever done that.

Fairly quickly, he hopped up, so I hung up my cell phone—too late. The 9-1-1 switchboard operator called and required me to give a location, as any call must be followed, whether or not completed. I explained, "I really think he's fine." But they insisted on coming.

Sirens blared as a fire truck and a paramedic van swooped in. By then, our little friend and I sat relaxed on the curb. Embarrassed when the firefighter asked the boy's name, address, and health history, I realized I knew only his name and that he lived in Egypt. The paramedics examined him, pronounced him fine, and left.

Trying to bring normalcy to the event, I explained, "In America, we have people to call with any medical problems we have, so don't worry. This is just an ordinary happening here in this country." I sheepishly drove him home, upset at myself for putting us both in a potentially dangerous situation without the parents' presence. Dr. Kahn and his wife were most gracious and understanding, and I thanked God no serious injury had occurred.

This incident reminded us of an interesting discussion we'd had with several Egyptian physicians, who had warned us that it would be disastrous to stop and to help at the site of an accident in Egypt. Since the authorities responding try to assign blame for any accident, especially one involving a death, they will jail anyone they associate with the calamity. Woe to those who have money, as the system works on bribes. Even physicians will not stop outside of their own locale, even though they have the medical knowledge to help.

On this, our first trip to Aswan, we met a German volunteer at the hospital, a dear older man named Klaus, who bore an uncanny resemblance to St. Nicholas. He planned to depart soon for Sudan with a team from the church in Aswan. Concerned that he seemed somewhat frail, I commented, "But isn't it dangerous to go into Sudan?"

He looked very soberly at me as his eyes twinkled. "Hmmph, it is also very hazardous to be in Germany, as people are dying daily in their beds...some possibly never having really lived!" That's become one of our truisms, as we take risks in countries around the world.

That reminded us of a quote by Harold Kushner:

I believe that it is not dying that people are afraid of. Something else. Something more unsettling and more tragic than dying frightens us. We're afraid of never having lived. Of coming to the end of our days with the sense that we were never really alive. That we never figured out what life was for.

Before we leave, we often give our young adults little speeches. "Now we know you might worry about us, but we are in God's hands and feel called to do this. We are proud of you all and realize you will make it fine without us if something unexpected happens. So, trust us to God. If we perish in a plane crash or an accident, understand we've loved serving together and, if we're taken together, rejoice that one of us won't have to go on alone. These mission opportunities have become our passion and are what God has for us to do right now. We're excited to know that we're still living our lives in service to others. That is the highest calling." We always add a P.S. "It's usually hard to call or email, so you probably won't be hearing from us."

How refreshing to allow tech detox! Once I heard a child in church praying the Lord's Prayer: "Deliver us from email (instead of 'evil')!" We always leave emergency numbers with our family and have only heard from them twice. We heard through family emails when my father died. One of our most memorable phone calls was when our oldest daughter called us in Egypt to announce her second pregnancy! The most exciting calls of our lives are when we get the announcement that another little one is joining our family.

How refreshing to allow tech detox!

A most dramatic story involved Dr. Akhen, the ENT doctor of the hospital. His scarred face is disfigured with a crooked smile, and he walks hunched over with a limp, while wearing his past as a point of inspiration and courage. He tells of overcoming numerous tragic circumstances as he felt pursued by God's relentless love. Both of his sons, ages nineteen and fifteen, have a genetic, degenerative disease, Muscular Duchane Dystrophy, which put them each in wheelchairs at around age six. A child in between died after one week of life.

To quote Dr. Akhen: "It occurred to me that, whether or not God chose to heal them, the boys would have a limited time on this earth. To obey God, to seek His glory, to extend His kingdom, is eternal. Those things last forever. God is worth it regardless of the pain or the sacrifices. No matter the cost, I will follow Him, especially since He gave me a second chance after the accidents."

Dr. Akhen survived two car accidents in which he should have died, the first one as a young man, when he knowingly resisted service to God. He sustained twenty-seven fractures in his face and one at the base of his skull. During his hospitalization he recalls a near-death experience where he believes he met Jesus with whom he pleaded for a second chance. Dr. Akhen promised he'd follow the right path, which he attempted with his whole being to accomplish.

Much later, Dr. Akhen thwarted a second accident in which he almost drowned. After staying up late one night to counsel friends, followed by a busy day in one of the outlying clinics, he fell asleep at the wheel of his car and crashed upside down in the Nile. Floating and trapped, he was saved by others' miraculous interventions.

At another interval, Dr. Akhen contracted Hepatitis C, where the treatment involved expensive injections for forty-eight weeks. This caused intense pain that kept him in bed for three days after each shot with side effects bringing severe depression.

Dr. Akhen summarized his life story after relating the many difficulties he'd encountered, admitting some problems resulted from his poor choices. "Filled with assurance and faith that God held everything in His hands and that He would accomplish His will, the presence of God became very real to me. One of my colleagues came into the office and seemed dazed as he looked at me. I asked him why he stared at me, and he said, 'I see an angel when I look at you.' "

Dr. Akhen witnesses to many, asserting that the power of God works through adversity. One night his family blessed our team by providing a lovely, Egyptian seafood meal at their home, where we enjoyed conversing with their two precious, wheel-chaired teenagers.

> "I see an angel
> when I look at you."

Nurse Mindy drove us through the chaotic streets as we visited the home of Dr. Deira, our dental colleague, and her lively, elderly mother. We settled into their small, elegant sitting room that contained plush chairs covered in plastic. This encasement was due to the dust from the streets and spewing ashes from the nearby sugar cane factory which covered the whole town. At the end of the visit, after we'd discussed our families and communities, Dr. Deira's mother startled us by asking about the condition of God's church in America. We assured her that many committed Christians remained, but, in the backs of our minds, we wondered if that wasn't changing some, as many Americans don't acknowledge God.

At the end of our visit, we prayed in three languages (Arabic, German, and English) for our countries together. We sang, "He is Lord" in all three languages, and we couldn't help but think that God smiled down on the five of us, representing Christians from three different continents.

Although we felt very close to our new friends at the hospital, two trips to Egypt seemed enough for us, especially since we'd accomplished our purposes of leaving the portable dental clinic there under the trained eyes of Dr. Deira and Nurse Mindy, who promised to manage the equipment for the outlying clinics. We relished a relaxing time on a cruise boat that traveled on the Nile for three days as we luxuriated in the gourmet food and the allure of the old temples and the rich history of Egypt.

*

Surprisingly, God called us once more to Egypt, just two months before the revolution that dramatically changed the country in January 2011. Even though we'd struggled with accompanying medical teams before, Mustafah sweet-talked us once again. Bob took two American dentists—one completely new to us and one on his second trip. Mustafah also convinced a cardiologist and a pulmonologist from our hometown to come along to teach the new residents at the Aswan hospital. A thirty-year-old occupational therapist (one of the dentist's daughters), and the pulmonologist's wife and her best friend, both fifty-something Christian women, accompanied the group. The team seemed diverse, but we kept cautiously optimistic. I soon realized I could have trusted my initial hesitant feelings. Several relationships would remain challenging throughout the trip.

While clearing customs at the Egyptian airport upon arrival on this third trip, we didn't feel as anxious as usual. However, we were perplexed when the officials diverted our dental bags to a separate section. We stayed with the bags as the rest of the team easily checked through. Mustafah waited outside, as he'd already been in Egypt for a week. On numerous occasions, custom personnel have questioned our bags of dental equipment and supplies, but we've never been denied entry. Most countries' officials are happy to let us through once they discover we plan to help their people voluntarily.

"No used equipment allowed in country—new law," one official explained in broken English.

Egypt apparently had encountered some problems with contaminated medical equipment entering the country and had recently instituted this seemingly inflexible mandate. The local custom officials, at the highest levels, wanted to allow us to take the equipment in, but their jobs were at stake if they broke the new ruling.

As an Egyptian medical doctor with many connections and an understanding of how things worked in Egypt, Mustafah was needed. We believed he, above all others, could persuade, and he attempted to slip them money…to no avail. Mustafah even called his friend, the Egyptian ambassador to the United States. But since we'd arrived late on this Saturday night, the dignitary could not be reached. After several hours of fruitless effort (and with the medical team members chafing at the delay), we realized the custom officials planned to keep the two dental operating units, while letting the rest of the dental equipment through.

They wrapped the two boxes in heavy string and placed paperwork on top, with melted wax sealing the envelope with a signet ring. It smacked of ancient Pharaonic times. They assured us the units would be safe and could be recovered as we left Egypt. Since we already had one unit in the country from our last visit and since our mission was primarily to train the four local dentists, we stayed optimistic in accomplishing our goal without the two units. The mix of patients (with most needing extractions rather than restorative work) made it possible for us to be productive without the extra machines. We kept the one dental unit continually humming with restorative cases, and the other two dental stations provided extractions.

Reclaiming the dental units from customs upon our departure stole several hours, and Bob paid five "tips" (bribes) and a storage fee before successfully retrieving the two units for the plane trip. In Egypt everything is accomplished with extra cash incentives, and everyone assists for a price. There are often extra steps to any task so many officials can be compensated, fostering much inefficiency.

> In Egypt everything is accomplished with extra cash incentives, and everyone assists for a price.

"It's a game to see how much they can get out of us!" Bob exclaimed. "You have to pay to get in the door of the airport, to get your bags to the airline, to use the bathroom, and to get water. Worse, there are no set fees." Service providers are usually supported by tips and not by their employers, so we *almost* had compassion for the individuals once we understood the system.

It's like paying a good waitress in a restaurant a reasonable tip for services rendered. We understand that a customary tip is part of their wage. But in Egypt, it's expected. Even if we didn't like it, we accepted it as a cultural norm.

On this third trip, we accompanied the team on the customary visit to the pyramids and risked riding camels as another memorable event.

EGYPT
Our team rides camels at the pyramids.

Our minds, however, were focused on fulfilling our chief dental goal of the trip. We were anxious to help the hospital at Aswan get the portable dental clinic operational, as we had heard they hadn't utilized Dr. Deira, the Egyptian dentist we'd trained our previous visit a year prior. The hospital administration had asked three other young, inexperienced dentists to join us this time, and Dr. Deira came as well. The dentists delighted in sharing professionally, and they promised to take turns providing dental services to the hospital. The hospital did hire Dr. Deira to care for patients in the outlying clinics, and the other dentists have helped on short-term trips. Our dental training in the use of the portable equipment turned out exceptionally well. Dr. Deira currently uses the dental clinic weekly to help in the villages.

It seemed to tax the hospital staff to handle our large and varied team. No one stepped forward to oversee the three women who came without distinct roles. As the only woman who'd visited Egypt before, I felt I should somehow cater to the other ladies on the trip. But it became difficult to assist Bob while simultaneously checking on the women, a sure recipe for ruin. The dental clinic rocked and wobbled with the three American dentists engrossed in treating patients and training the four Egyptian dentists who also acted as interpreters. I kept busy sterilizing as Bob didn't need me chairside.

Meanwhile, the other women on the trip tried to find a place to fit in and were understandably discouraged about their lack of roles as they hung around the dental team, often as a distraction. The small hospital, on this occasion, did not provide leadership to utilize effectively the extra helpers, although they needed the physicians and dentists.

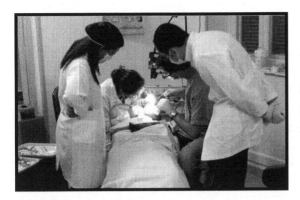

Egypt

Our team trained four Egyptian Dentists.

I always depend on Bob to right my world whenever it tips, but this time he remained busy. The team members' needs were spinning out of control. It became the most difficult trip with its undercurrent of dissatisfaction from the other women. I allowed one lady to help in the clinic the first day, but it didn't work well. When the lady's friend found there wasn't a job for her in the medical clinic, she showed up at the dental clinic too.

"I feel like we're dogs snarling over the same bone," I commiserated to Bob. "I know they want something to do, but I must stay here to help you and don't have enough to keep them busy, too." With so much happening, and our dental roles clearly defined, it wasn't something I could fix.

Bob whispered, "Idle hands and extra chatter in a busy, confined space is disrupting the clinic's harmony and efficiency. We are trying to teach dentists while treating anxious patients. I don't know what to suggest for them." Finally he came to my rescue by kindly advising the women that there wasn't enough room for everyone and that he really needed me to focus. How true that was!

But to me, the scenario became a source of guilt, my default response to any less-than-perfect outcome. I know one of the deepest principles of nature is that we all have a craving to be appreciated, and the worst punishment is to be ignored or abandoned. I was truly sorry for the women team members.

Although the other ladies rode along on our visit to the outlying clinics, they were restless there as well. They didn't appreciate the suggestion from the hospital administrator's wife (who came to see her ophthalmology patients) that they wash windows.

*

The next morning, Bob suggested Nurse Felicia take them out to the village for a diversion, although we also desired her nursing assistance. That backfired as some local children threw stones at them. Since Nurse Felicia had a thirty-year reputation at stake, she marched into the school and asked the administrator to take action on the perpetrators, as "racial and religious hate should not be tolerated anywhere!" Felicia's power and influence in the village impressed us, but we grieved over the divisions in the world.

I flashed back to my first brush with racial prejudice that occurred merely months after our wedding, over twenty-five years prior. Thereafter, I'd vowed to fight discrimination wherever I encountered it.

Our African-American neighbors hailed from the South and were part of the enlisted soldiers' ranks. In the Army there is a distinction in socialization between the enlisted and the officer corps. Because the officer may sometimes have to "pull rank" on an enlisted soldier, socializing between the two groups is discouraged, except for whole unit events. I didn't understand these norms when I first associated with the Army after marrying Bob. Even within the officer corps, respect for the wives of the senior officers took on great importance, as evidenced by my first ladies' group meeting where all the women stood when the wife of the commander walked in. The leader's wife was addressed as "Mrs. Stone," although everyone else used first names.

I still don't relish the stratification in the Army, although I can't change age-old traditions. Before comprehending these dynamics, I invited several enlisted men's African-American wives from the neighborhood to a craft party with some of the Caucasian officer's wives in Bob's unit who had also grown up in the South.

Despite my innocence, it didn't take long to realize something seemed very wrong. The two groups refused to interact, and several women left before the refreshments were served. Socio-economic, race, and husbands' rank issues all came into play. I still insist that laundry is the only thing that should be separated by color! I don't want to be involved with anything or anyone who won't have *everyone* as an accepted member, though that seems simplistic in today's world.

> I still insist that laundry is the only thing
> that should be separated by color!

Another difficulty that transpired on this Egyptian trip occurred when a substantial amount of the team money disappeared (probably stolen) due to a team member's disregard for the established safety measures. We got the impression he thought Bob had miscounted or short-changed him. Whenever a large amount of cash is carried into the country, it is wise to split it among the team. We learned to never assume the carriers will count the money when they agree to transport cash, which after this instance we insist upon.

A team member also brought a laptop computer that he planned to leave for the medical residents. When he did not follow through on his offer, the director of the Egyptian medical residency program was dismayed. When Bob asked the man why he didn't leave the computer, he replied, "Oh, I don't have time to take my personal stuff off it, so I'll just take it back to America."

We bit our tongues when watching these mistakes and gaffes. Not only do we try to guide but also to extend the grace of "freebies," where we give people breaks when they act irresponsibly due to lack of cross-cultural experience.

*

After living a stone's throw from the river for a week in Aswan while we worked on dental patients, the idea of a Nile cruise beckoned. As one of the

240 riverboats available, we walked to our luxurious, three-deck cruise ship docked across from our hotel. It featured a large dining room and an open top deck for sunbathing and sightseeing. We checked into our private room that held a huge, picture-window view of the Nile. Our tour included an English-speaking guide assigned to direct and to instruct our team during our travels through ancient Egyptian ruins.

We ate and slept on the riverboat for two nights but spent most of our time at the major archaeological sites along the Nile, ending in Luxor, where we caught our flight home.

Following the construction of the first dam at Aswan in 1904, the Philae temple was underwater, forcing relocation to a nearby island for preservation. This temple, sacred to the goddess Isis (giver of magic and life), is one of the best preserved Ptolemaic temples in Egypt. At the Kom Ombo temple—dedicated to Sobek, the crocodile god and Horoeris, the winged god of medicine—we noted the wall reliefs showing ancient surgical and dental tools. The temple of Edfu, the best preserved of all Pharaonic relics, is dedicated to the falcon-headed god, Horus.

Egypt

I hold a live
Nile crocodile.

In 1922, King Tutankhmon's tomb was discovered in the valley of the Kings on the mountainside behind Thebes. Although the tomb had long ago been pillaged and plundered by robbers (as occurred in most of the graves), King Tut became famous for the enormous amount of treasure found in the burial chamber, fortunately missed by thieves. Queen Hatshepsut's funerary monument at Deir El-bahari was another architectural masterpiece. The Karnak temple, with its majestic avenue of ram-headed sphinxes, and the Luxor temple complexes remained the capital for the wealthy Egyptian Kingdom for centuries. A dazzling sound and light show within the remains of Luxor dramatically illustrated a glorious kingdom long ago lost, although well preserved through the centuries in many impressive ruins.

After the strenuous walking tours of the temples and historic sites in the blistering, dry heat, the group was overwhelmed with the information deluge. Although a fascinating excursion into the past, the Egyptian tourism trade was drastically curtailed with the revolution, hopefully temporarily.

A doctor and a wife from America, who'd served at the hospital for several weeks before we arrived, attached to our group for the cruise. When the expected tips were to be given to the cruise boat crew and our very helpful guide, they refused to contribute.

"I don't know what to say to them," Bob confided to me. "I told them it's the only income the workers will receive and is required as a regular charge would be. They just don't get it. They don't want to pay it, even though they admit the service was adequate. They wouldn't give me a reason why they wouldn't pay."

"Hmmph! They told us they're planning on serving on other missions, so this is something they need to learn. They can't be rude to the locals by not giving the expected wages that come in the way of tips," I insisted.

However, the American couple, miffed and cold toward Bob's comments and guidance, still refused to give their portion. Since we refused to insult the workers in any way, we took what they owed out of our team's fund, already short due to the stolen cash loss. It was another painful ordeal for Bob. There had been more than the usual stresses this trip.

*

In March 2011, we received an email plea from our "Mother Theresa of Egypt" (the Christian woman who ran the Sudanese refugee school and many other community-aid projects) about the effects of the revolution that had overthrown Mubarak's government in January 2011. It brought great concern to our hearts, now inextricably woven with Egypt after our three trips.

She pleaded, "Please pray for the people in our neighborhood who have experienced loss through violence and death. Over 130 people were injured and ten died as a result of a well-organized and deliberate attack on Christians in general and people in the garbage community in particular. Please pray that the village Christians will not seek revenge. Egypt is going through very tough times, with a crumbling system of law and order.

"Although the revolution brought some good and necessary changes, it also caused quite a collapse in the fabric of society, including the economic system. Millions of people are out of work, partly because foreign companies, investors, and tourists have not returned. Naturally, this is causing great social unrest for people who are trying—in vain—to feed their families. So, we need prayer, dear friends—lots and lots of it! We hate to see our beloved country collapsing like this, people going hungry, and Christians possibly becoming scapegoats for all ills. Thank you in advance for praying. Love to you all."

Our thoughts and prayers often have been with Egypt during these difficult years. After the revolution, one of the darling dentists we trained that last trip visited us in Colorado. Her relatives in Pennsylvania wanted her to stay in America, but she felt it important for Christians to not abandon Egypt. She planned to continue working and speaking for God there, including joining Dr. Deira at the village clinics around Aswan.

Sometimes childhood dreams and visions play into our destiny, as they had for me in Egypt. It would occur again on our next trip to Africa.

MOZAMBIQUE AND SWAZILAND

Africa, AIDS, and Aspirations

* * *

"I'VE PONDERED THE NURSES' LIVES in Egypt, and it looks like I'll have more déjà vu moments from my girlhood aspirations on our next mission," I warned Bob. "Swaziland has the church hospital I heard about all through my childhood. I even attended college with a young man who grew up there, so it's been in the back of my mind for years. That hospital became one of the most inspirational factors in my career choice of nursing. I'd often thought about being a missionary nurse there!"

"You were not a child without ambition...and you've often been my visionary," Bob sweet-talked.

"Well, I've always believed that from a little spark a mighty flame might burst forth. Although we've done well with our family, I think we have a lot in us to accomplish yet." I hesitated. "Not that I know many facts," I remarked as I saw Bob scanning the guide book as we flew on the eighteen-hour plane flight. "You're my researcher. Give me a run-down on the country."

"Okay," Bob replied. "Swaziland is a small, land-locked kingdom surrounded by Mozambique on the east and the Republic of South Africa in the other three directions. It is about the size of New Jersey and is a monarchy, where the Ngwenyama (hereditary leader) rules the country as king. He appoints other leaders, and some are elected. About three quarters of the population work at subsistence farming, and 60 percent of the people live on less than $1.25 per day. Now it is early winter, where the average high temperatures are around 60 degrees Fahrenheit."

"That'll be cool weather. How bad is the HIV/AIDS epidemic here? I've heard it's not pretty."

"Swaziland is critically affected by the AIDS pandemic, having the highest HIV infection rate in the world—26 percent of all adults and over 50 percent of those in their twenties, with the lowest life expectancy on the planet at thirty-two years. Half of the country's population is under seventeen years of age."

We traveled with Sir, his wife and son, along with another dentist and his assistant. Sir had previously worked in both these countries, traveling to that part of the world various times in his illustrious church financial career. Flying into Johannesburg, South Africa, we rented a van that Sir drove to Swaziland, several hours away.

*

We arrived at the Memorial Hospital, a 350-bed regional referral and teaching hospital situated in Manzini, the populous hub of Swaziland. With sprawling buildings, the hospital contained specialty wards, operating rooms, and outpatient clinics servicing 500 patients daily. Founded in 1926 by an American Protestant church as an emergency intervention center, its expansion over the years included a college of nursing and other health-training institutions.

After he returned from meeting the administrator at the hospital, Bob informed me, "Hey, you're goin' to love this! We're actually setting up our dental clinic in the current nursing school, since there's a break for students right now. I guess your vision of serving in the nursing school is coming true, in a weird turn of events!"

"I always dreamed of this." I laughed. "Thanks for making it happen, Sweetheart!"

"Well, save your excitement for a week or so," Bob reminded me. "We're heading over to Mozambique first and should be there by dinner." Mozambique had a more civilized feel than Swaziland.

"It's a huge country—twice the size of California," Sir said.

*

Mozambique

We spent a week at a seminary compound in Mozambique, where the rural acreage contained a currently vacant dorm, where we set up our dental clinic. The rooms had large windows that looked out onto a grassy plain where tall, striking black women strolled gracefully, often carrying burdens on their heads as scampering little children shadowed behind. Just down the hall from the dental rooms were bathrooms with sinks and running water, which is always a blessing. (So many times we must carry water some distance to use for our sterilization.)

One challenge lay in attracting patients at their scheduled times, as they'd often show up late or even the next day. We related soon to a common local expression often repeated: "It's ten until it's eleven" (meaning the person wasn't late until the hour had passed).

"The trouble with being punctual in these countries is that there's no one here to appreciate it!" We laughed.

Treating the students and their families became our goal at the seminary; and, for almost the first time, we kept a select and *limited* patient population for which we could provide comprehensive care. We often treated multiple problems that required several dental visits. Completing all the current dental needs for each person living on the compound was a rare and wonderful feeling.

Our best case involved an elderly, tall, distinguished man who showed up unannounced one afternoon.

"How did you lose your front teeth?" Bob questioned, using the interpreter.

The man bowed his head as Sir stepped forward and quietly elaborated, "This is the church district superintendent for the entire country. In a political uprising about fifteen years ago, he withstood torture and persecution for being a Christian. The abductors knocked out his teeth."

Shocked he'd been without teeth all those years, Bob couldn't wait to make him a front partial. We thrilled to his quiet elation, marveling at his humble acceptance of the circumstances of his life. It brought tears to our eyes to realize what he'd been through and to see his strong character developed through life experiences.

My niece, newly graduated from college, planned to spend the summer doing mission work with children wherever her church sent her. Ironically, she showed up at the same compound and her first week overlapped our visit. The four fresh and vibrant college students who volunteered for the mission enriched our stay immensely. Feeling a little uncomfortable with the safety of the compound, we felt conflicted about leaving the young people there. The only English-speaking missionaries planned to be gone for the majority of their visit that would extend for several months. I felt protective of my niece but realized we had to trust it would be all right, although we longed to scoop her up and take her with us. Later, we heard all had gone well, and she'd treasured her summer experience, much to our relief.

The leaders of the seminary served a wonderful dinner for us on our last night and surprised the women of our group with African headdresses and tied skirts. Since I loved dressing up, I strutted as if I walked a fashion runway, showing off for my niece. The young seminary students guffawed, embarrassing me with their boisterous laughter.

We truly felt warmed by the love of those we'd served, but we were a little taken aback when the American missionaries who had directed the seminary there for years commented, "They view you as a cross between Superman and Santa Claus, due to your status as Americans. You are like Superman because you bring this high-tech, dental equipment that creates marvelous end results, and because you give it without charge you are like Santa Claus!"

> "They view you as a cross between Superman and Santa Claus, due to your status as Americans."

It humbled us, as we realized we were only able to bless others because of the wondrous way we'd been favored by our opportunities in America.

*

Swaziland

After lunch, we arrived back in Swaziland and found that the house that had been reserved for us on the hospital compound would now be shared with other American medical personnel who'd showed up unexpectedly during the prior week to help at the hospital during their summer breaks. Although they claimed the nice bedroom, our team squeezed in, but one person slept on the screened porch.

Sir's wife laid out our breakfasts of fruit, cereal, toast, and hard-boiled eggs. We had rice and a meat topping in the hospital cafeteria for our lunches, and Sir's wife cooked several meals for us at the house. We enjoyed a great restaurant several times. Their specialty was Cordon Bleu, a breaded pork, ham, and cheese rolled-up delicacy.

Staff meetings in the medical library initiated each day, as we read the Bible and sang together. We treated dental patients for four days, including the neediest hospital staff members from the head administrative doctor on down to the maintenance workers. Since the workers numbered around 400, it disappointed us that we didn't have time to treat everyone. Each hospital department could send their five neediest patients. English speakers were more common here because of Great Britain's control of the country from the late 1800s until the 1960s. Since SiSwati is the language many of the citizens spoke, we still needed translators most of the time.

It shocked us to hear that only eight national dentists in the entire country provided care, and we were honored to hear that one wanted to meet us. He watched us work in the clinic and then followed us to the house where we stayed. Some Christian benefactors had generously supported him for his dental education in Canada; but, unlike many dentists who'd left, he had returned to help his country. His wife, one of the few trained dental hygienists in Swaziland, cleaned and pulled teeth. Her sister had become one of the King's eleven (at least) wives.

> Only eight national dentists
> in the entire country provided care.

We met other fascinating people striving to make a difference. One American couple moved to the country to start a caring ministry. He is a doctor of pediatrics and internal medicine, and she'd trained as a physician's assistant (P.A.). Educated in America, both came to faith in God as children and felt called to use their medical skills overseas. We could not think of a needier place than Swaziland.

They arrived with their eight-year-old triplet sons, and had a five-year-old son and a baby daughter born in Africa. A newborn girl, abandoned on their doorstep a day before we came, became the center of attention. We took turns holding the baby, knowing she probably was infected with AIDS. This medical couple works with a team of fifteen Swazis they have trained to conduct medical care clinics to 25,000 rural patients a year. They serve communities with limited access to healthcare services and are based at the hospital, where clients can access relief and reduction HIV/AIDS programs.

"Could you train us to help with dental problems? We see them all the time and are at a loss," the American pediatrician and his P.A. wife asked.

"We'd love to!" Bob responded, knowing that often medical personnel can be capably trained to help patients dentally, especially with extractions of infected teeth.

BELIZE
I hold an abandoned infant found on the doorstep
of this medical mission family.

The couple spent a day in the clinic thinking they could quickly learn enough about dentistry in a few hours to expand their services. After only a short time with us, they realized dentistry was much more demanding and difficult than they had envisioned.

"I don't think we can do dentistry and doctoring, too. But maybe we can provide the administrative and the logistical support for dentists to come to help us at our clinics."

With this in mind we decided to split the cost of a portable dental clinic, which we left for other dental providers to use. We connected them with the dentist who had been trained in Canada, in hopes that he could be persuaded to help with humanitarian work in his country. We treated both couples to dinner, but at the end of the meal, our Swaziland dentist said, "I just don't have the time to help. Do you know we're supporting almost ten children ourselves? They're all young ones of our brothers and sisters who have died of AIDS."

We felt sorry for the terrible needs and have followed the ministry of this medical couple who have occasional visits from dentists. We're planning another trip there and hope to connect again.

The current King of Swaziland, King Mswati III, was born at the Memorial Hospital, which has the highest number of hospital newborn deliveries in the country, with approximately one baby born every hour. The maternity ward consists of a large rectangular room, with twenty beds lining the sides of the room with a middle walkway. Sometimes the beds had to be shared when it became crowded, and frequently the babies were delivered there in the room, with all the other patients watching.

An American nurse said we'd be quite taken aback at the methods of treatment patients received during labor. She witnessed local workers speaking punitive statements to the patients in harsh voices. "Quiet down! This isn't hard, and you must cooperate!"

It did seem to be a place of extraordinarily chaotic activity as we walked through. Right outside the windows a grassy courtyard held family members who camped out on the site and used small, open fires for food preparation.

"It's really dark out there," I told Bob one night after we'd stayed late at the dental clinic. "Sir told us to call for a ride when we finished."

"I hate to bother anyone," Bob replied. We easily walked home along the one-mile dirt path that we followed each morning to the clinic. Laughing and chatting along the way, we reached our house, where we discovered the gate and the high fence locked. We had to scale the ten-foot enclosure.

Then, upon entering the house, we found out there had been recent stabbings along the path we'd just traversed. Sir crisply told us we should not have taken the chance in the dark. Once again we're sure our angels shake their heads over our stupidity as they keep us from harm!

*

We'd been definitely on a roll with our missions, which came to a sudden stop when our next mission fell through. Although we'd planned to go to Nigeria with a group who taught indigenous people to perform simple dental procedures, the leaders cancelled due to the religious persecution of Christians. It would be foolishly dangerous to go, as 300 Christians had been killed recently,; and our sponsoring pastor hid against threats on his life. Instead, our next assignment came in a most unusual and affirming way.

Bob received the national "Dental Volunteer of the Year Award" from the Christian Dental Society, and we attended their conference for the first time. The organization served us well by connecting us to an astounding family who'd been at the core of many outreach adventures in India, relaying one of the most awe-inspiring stories we'd ever heard!

INDIA

Hardships and Miracles

* * *

AT THE CHRISTIAN DENTAL SOCIETY CONVENTION, we heard a speaker with a most magnetic personality. Thomas told dramatic stories of God's work in India, a country high on our "bucket list" (places we want to go to before we "kick the bucket"). Due to the fallout of Nigeria, we had the following February free and hoped for a mission opportunity during that time frame.

"Wanna go?" Bob asked me.

"Sultan-ly!" I grinned.

"Thomas, your story has stirred our heartstrings," we told him during the break. "Would it be possible to visit?"

"February would be the best time for us, and the weather would be good for you," he replied without our prompting, totally confirming our decision to go. He continued, "One billion people live in India. Yet, there are over 500,000 villages that have never heard about salvation through Jesus Christ. Although they believe in gods and know they are sinners, they rely on rituals and pilgrimages to take away sin's penalty. Out of the world's total of 900,000,000 Hindus, approximately 700,000,000 live in India. Hinduism is formed of diverse traditions of millions of gods, with no single founder."

Thomas related the story of his family at the conference that day. As a young man, Thomas's Christian father, Paul, searched for the reason why the church hadn't preached the gospel to the millions of unreached people in India. Paul decided that most Christians do not have the willingness to leave their homes to work in needy places. When he inventoried his life, Paul realized he owned nothing to give but himself, and he made a commitment that he'd follow after God no matter the price. Paul felt led to reach all the unsaved people he could by showing them a film on Jesus' life, and he purchased a projector by donating his blood.

At a marriageable age, Paul wanted a girl who'd love God above all else. He even considered marrying an orphan, since he disagreed with the dowry requirements by which the girl's family must pay a great deal to obtain a husband for the daughter. He felt this system treated women as merchandise, considered only of value according to the amount of dowry the man's family could obtain. "So many times I've seen people marry for the wrong reasons," Paul told us. "Because of lust or because they think the person is beautiful or can bring them popularity or wealth. It's much better to be in God's will and to be happy than to be miserable with someone who's not in God's will. A poor marriage choice will affect your children and grandchildren."

We agreed with his analysis. Paul found a wonderful orphan named Aja, who gave birth to their first child, Thomas, our new friend.

With no vehicle of their own, for years they used the public bus to haul around their small children, the projector, Bibles, Christian literature, their belongings and the rest of the team. "Sometimes the bus pulled in, looked at the group, and then quickly left us standing there!" Thomas laughed as he related the story to us. "Each adult loaded a parcel of sixty pounds of brochures on his or her head and worked all day until the materials had been given away. We'd show the *Jesus* film in the evenings, touching many people, although we were often ridiculed and persecuted."

Each night they sought shelter, sleeping on the beach, at a bus or a train station, taking baths when they found water. They couldn't afford to buy milk powder or much food for their children, who picked up sicknesses and skin problems with the constant moving around. Opposition stayed strong, and many times their enemies defecated around where they slept. They recounted miraculous outcomes when they were threatened by others or became ill to the point of death.

> Each night they sought shelter, sleeping on the beach, at a bus or a train station, taking baths when they found water.

"How can we believe all these seemingly supernatural events?" we questioned as Thomas told the story in dynamic detail at the conference, passing out a book that recounted their survival in many dangerous places.

"Americans today don't often experience such dramatic evidence of the power of God," Bob noted.

"Why not validate Thomas's narrative for ourselves?" I asked.

We'd been caught up in the story. A dentist and his wife from a small town in Indiana were inspired to accompany us.

*

We arrived in India that February after a two-day flight and rattled along rocky, bumpy roads in a van for eight hours on a trip that seemed endless. One of our bags hadn't arrived, but luckily it had contained only our uniforms and the items, including a kitchen sink, that Thomas requested. We've often been asked to bring items for missionaries and thought we'd heard it all. Thomas needed the basin to equip the camping vehicle he'd been assembling for his family's use as they visited villages all over India. We laughed when it was delivered to our Colorado home. Thankfully, all the other bags that contained the essential supplies for the dental clinics arrived safely in baggage claim. We've never lost a bag or been without the dental equipment we've needed on over thirty trips. What a record!

How overwhelmingly sad it was to see a village decimated by the tsunami. Although six years had passed, evidence of the disaster still existed in the rotting boat skeletons that littered areas at least a mile from the sea. The absolute devastation of the December 26, 2004, tsunami resulted in almost 200,000 people dead or missing. Within minutes of the deluge, the victims left behind fractured families, resulting in ruined homes, destroyed businesses, and a demolished infrastructure.

> Evidence of the disaster still existed in the rotting boat skeletons that littered areas at least a mile from the sea.

The first wave of the tsunami wasn't the worst of it, however. Many survivors of the initial crest saw the abundance of fish washed up on the beaches as the gigantic first swell receded. As they rushed in excitedly to scoop up the huge killing, they were oblivious to the second crushing tide that soon swept in to drown them. Afterwards, many men tried to provide for the disproportionate number of widows by marrying multiple women.

The dental clinic was held in a community center built with government relief money in a neighborhood of recently constructed, look-alike apartments that attempted to house the homeless. Our presence, announced with a flyer in Hindi, generated an unusual excitement since the availability of dental care was nonexistent in that area.

Our greatest success involved the chance to remove a pretty widow's severely decayed front teeth and to provide new incisors. She thought her new appearance would help her find acceptance and possibly a husband. A reporter recorded her story and our intervention for the local news.

India

The power of
prayer
begins each day.

"Look at the adorable children!" I said on our second day and immediately embraced the loving orphans, many of whom were parentless after the tsunami. They happily played in a shady area in front of large, one-story dorms. We set up in a room and the Indiana dentist did extractions in his balmy office on the porch. The inconsistent and low power of the available electricity required a generator. Due to energy fluctuations, our amalgamator and the goose-neck light burned out. Fortunately, Bob had a back-up light and used composite fillings as we continued working.

The village of our third clinic posted a banner at the front gate announcing our arrival. A weathered, fragile older woman named Sabiya came to greet us first. Distinguished and radiant in a white sari—a strip of unstitched cloth, from three to nine yards long that Indian women drape over their bodies like gowns—Sabiya came forward tearfully.

"I've prayed for thirty years for missionaries to come to my village." Sabiya gripped our hands in her surprisingly hearty handshake, "You are the first foreign Christians!"

That humbled us so completely that we stopped in our tracks at the thought of this little widow of simplicity and tiny stature so powerfully dedicated to prayer for her family and community. Through a translator, Sabiya related the story concerning her small home where she prays throughout the day. She initially felt God's calling to work among the poor and the destitute, specifically the sick and the dying. She spent the majority of her time at a local hospital, where she prayed for patients and witnessed a variety of miraculous healings. Sabiya claimed she'd even seen deliverance for patients who came as HIV positive. News about her effective prayers quickly spread in her community, and people began postponing their hospital visits and traveling to Sabiya's home with the hopes of a miraculous healing. Soon, Sabiya's home became like a small church. Her prayers began early in the morning, creating a ruckus that became untenable for her devout Hindu neighbor to handle. Frustrated with the noise and all it represented, he sought counsel from his Hindu friends.

"Build a temple in your backyard, equipped with a loud horn to counteract the noise rising from Sabiya's property," the Hindu friends advised. "Sound the horn when she starts praying."

The Hindu man purchased the supplies, including sand, bricks, and idols that would be displayed throughout the backyard. As the temple construction began, Sabiya watched from her back window, thoroughly aware of his intentions. She immediately vowed aloud, "My God will change this situation." With that, she prayed relentlessly until 2:00 a.m., when she felt an overwhelming peace and fell asleep.

BELIZE
The older woman in the center of the photo (wearing white)
prayed thirty years for Christian missionaries to come to her village.

In the early morning, Sabiya woke to the sounds of heavy monsoon rains. She peered out her back window to see rushing floodwaters carrying away her

Hindu neighbor's construction materials. The idols, collapsed and broken, became armless and legless statues of stone staring helplessly toward the sky.

The Hindu man, furious upon the destruction of his recently purchased materials, also became fearful of what the broken idols might mean. Seeking counsel, he approached a local Hindu priest and asked if the destroyed statues might represent a curse or his imminent death. The priest advised him not to build the planned temple. To confirm, the Hindu man decided to visit a witch doctor, who asked, "Do you have any Christians living near you?"

"Yes. Next door. That is why I was building the temple in the first place!"

"Do the Christians living near you pray?" the witch doctor probed.

"Every day! They pray all the time!"

The witch doctor realized the power in Sabiya's prayers and counseled, "You'd better move and leave that area completely." Out of fear, the Hindu man did just that.

With the Hindu man gone, Sabiya continued her ministry with no distractions or threats to this day.

"Wow, just think how the world could literally be turned upside down if believers had Sabiya's faith and heart for intercession." Our Indiana dental friends shook their heads. "She is a humble widow with a giant faith."

Sabiya admitted she'd prayed long and hard for her son-in-law, Valin, a man very opposed to God. As a renowned gang leader with an intimidatingly large frame and an affinity for tobacco (chewing around fifty packets a day), he caused many to fear his presence. His wife and Sabiya prayed daily for Valin's cruelty toward believers and cynicism toward Christianity to end. After several years of coaxing, and to appease them, Valin began attending nearby Sunday services at Pastor Kirsi's church, although he'd sneak out to catch a movie at the nearby cinema while the three-hour service continued. Just before the end of the sermon, Valin weaseled his way back in, creating the illusion that he'd worshipped with the congregation.

"She is a humble widow with a giant faith."

Valin attempted several different lines of work, all which seemed to be disastrous. As a bus conductor, accidents occurred every time he drove. Frustrated, he moved on to shop keeping. With a knack for swindling, he felt sure he'd succeed in this field, only to find failure yet again. As Valin's family continued to pray faithfully, his wife recommended that he be baptized. Though Valin spoke adamantly against the idea, Pastor Kirsi baptized him anyway.

Valin miraculously changed on that day. Soon after, Valin saw a clear vision where he carried a basket of fish and tomatoes on his head toward a nearby village where he'd lived previously. Three families from that close village, who attended Pastor Kirsi's church, had a similar vision about Valin. In this way, God confirmed Valin's calling to begin ministering to that particular area. Though a recent believer, Valin obediently followed his new assignment and started visiting that village three times a week until, eventually, he moved his family there. In the past three years, 150 people have been baptized and touched by his powerful story of transformation. "If God could change me," Valin affirmed, "God can change anyone."

Into this village we came to set up our dental clinic and met Valin, now a helpful and humble pastor. Valin's two teenage daughters translated for us. They provided lunch in their family home, which consisted of one room attached to the back of the church. Four mattresses on the floor showed where they slept. A kitchen nook in disrepair contained open shelves with sparse items, a table, an assortment of chairs, and several old utensils. They appeared as clean and gracious people, even though they hauled their water from a well some distance from the home.

"If God could change me...God can change anyone."

When we asked for a restroom, they indicated a sandpit behind a branch-constructed screen that barely offered privacy, their only toilet facilities for the church and the home. Our team felt saddened by their lack of sanitation facilities and offered cash for their "bathroom fund." We boarded the bus, thinking we'd leave before they opened the gift. Suddenly, the whole family and some church members climbed into our little bus and hugged and kissed us as we told them the thanks belonged to God, who provides for us all.

*

In India we witnessed the elaborately carved stone towers of Hindu temples with hundreds of diverse gods depicted. Monuments to countless gods dotted the countryside. The impersonal religion is determined by the law of Karma, characterized by belief in reincarnation. Salvation is freedom from the cycle of repeated birth and death. India, as a whole, has about 50,000,000 people still living a primitive tribal existence. They reside in isolation and have yet to be impacted by modern civilization. They wear little or no clothing, and many are plagued by warfare and cannibalism.

Bob preached in a nearby church, a building completely packed with many women sitting on the floor, appearing as a rainbow of beautifully arrayed colored saris and caring, glowing faces. During meetings, men sit on one side of the room and women on the other. Guided to special chairs on the platform as honored guests, we felt the crush of people.

Bob spoke on "Hope in Christ," after which the congregants presented us gifts of brightly colored scarves. In most Christian churches in India, and around the world, more women than men attend because the gospel message is one of liberation and acceptance, a message that is powerful and esteem building to women in the midst of cultures that remains oppressive and devaluing.

INDIA
A packed church service where Bob preached on "Hope in Christ"

I greeted the group and told them that God had blessed me as the mother of three and the grandmother of five. The Indian women gasped in surprise, thinking I appeared younger. I thought of my habit of using chemicals to cover up the gray in my hair, as many American women do. Gray hair is respected and honored in many developing cultures such as these.

Thomas told us, "Public worship among the disciples of Jesus in India is generally far more exuberant, loud, and fervent than in American congregations. Try to forget yourselves and get right into it. It is very common for American believers to experience rather dramatic epiphanies during their sojourns among the churches in India and to see and to experience spiritual dimensions which they have only previously read about in the Bible."

We were certainly seeing spirituality in a different way in this country, which brought reflection. We wondered if Americans, with our self-sufficiency and independence, feel we don't need to rely upon God to help us. In this environment, our skepticism on the miracles had completely dissolved.

After Bob preached, a follow-up talk by the pastor seemed quite intense, and, because we couldn't understand the words, we later asked Thomas what had transpired. "The pastor told the people that you had come so far to show God's love, risking your lives and using your own money. He pressed the congregation to be willing to at least go out to their neighbors and surrounding villages to share the love of God." To think that our actions might have produced a small ripple effect brought us great encouragement.

India, although fascinating, exciting, and mind-boggling, had absolutely the worst driving of any of the countries we've encountered, although we've white-knuckled it many times before. They "drove on the wrong side of the road," British-style. With breakneck speeds and bizarre passing, survival depended on drivers understanding the unwritten rules of the road. It was not unusual for oncoming traffic, and a vehicle being passed by another, to brake and move over to enable the three vehicles to wedge through a narrow place simultaneously, with inches separating all from disaster.

Ever-present pedestrians, bikes, and animals headed to the almost nonexistent shoulders while horns blared incessantly. Seemingly impossible paths opened up while the van's speed barely diminished. The windshield on our van was so dirty and cracked, we wondered about visibility. "Our driver's maneuvers seem so dangerous and absurd, I wonder if he gets a season ticket from the police," Bob whispered to me sarcastically.

Although we did not see speed limits in India, I muttered, "He'd get stopped in America for going 52 in a 25-mile zone—which is about what he's doing. I guess he could try the excuse that he's dyslexic!"

> "Our driver's maneuvers seem so dangerous and absurd,
> I wonder if he gets a season ticket from the police."

Congested roads accommodated people, bicycles, motorcycles, carts, wandering sacred cows, and even a huge elephant walking down the middle of the road at one point. In fact, we'd often see bikes with multiple items hanging off them. These stacks of gadgets and plastic containers eight to ten feet high obscured the bike completely, as Thomas laughingly called it, "Walmart on a bike."

Roads around villages held mature, dried rice plants piled on the streets so that vehicles driving over them threshed the rice, removing the kernels from the chaff. Did anyone care if a little petroleum or dirt mixed into the rice?! I wondered. Our driver careened around corners, missing oncoming vehicles by inches. Sometimes we peered between our fingers as we avoided watching the erratic encounters seemingly destined for collision.

Thomas laughingly called it,
"Walmart on a bike."

Thomas warned us in early emails that there are only three seasons in South India: "hot, hotter, and hottest!" Though we were thankful we'd come in the coolest season, the temperatures still challenged us. Although the ministry had hired a male chef who accompanied us the entire time, we decided his meals reflected the same scale: spicy, spicier, and spiciest! Still, we enjoyed the jovial cook. His devotion reminded me of the saying on an old kitchen plaque of mine: "Cooking is like love...it should be entered into with abandon or not at all!" We pushed the food around on our plates to look like we had eaten. We resorted to ordering plain yogurt to mix with our dishes when we went to restaurants, trying with little avail to dilute the caustic (to us) seasonings.

"These food establishments need a sign that says: 'Don't just stand there outside and be hungry. Come on in and get fed up!'" Bob joked to me quietly. "I haven't found anything I like to eat here."

Once, in between villages, Thomas dropped us to rest for a day at a first-class hotel that catered to foreigners, complete with a gorgeous buffet. Bob asked the waiter which of the foods were milder, but we still found them almost impossible to eat.

"How is it, sir?" The excellent waiter returned to ask if Bob liked the food.

"Honestly," Bob said, "I just can't eat it."

"Ah, you have a baby stomach." The waiter twinkled, to which Bob readily agreed. In a short time the head chef came out with a specially prepared plate of what he called "KFC chicken nuggets and French fries," and Bob smiled at a meal for the first and only time in India. We resolved to bring our own food if we ever came again.

For most meals in India, except for fancy restaurants, people ate using the fingers of their right hands, sometimes scooping the food off large leaves that substituted for plates. A nearby bowl or sink provided hand washing. One never extends a left hand to anyone for any reason, even to give or to receive an item. This is a practical custom in India and many other countries, stemming from the realities of toilets without paper, where the left hand and a bucket of water suffice.

The accepted greeting of respect among adults in India is to press hands together with fingertips under the chin and to bow forward one time. We addressed others by their title, finding that the use of a single name would appear disrespectful or condescending. If we didn't know or couldn't recall a name, we were instructed to call them "Uncle" or "Auntie." To show they intently listened while others talked to them, the Indians moved their heads so they neither shook nor nodded but displayed smoothly executed "bobbles" to acknowledge their attention. The motion distracted and entertained us, and I often struggled to keep a straight face.

Throughout most of Asia, there is a recurring custom against saying "no" to any appeal from an adult, especially from a guest. Thomas informed us that if we made a request of any sort, we must keep in mind that a hesitant or bland version of "yes" probably means something a little closer to "no." There is also a conflicting cultural stigma about saying "yes" too quickly.

> A hesitant or bland version of "yes"
> probably means something a little closer to "no."

When invited for dinner, for example, the initial response is always expected to be "no," even if one wants to go. To be polite, one has to be asked at least three times and then it is acceptable to say yes. It is often difficult for us to understand when a "yes" means "yes" and a "no" means "no" in various cultures. We often have to depend upon our host to decipher cultural norms to avoid hurt feelings. Usually nationals kindly give us latitude since we are strangers in a foreign land. Saying a firm "enough" proved sufficient in deterring further advances of food, which we learned rather quickly as we never wanted seconds.

As is a common request in most developing countries, we were asked not to wear elaborate outward adornments, such as jewelry, paint, piercings, and cosmetics, as they are showy and possibly also representative of pagan religions. The instructional email read: *Regardless, you may feel free to bring your tattoos along, but keep them covered as much as is practical.* Too funny!

Our last dental clinic ran for several days at the sprawling Christian center that Paul's family started on a southern island between India and Sri Lanka, the second holiest site in Hinduism. Once again we heard an amazing history.

After over fifteen years of ministry all over India, Paul felt that God wanted him to take a break and to spend forty days in prayer and fasting, which he did. On the fortieth day, Paul says, "God showed up! The way I saw Him was awesome and almost indescribable. The light in my room seemed to come from the light of 100,000 suns on that day! I could not sit or stand in the awesome light, and I just fell prostrate on the floor. I have never been the same and my ministry changed."

Paul and his family believe that God told them to relocate to the southern island of Rameswaram, but they had nothing of material means. God sent people with money and others who provided shelter. At first they received a room six feet by six feet and later a shack where they could sleep at night. They accepted the shack, which was used for cleaning fish by day. They now had five children who minimally subsisted, experiencing frequent hunger. Paul and Aja felt the importance of learning to be content no matter their circumstances, wanting to train others to follow by attesting to the fact that God always provided in time to meet their needs.

Paul reminisced, "In the early 1990s we began reaching out to refugees from the war in Sri Lanka, often feeding 4,000 people a day. Many accepted God because of the kindness they received. We decided to expand and to build a Christian center on the island. God provided unsalted water in the wells we dug, allowing us the only fresh water on the island today. Seventy-five families come on a daily basis to get safe water." Persecution remains a persistent problem, however. Radical Hindu groups burned their structures several times, causing them to build currently with cement and brick.

The scourge of femicide among the villages of India often occurs when families discretely kill their newborn daughters. By scalding and drowning them in a boiling bucket of water, families hope to escape the requirement of a bridal dowry years later. This horrible practice still occurs, and in some regions boys now out-number girls by as much as 20 percent. Pastors associated with Paul's ministry stay watchful for any chance to intervene in this tragedy, offering to take the newborn daughters to be raised in Christian homes. On Paul's compound there is now a Rescue Nursery, complete with a nurse's station and air-conditioning. It's clean and accommodating, with sweet people running it. Paul's ministry clothes, feeds, and provides shelter for about fifty orphans.

While I was there, a tiny girl named Diane stole my heart. Baby Diane's family didn't have the resources to raise her, but they would not allow her to be adopted. That is often the case in institutions we've visited around the world. The compound also supported the King of Kings English elementary school, a three-story building that accommodates 350 students. A North Carolina church helps support it and sends young people to teach English and other subjects, resulting in test scores unmatched by any other school in the area. Recently, some of the anti-Christian priests have started sending their children to the school because of its excellent reputation.

While touring the school, the teachers presented me with a lovely linen shawl. We walked through the many clean, airy rooms that housed polite young people in burgundy and green plaid uniforms. I felt honored when asked to pray aloud for each class, as they would soon take their qualifying tests for the year. The educators related that the extensive subject matter caused anxiety and stress for many of the students.

On our last afternoon, a student rushed into the clinic and requested our immediate presence in the large meeting room at the school. As we quickly complied, we were surprised to find the entire student body sitting on the floor according to age groups. Outfitted in colorful saris and bright smiles, they performed a stunning concert of song and dance, presenting us with beautiful, homemade bouquets of flowers and kind words.

We presented aprons that I'd sewed to several of the ladies who helped us and to the chef, who had labored so diligently on our behalf. Even though the food did not suit us, we realized we might have endured much worse without a chef who had tried to cater to our relatively weak Western stomachs. Rarely do we lose weight on a trip, but this time we did. We arrived home with cases of Giardia, a parasite from contaminated food and water.

On the huge compound stood the shell of a five-story, gigantic training center, as large as a stadium and as ornate as the Greek Parthenon. It is awaiting completion as donations continue. The immense and stunning white building arrests the attention of the hundreds of thousands of Hindus who walk past on the road to the famous pilgrimage site annually. The center features several floors of finished dorm rooms and classrooms. One bathroom oddity we'd seen nowhere else involved a special toilet seat that had places for feet on the sides of the rim. It allowed one the option of standing or squatting on the toilet so cleanliness could be maintained. Many groups believe the "squatty potties" (holes in cement) are cleaner because no part of the body except the feet touches the toilet area.

Over the years, 1,000 national missionaries have trained at the center, and have migrated to show love to unreached people all over India and surrounding countries. On the bottom floor, a dental clinic is being developed by the dentist who'd arranged to have Thomas speak to the dental conference that'd hooked us. He had been leading dental missions for years and had received the American Dental Association (ADA) Humanitarian Award designated to recognize an individual who has made a lasting impact on the oral health of their fellow human beings. He used the $5,000 awarded him by the ADA for charity, to help establish the new dental clinic which we used. Because the clinic was not yet finished, Bob and the Indiana dentist helped Thomas with some dental-specific ideas for the clinic.

India

Bob consults on dental clinic construction plans.

Bob and the Indiana dentist were excited to be the first to use the new deluxe dental chairs that had just been delivered. We were especially pleased when Paul received the first dental care in the new chair, followed by his many family members. Bob also repaired the broken partial denture of Aja, Paul's wife. Some radicals riding horses left her bruised, bloodied, and without front teeth during a raid to discourage their Christian work. Bob added a tooth to a space in Aja's smile, fixing what she'd lived with for years due to her persecutors' assaults.

Paul and the workers in his ministry have seen millions of Hindu pilgrims come to bathe in the ocean, attempting to wash away their sins and to receive pardon and peace. We drove the few miles to the beach of the Indian Ocean and toured side buildings, where pilgrims were shaving their heads for the ceremonies. Some worshipers drank the urine of cow gods, believing it to be a shower of blessing. I waded into the surf, where people dunked close to cows that facilitated the worship. Contaminated with city sewage, the filthy water seemed a contrast to its sacred purposes.

In another town we visited a large Hindu temple that kept a living elephant inside.

The Hindus in India have many festivals, including "Cavadi," where millions of people try to save themselves by making personal sacrifices. One sacrifice requires the pilgrim to pierce his flesh with four hooks placed in his back that are then tied to ropes and attached to a chariot that weighs approximately 200 pounds. The pilgrim's task is to pull the contraption six miles to the temple, which tears at his flesh the entire way. Another pilgrim sacrifice involves placing a three-to-five pound iron rod through the cheeks. After reaching the temple, the pilgrim pulls the rod out, causing profuse bleeding. In yet another sacrifice, the pilgrim places eight hooks in his back to hang from an ox cart, usually for about four hours.

> We visited a large Hindu temple
> that kept a living elephant inside.

"They believe they can save themselves and their households through rituals that only make them bloodied and desperate," Thomas said. "It's incredibly sad that they must endure these unnecessary and painful practices."

Tears sprang to my eyes. "It's a difficult thing to see. We believe in the one-time sacrifice of Jesus on the cross for our sins. It makes me realize how great the grace of God is in our lives. I wish we could reach these struggling souls."

Pilgrims from all over India visit Ramaswaram at least once in a lifetime, and the ones with mentally challenged relatives often use this opportunity to dispose of their ill ones. Dumping them in the so-called "holy place" gives them a peace of mind that they have left the hopeless ones at the entrance of "Moksha," the gate to eternity (according to Hindu mythology). With no roof over their heads, these special-needs people are often mistreated and can feed on nothing but the waste dumped from the vegetarian restaurants.

Paul's ministry reaches out to these desperate souls, giving long-overdue haircuts, baths, clean clothes, nail trimmings, and decent food. The lives of these poor people, often transformed with the love shown them, catches the curiosity of the anti-Christian priests and the police.

"Relief work in India is totally unheard of," Paul explained. "In fact, the temple priests often declare, 'If this is what the Christians are doing now, then eventually this whole island will become Christian. '"

"Relief work in India is totally unheard of."

Until 1998, government policy stood against open violence, but that changed with new national elections. A Hindu political party—which opposes Christian influence in India—gained control over the national government, and now turns a blind eye toward violence against Christians. While in India, we found that one of the village churches had a banner posted where the face of the pastor had been slashed off. The warning read: *This will happen to him if he doesn't stop preaching about Christ!* We wondered at our own safety but continued to trust in God's protection.

The Tsunami of 2004 completely missed the area where the training center stood. Thomas told us that Ezra, an old prophet who lived nearby, claimed to have been awakened around 3:00 a.m. on December 26, 2004, by the startling vision of the "angel of death." The angel declared he had claimed the Island of Rameswaram, which would soon be utterly destroyed. Ezra quickly rose and called church leaders around the region, begging them to join him in prayer through the night that God would spare the island from destruction.

At about 7:00 a.m. the following morning, massive tidal waves struck the entire east coast of India, Sri Lanka, and many other nations. The devastation miraculously bypassed the island of Rameswaram. The mayor later declared that "we didn't even lose a chicken!"

Just twenty miles to the north, death and desolation occurred along the 1,000 miles of coastline, with entire villages swept out to sea and millions left homeless. To the south of Rameswaram, the devastation of the cape of India left thousands of bodies to be buried in mass graves.

Two days before the tidal waves, petitions had come from a high government official and radical Hindus to Paul and Thomas, ordering the construction of the training center be stopped.

Immediately following the tidal waves, the official contacted Thomas, saying, "I apologize for my hasty edict. I did not realize the importance of your new building as the only structure in this region suitable for large-scale assistance. I hope you can help with the staggering numbers of displaced people among the coastal population."

The Indian government largely obstructed foreign-aid agencies from reaching the stricken villages, appeasing the Hindu radicals who claimed offense at assistance from "foreign religions." However, since Paul's work was an Indian ministry with years of experience in refugee work, they stayed at liberty to organize relief work and to present the Gospel.

India espouses the caste system, which brings social stratification and restriction in India, with four well-known categories: Brahmins (scholars, teachers, priests), Kshatriyas (kings, warriors, law enforcers, administrators), Vaishyas (agriculturists, cattle raisers, traders, bankers, artisans) and Shudras (laborers, craftsmen, service providers). Certain people remain excluded altogether with the label "untouchables" (called Dalits or Outcasts) which is unique in its extreme rigidity.

Tradition points to an Aryan migration from Eastern Europe several thousand years ago, which eventually dominated the indigenous dark-skinned Dravidians of India, causing society rules to be executed by a detailed system of unchangeable strata, defined by skin color, birth-family status, occupation, and other factors. Common people often make gods of those with paler skin. (Thomas once had a remote village offer to worship him due to his lighter skin shade.) Others act more prejudiced toward those with darker skin, ignorantly basing assumptions on their exposure to 2,000 years of race-determined Hindu religious fables.

Common people often make gods of those with paler skin.

Although India's national constitution of 1950 sought to abolish caste discrimination, especially the practice toward Outcasts, the caste system remains deeply entrenched in Hindu culture and is still widespread throughout southern Asia, especially in rural India. In what is labeled India's "hidden apartheid," entire villages in many Indian states remain completely segregated by caste. Representing about 15 percent of India's population—some 160,000,000 people—the widely scattered Outcasts endure almost complete social isolation, humiliation, and discrimination based exclusively on their birth status. Even an Outcast's shadow is believed to pollute the upper classes. They may not cross the line dividing their part of the village from that occupied by higher castes, drink water from public wells, or visit the same temples as the higher castes.

We encountered beggars and outcasts, but customs in India require that only rupees be offered to them, but not food. Even if they appear hungry, to be seen taking food would seriously shame them, even among the other beggars. Since a typical wage for unskilled labor in India is the equivalent of $1 per day, tips and gifts must be small. Beggars in India are even unionized, especially in the holy places. Each beggar staked his or her territory on the street and would not tolerate violations by others.

India truly surpassed our expectations as an exotic and interesting place. We breathed a sigh of relief to have survived the experience. It was one of the most difficult places to serve. Paul told us that at graduation, right before they send their teams all over Asia to spread the gospel, he takes the newly trained ministers to the cemetery to visit the graves of past foreign missionaries.

He said, "I use them as an example to explain the sacrifice these men and women made to bring the gospel to unknown people. Over a century ago they came to India, taking months of travel from England and America. They came to a foreign place leaving behind everything familiar, not knowing the language, culture, food, or weather. Their passion for Jesus and the burden they carried for the lost caused them to leave behind their warm, comfortable lives to come to this place. They brought all their belongings in a coffin because they knew they'd lay down their lives for the furtherance of the gospel. They committed to stay in India until death, a lot of them spilling their blood on Asian soil, many as martyrs."

The stark challenges of the country forever impressed us. We'll never forget the committed souls and the spiritual giants we grew to love and to admire. Remembering the sobering needs of that great continent, we hope to impact it again in some small way in the future. We would experience an almost identical culture in Bangladesh several years later.

A day after we returned home, we unexpectedly received a phone call destined to change our mission focus dramatically.

HONDURAS AND DOMINICAN REPUBLIC

It's All About the Kids

* * *

"MAY I BRING SOMEONE OVER WHO HAS A HUGE DESIRE to take dentistry to children around the world?" Dr. Jerome called us upon our arrival home from India.

Bleary-eyed and sick, but available, it intrigued us to be sought out by a ministry group, as usually we'd found our own contacts. That life-changing encounter brought a network for our next four missions. That same day Dr. Jerome and Colin, a vice-president of an organization that provided sponsorship for needy children around the world, came to our home.

"Our hearts have been touched over the years with the injustices we have seen concerning the little, helpless, innocent, vulnerable, and most trusting members of our human family," Bob told Colin. "Children often pay the greatest price for the evils and the simple neglect that are perpetrated in our world. Because kids are powerless and voiceless, they are often marginalized."

"My background with little ones in America makes me sympathetic to the plight of little ones even here," I added. "Children must be nurtured, treasured, and esteemed as beautiful, exquisite works of creation. They are little pieces of innocence that require unequivocal love."

Colin agreed. "Most people who become Christians do so usually before the age of fourteen. If people haven't accepted God as youths, studies show that the probability that they will come to faith is around 23 percent. It is better to build children than to repair men!"

His mission group, headquartered in Colorado Springs, works with local evangelical churches in seventeen countries. They coordinate church partnerships between American churches and foreign churches, where the Americans take on support of about 100 orphaned, homeless or more often, abandoned children (those whose father or mother has left the home, leaving the child with irregular resources). This child sponsorship group had become especially interested in beginning a dental ministry to help their 40,000 sponsored children around the world. Colin's words pulled us in pronto!

Since the child sponsorship group knew a local dentist in Honduras who'd agreed to help the project children there, they wanted us to set up a portable clinic with a recent donation they'd received of $4,000 for that purpose. Since Colin planned a trip into Honduras the next weekend, Bob arranged for him to take a portable dental chair and some equipment with his checked bags, as that would save shipping costs.

Over the next several months, Bob assembled a complete dental clinic by soliciting contributions of supplies and through purchases of essential items. To ensure the new clinic and the local dentist could function properly, we planned a quick trip to Honduras to coordinate and to test the clinic operation. In an advisory capacity to a dental company while still in the Army, Bob had continued to help develop new portable dental equipment. He desired to "field test" a new portable dental operating unit, as well.

Another purpose for traveling to Honduras was to check out the country for a larger team, which we planned to take for the child sponsorship organization within the next six months.

*

Honduras

Flying into the Honduran capital, Tegucigalpa, with a little trepidation, we knew the country's political instability had resurfaced, with recent airport closures at the drop of a sombrero. Colin, attempting to gain entrance into the country just a few weeks prior, finally took a boat from Mexico into a Honduran harbor. His stolen passport also caused him duress; therefore we questioned the timing of our trip. However, we made it in without incident and connected with a small plane that transported us to La Ceiba, a Caribbean coastal town on the north side of the country.

During four days in one location, we treated children and staff in need, all from the four churches sponsored with our mission group in that area. We performed many extractions and fillings, and had a run of black holes on front teeth we fixed on a half-dozen youngsters.

Bob liked sharing ideas with the Honduran dentist, Dr. Dulcia, a lovely woman who would marry Colin within the year. As for me, I so enjoyed the romance!

Dr. Dulcia, like most recent dentists, found it difficult to acquire practical experience or to set up a dental practice in Honduras because of lack of resources. Even in dental school, students were forced to photocopy learning materials from the Internet, as textbooks cost too much. We enjoyed Dr. Dulcia's twenty-four-year-old sister who translated for us, and the adorable children and staff whom we treated.

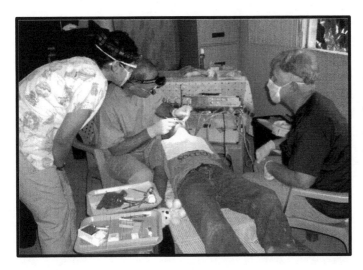

Honduras

Treating children while teaching a local dentist.

The weather stayed warm and balmy, and we toured the lush, green, and flourishing countryside. Many of the homes in the country seemed fairly well maintained, contrasting with the hovels and crowding in town. We visited stunning falls and caught a canoe ride on a lagoon that led to a calm bay on the Caribbean, where monkeys sang to us from the trees. The water lay still, pristine and lazy, with thick, drooping trees on the shoreline.

"Float away with me forever!" Bob swooned to me, as we drowsily watched the soft, rolling terrain of the shore as it flowed to the sparkling bay.

Only later did Bob realize that mosquitos had feasted on his feet, which took several weeks to heal. We toured an attractive, uncrowded, "all-inclusive" resort that catered to tourists. The sunny, vivid days fostered happy feelings of contentment through contributing to others, creating an easy and fulfilling trip.

One of the dental clinic pictures graced our Christmas card photo, as I thought we both looked radiant (or was that sweat?!). Some tell us that we look quite photogenic in our mission scenes, a fact that I contribute to finding our true sweet spots, very satisfying times of our lives.

"What a great introduction to the child sponsorship organization!" Bob enthused. "You know, I've been approached at church by an orthodontist who'd like to take his family on a dental trip. We could put together a team of families, as I've had other recent contacts from parents wanting to expose their older children to missions. Because of the political instability of Honduras, I don't think we'll take an inexperienced team there. But Colin tells me there are needs in the Dominican Republic (D.R.), which might be a perfect spot."

Colin passed us off to one of their most fascinating staff members, Nita, who represented D.R. Nita, originally from Ecuador, is a vibrant, caring Latino pastor's wife and grandmother, a long-haired, petite, and dark beauty. Her compassion for the needy is boundless, and she works tirelessly for the rights of people everywhere as a special crusader and champion for children. She dispenses motherly energy to everything she touches. Since we'd been saddened recently by the loss of Lola (our previous Guatemalan pastor's wife) who'd succumbed to death from cancer, we felt God gave us Nita, whom we'd work closely with on upcoming missions.

> Her compassion for the needy is boundless.

The orthodontist and his wife brought their eighteen-year-old son, Jared, and ten-year-old daughter, Jenny. Jared had graduated from high school several days before the trip and assumed the aura of an aspiring renegade, making a valiant attempt to be a cool dude in a loose mood. Since Jared was considering humanitarian work for a year before diving into college, this family trip stood as a safety test Jared's parents had concocted, uncertain if his maturity level was sufficient to traipse the world on his own.

Their valid concerns came to light several times on the trip, starting with a nabbing Jared received in the Denver airport as we all processed through the security checks. He'd packed his own backpack for the trip, "forgetting" to take out some long knives from a campout the prior week. Of course, knives will cause a serious disturbance if trying to go through airport security! With his parents present he escaped arrest but filled out paperwork, endured photographs, left the knives, and circumvented the threat of large fines.

"I want to do something for the trip," young Jenny shared. "Did you say these little children have never been to the dentist before? Maybe I can make their experience a little better."

Before we knew it, she'd gathered new and gently used stuffed animals through her taekwondo classes, school, and church, collecting over 1,000 animals. Although not all would fit in our bags, they could be used for subsequent trips. A local newspaper printed the story with front-page coverage. The toys, well received by the children, gave a marvelous purpose for our youngest member of the team as she loved sitting at a table to pass them out along with a toothbrush and toothpaste to everyone.

Our frequent flyer couple, Dr. Frank and Shelly (who'd come with us to three countries already) brought their daughter (who'd recently become a dentist) and her new husband for their first trip. The young dentist's husband planned to help with construction, positive he'd never set foot in the clinic. Later in the week, when we needed to shift people around because Jenny was in need of her mother's full attention, the new dentist begged her recent husband to help her. He loved it! On a later trip, he insisted on assisting again, saying it'd given him a whole new appreciation for his wife's profession and the exertion it took.

A German foreign exchange student, Alyson, became our most flamboyant team member, sent by her sponsoring couple who probably welcomed the break. Alyson, a true adventurer at seventeen years old (we thought her to be eighteen until the end of the trip), seemed always party ready. Having lived in several countries with her parents, she appeared to be quite independent. We hoped all the young men around would have high boiling points, since this beautiful, material-girl blonde certainly sizzled. Her alluring face easily vacillated between demure and provocative, and she definitely knew the power of her eyelashes.

The comments at our meetings about simple, modest dress never registered with her. Alyson made her entrance at the airport in a backless, tight, halter top that caused me to spend most of the airline trip wondering what to do. Finally, as the airplane descended, I leaned across and suggested that Alyson wear her jacket to avoid unwanted attention. Unfortunately, her fleece jacket looked inappropriate in the 100-degrees-Fahrenheit heat, but she complied.

Later on, it became obvious something other than chance had put the team together, though it seemed easy to doubt at first. I sang in the church choir and mentioned the proposed trip to Dominican Republic. Undetected, a hefty, gray-haired schoolteacher stood nearby. She suddenly entered the conversation, announcing that she wanted to go to the meeting.

> It became obvious something other than chance
> had put the team together.

"We can't take just anyone who wants to go. We already have a big, almost untenable team," Bob argued heatedly when I told him about the encounter.

I held back in telling him that the lady struggled with walking and high blood pressure problems as well. We didn't know what to do but decided to let it work out. At the first meeting, Dr. Frank brought his office dental hygienist, another person who totally surprised us. She and our schoolteacher, both in their fifties, had humor and unhappy male relationship troubles in common. These last two team members became the perfect pair, as they ended up as closely matched roommates and worked as a team for the preventive area and hygiene station. It was meant to be.

During the clinic, we received a little patient who couldn't hear or speak. The teacher, who had worked with special-education kids for years, could communicate with him due to her knowledge of universal sign language, easing his stress and anxiety greatly. We often encourage young people to learn at every opportunity, as one never knows when a bit of experience or knowledge may be beneficial. We didn't know the teacher possessed those gifts and were thankful she'd come as she assisted in many cheerful ways.

"If there's one thing I can't stand, it's a smart teacher." Her roommate, the hygienist, smirked.

"Sounds like you need a compliment, too," I said. "When you cleaned the pastor's teeth today, he told me he wasn't going to eat for three days, as he loved the clean, smooth feeling of his teeth. By the way...do you know what the hygienist of the year gets?"

The hygienist shook her head.

"A little plaque..."

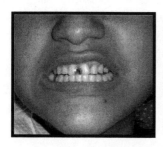 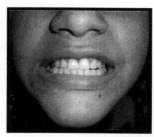

Honduras

Fixing front teeth (before and after) gives hope to a young girl.

Everyone around groaned, and our hygienist walked away grinning.

Since we'd geared this trip for all ages, one other family accompanied us. They'd been interested before but had high school students involved in sports, advanced studies, and varied distractions. They also hesitated due to the risk involved of travel in developing countries, especially as the mother worked as a lawyer (which explained the safety and liability concerns). The father, an excellent dentist, showed capabilities in all general procedures. With a daughter just graduated from high school and a fifteen-year old son, they felt it might be their first and last chance to go on a mission trip together as a family before the daughter left for college. This didn't prove true. They loved it so much they signed up the following summer for Africa.

Our last team member came to us serendipitously through a supposedly chance meeting, though we've come to believe there's no such thing. A family party in Colorado Springs led to an encounter with a father who overheard we'd soon visit Dominican Republic. His twenty-two-year old, pre-law son, Michael, happened to be there on a Spanish-immersion trip for six months. Michael, complaining of boredom, asked his father to ship some law books. Attempting to hide our grudging assent, we agreed to find space for them.

*

Dominican Republic

On our first night in Santiago, Michael showed up to meet us and to obtain the books. His friendly personality, heart-throb looks, and height gave off an immediate clean-cut appeal. His homesickness, as evident as his boredom, captivated the attention of our young people. Michael rode along to church with us the next day and became our new best friend.

DOMINICAN REPUBLIC
Five dentists, a hygienist, and the support team arrives.

131

The entire trip Michael stuck like Velcro, with a fine attitude, quickly burrowing his way into the fabric of the team. We found out later that he'd been somewhat estranged from his family's faith, and these encounters seemed timely for him. He debated with us whether he belonged in the law profession and accepted advice from the lawyer mother on the team.

Michael told us that one day shortly after our team left Dominican Republic, he walked downtown to the bank, asking God to show him a sign of His presence, as he doubted the existence of a caring God. When Michael came out of the bank, a huge rainbow spanned the sky, especially uncanny as the conditions weren't conducive to its presence. He asked the security guard what the Spanish was for "rainbow" and felt God's presence very near to him.

"I started thinking," Michael told us later, "is it really possible that all the religious people I've known and studied about are wrong? My whole generational line-up consists of strong believers, missionaries, and Christians. Was I willing to go against the many people in history who have lived well for God? I've pretty much been a white sheep in the family. Why change now and cause all that conflict? Maybe my life can become one of satisfying service." He thrilled Bob a year later when he requested a recommendation letter for his application to medical school. The school accepted Michael, and he is pursuing his physician training.

"Maybe my life can become one of satisfying service."

Nita, our lovely leader from the child sponsorship organization and Ecuadorian pastor's wife, left for D.R. a day before we did, as she preferred to check details in readiness for the team of eighteen. Since she needed little luggage and we overflowed, we gave her a suitcase of toothpaste and toothbrushes, knowing that, if questioned, she could handle that over more technical dental equipment.

"They gave me a very hard time," she called back to us as we left. "Maybe they wanted to confiscate such a fine stash of toothbrushes to be sold easily on the black market. I finally got through only because I pretended I didn't speak Spanish, repeatedly saying in English that I carried them for our project's needy children."

Because of this confrontation, Nita prayed intently for our group's luggage, which contained an entire six-chair dental clinic that would arrive with us the next day. When our team showed up—looking like a group of tourists—the customs people just waved us all by, not even requiring that our bags go through the x-ray machine.

The Pizza Hut next door to our hotel in downtown Santiago offered easy food to us, since most hadn't slept on the overnight flight. Jared, always ready to push the envelope, didn't want to eat there. "I want authentic food." We would have preferred to find a harmless "slow-food" local restaurant for everyone to experience, but it just wasn't available. "Fast-food" chain places from the developed world often offer a solution to survival in uncertain areas. Even in America a quick dinner out has come far from being merely a treat or a reward, as families in America often develop dependence on "Colonel McWendy's King."

We needed to educate about "safe" restaurants for Americans. Some of our inexperienced team members did not understand the dangers of food poisoning in developing countries. The clean and decent hotel offered a safe and beautiful breakfast buffet of mangu (mashed plantains, similar to bananas), rice, black beans, and fresh fruit (including mangos, pineapple, and papaya), as well as traditional American breakfast food (eggs, pancakes etc.) since the hotel catered to foreigners.

> Some of our inexperienced team members did not understand the dangers of food poisoning in developing countries.

On our first day, Sunday, the streets held a cacophony of horns and roaring motorcycles, which leant an air of industry to the little storefront shops that lined the narrow, two-lane roads. The bikes passed on both the right and the left sides of the bus. Our driver felt his way along, often braking for animals or pedestrians. Women carried tall loads on their heads. One intersection displayed a collection of homemade cages filled with live chickens that held the promise of a special dinner for lucky families. Several places along the road displayed sausages curing, hanging like emasculated snakes.

Often buildings looked only partially constructed, with tall, angled rods of steel (rebar) sticking up from the first floor, begging for the completion of a second floor. An occasional nice home featured concrete fences surrounding the yard, with a layer or two of cut glass or barbed wire at a level between eight and nine feet high. We left downtown Santiago for more open spaces, where the shacks became shabbier and thriving fields of swampy, vibrant-green rice plants provided eye candy.

"The location of our project community is considered a no-man's land in the city," Nita informed us. "It's home to some Haitian refugees and many desperately poor people who have migrated over the years, even before the devastating quake in Haiti that hit six months ago. The local government won't assist them since the people aren't legal residents. The children don't receive schooling from the government, and the residents don't qualify for public assistance, minimal though it would be anyway. Richer Dominicans hire these undocumented Haitians for the equivalent of about $5 each day."

"That must be hard to live on," we responded.

"That's exactly why we're here," Nita said. "These poor children seriously need us. Dominicans call them names and treat them with disdain. There is a social pyramid defined by skin color where whites hold higher status and black-skinned people—like the Haitians—are at the bottom."

Hmm...this rang familiar after the caste system in India and even the racial prejudices in America. *Why must prejudice be part of the human condition?* I wondered.

> There is a social pyramid defined by skin color where whites hold higher status and black-skinned people— like the Haitians—are at the bottom."

Nita continued, "Trujillo, the tyrannical dictator for thirty years, showed fanaticism about skin color and affected the country adversely by his cruel leadership and repressive control. He encouraged Jews and Nazi Germans that hid out around the world to come to D.R. so intermarriage would lighten the skin color of the general population. Most D.R. people remain prejudicial against the Haitians stemming from years of war and injustices on both sides."

Since we had time in the bus on our way to church, Bob urged Nita to tell us more about the history of the area. Nita, an articulate woman who'd been to D.R. many times, complied.

"The Dominican Republic is a fairly young democracy, as it has endured long and brutal dictatorships in the past. General Trujillo's assassination in 1961, with American assistance, brought a dark period of the country's history to a close, but it created a power vacuum."

"Didn't some want to slide into communism, like Cuba?" Bob asked.

"Oh, yes. Many feared that," Nita answered. "A military coup and civil war raged through the capital in 1965, and America intervened, sending 23,000 troops to install a temporary government. The 1966 elections were won by Joaquin Balaguer, a former president and collaborator with Trujillo since 1930. With American aid and military force, Balaguer succeeded in restoring some order, strengthened the economy, and maintained an outward semblance of peace. He held power off and on for the rest of the century, hugely influential until his death in 2002. The 2004 elections seemed fair, and we can only hope the country stays free of dictators."

"Is this a fairly stable country now?" we asked Nita.

"Well, there are still problems with the power structure, and political and economic reforms are badly needed. Hindered by corruption, financial scandals continue with the economy in tatters. Half the population still lives in poverty, with a third hoping for better employment. The safety valve for this economic pressure is immigration, which is ongoing as people seek a new life elsewhere. About one million legal and illegal Dominicans live in America, the largest Latino group in the U.S. after Mexicans. Much of the money earned by migrants in America returns to D.R. in the form of regular payments to relatives, but the children we service remain basically abandoned. They may live with a poor relative, but they have little sustenance."

"So, tell us some more about the projects," we encouraged Nita.

We'd had an overview in our pre-mission meetings, but we've always found that facts of countries become much more relevant as we visit and visualize the communities.

"This poverty-stricken neighborhood holds 128 project children, of which about a quarter are members of the church and three quarters are nonbelievers. Dominican Republic fans revere the sport of baseball, with some Dominicans making it to American teams to become sensational baseball players. The school center, the church, and the basketball court are all provided by professional American baseball players with roots in the D.R."

The large, scruffy baseball field was plush and green, bordered by a crayon blue, open-air church that consisted of a cement floor and a frame holding up a metal roof. Many skinny, bright-eyed children ran around the sun-washed field bordered with immense mango trees, bushy banana thickets, and a fragrant tangle of dense shrubs and yucca plants.

Occasional breaks in the vegetation showed the community of small shacks with tiny windows, where shutters hung askew with frayed curtains gently blowing in the breeze. Sagging porches drooped under a variety of patched materials that provided overhangs.

> Skinny, bright-eyed children ran around the sun-washed field bordered with immense mango trees.

Women in cotton house dresses and older men in baggy cotton pants or jeans hung around the packed dirt yards, lounging in cheap, plastic lawn chairs of various colors. Clotheslines stretched above beat-up motorcycles or bikes laying on the untrimmed grass. Chickens scratched freely for bugs, and an occasional goat or scraggly cow foraged in the plenteous greenery, while mangy dogs prowled about.

A happy, relaxed existence seemed the norm in the shady neighborhood, as the sounds of gentle animals, an occasional baby's cry, and the gleeful laughter of child's play were pierced intermittently by the sputtering start-up of a motorcycle.

A happy, relaxed existence seemed the norm in the shady neighborhood.

Bob presented the sermon at church, which seemed to go well with interpretation, while our group sang as a team, which went horribly. Although we'd practiced some before we left home and one team member played the piano, it just didn't work that morning. Without confident singers, the music dragged along sadly. It didn't help that the local song team performed afterwards with choreographed music and a back-up band. Never again! Our gift is dentistry, not singing.

After church we toured the community where our patients lived. The tropical heat sweltered, and Nita laughed about a child who'd written his Christian sponsor a letter, saying, "It's hotter than hell here right now!" We followed a narrow, poorly graveled road into a shaded area of small homes. At the first sod-packed yard, we greeted a grandmother who cared for her young grandson.

"The grandson is one of those sponsored by a professional baseball player from the Boston Red Sox, who grew up in D.R. Abandoned by his father and a mother who simply disappeared, the grandmother took him in although she has little. These families have no governmental safety nets like those available in America: Medicaid, food stamps, social service agencies, foster child care…*nada!* Sympathetic family members are a child's best hope."

When we were out of hearing range, Nita elaborated. "Unemployment is at 16 percent and a third of the people in the country live below the poverty line. Our sponsoring organization also provides vocational training in English, sewing, computers, and beauty school."

A motorcycle roared past, driven by a young man who looked barely able to subdue it.

Nita explained, "Many use their motorcycles to give rides for income."

"*Donor* cycles, they should be called," Bob whispered to me. "Remember when you made me give up mine when our first baby came? We used the money to buy a washer and a dryer—but I really think you were just afraid I'd get hurt on it."

"Hey, not me! Who looked the other way all your soldier years while you jumped out of planes, repelled, blew up things, and so on?"

The next week we saw a motorcycle with a girl clinging to the driver in northern D.R. The young man steered with one hand and held an intravenous bag attached to tubing with a needle in his passenger's arm. We often saw up to four young people (often holding children) on a cycle at one time. We worry about the safety of motorcyclists everywhere, especially in countries with absurd driving habits and no helmet laws.

On our neighborhood tour, we arrived at a neat, little wooden cottage set somewhat back from the road in a lovely grove of banana trees. Sweeping the porch with a homemade broom of straw and twine stood a slight, exotically beautiful woman. Two little girls played at catching grasshoppers and flies.

"One of our church teams came and helped Marisol build this cute house," Nita explained. "She is a single mom, abandoned by the father of these adorable girls. Generally, males in this culture feel like they are the conquistadores of women and expect females to adopt a submissive role. But the big problem is that many men assume little responsibility for fatherhood, and common-law or free unions far outnumber marriage among the poor."

> Males in this culture feel like
> they are the conquistadores of women.

"I've read about Latino machismo," I said. "To me it seems like bad daditudes!"

"That's close." Nita laughed wryly. "*Machismo* describes a man's attitude of exaggerated masculinity, which allows or excuses him to have free reign in relationships with a variety of women, coming and going as he pleases. Men exhibit transitory lifestyles, often immigrating to other places like Puerto Rico or New York to look for work. They may send some money back to their families for a while, but as likely as not, will disappear after a few years. They usually fall into another relationship and begin another family somewhere.

"Many of the children have a very loose affiliation with their fathers and some never see them again. That is why the term *abandoned* is used. Many children have several adults whom they are blood-related to in their lives, but the family structure is very fluid and temporary. It's disruptive to any kind of functional family, and the children, again, are the ones to suffer."

"I remember reading a book called *The Shack*, which mentioned that the emphasis in the Bible on fathering is necessary because of the enormity of the absence of true fathering in life."

"So true!" Nita nodded.

Marisol gestured to several plastic chairs in the yard. She invited us to tour the two-room wooden structure in groups. The kitchen, the size of a small bathroom in America, contained a tiny sink and a small stove, with some open shelves that held simple dishes and pots. An adjacent door led to a tiny room that held a bed, some wooden chairs, and a ragged rug. Although dark and stuffy, the bedroom looked clean.

We'd progressed down the road a short way when a gray-haired woman with many missing teeth and a deeply lined face waved us into her yard, once again inviting us to a half circle of mismatched, plastic chairs. A couple of old men joined us from nearby. The older lady told us she had ten children and twenty-four grandchildren, but no present husband. She praised the sponsorship project's positive influence on the children in the neighborhood, especially teaching them obedience and spirituality. "The children even remind their parents to pray before meals and bedtime and to brush their teeth!" She laughed.

"Tell us about the diet here," I asked Nita.

"The normal fare for a D.R. family includes protein about once every fifteen days. Beans are usually too expensive for them, as well. They often exist on nutritionally deficient green bananas. Now, due to the sponsorship funds, children's lunches include a daily small serving of protein, beans, rice, local fruit, and fresh juice. We work with the kids as they acquire a taste for salads and carrots, something they have not grown up with. The children receive a healthy breakfast of oats with milk and are given fluoride, vitamins, and de-worming medicines. The project meetings held after school three times a week feature talks on healthy habits, nutrition, literacy, and Bible lessons."

> "The normal fare for a D.R. family includes protein about once every fifteen days."

Even though we came back parched and worn out from our tour of the neighborhood, we needed to set up the clinic for the next day. Since only Dr. Frank and Shelly had participated in a short-term mission before, it was important to take the time to thoroughly orient everyone to the setting and the routine.

We transformed the first floor of the two-story building (next to the baseball fields and built with the professional players' money) into a dental clinic. It usually served as classrooms for the child sponsorship project. The ground floor held a kitchen, bathrooms, and four rooms on each side of a large open area. Each classroom was a third of the size of a normal school room in America, but all had large windows and smooth, cement floors. Each dentist and the hygienist received his or her own room to work in, while Bob and the orthodontist took the largest room together so that Bob could help the orthodontist with any questions he might have. Although he'd started with general dental patients early in his career, the orthodontist had dealt only with braces on patients in recent years. He did an impressive job, and his wife enjoyed assisting, since she'd never been part of his dental career at home.

Later that evening we bussed to the Monumento a los Heroes de la Restauracion, which stood at the highest point in the city. We climbed to the top of the 230-foot pillar by a staircase spiraling upwards like a candy stick, with an allegorical figure of an angel of Victory balancing atop. A panoramic view of the city greeted us, with spectacular sights to the surrounding countryside and mountains. Trujillo, the egomaniac dictator, had commissioned a mural by a Spanish artist to reflect his own honor. Instead, illustrated scenes of peasants and laborers striving for freedom decorated the marble edifice that'd been rededicated after Trujillo's death to heroes of the Wars of Independence. Even self-important leaders grasping for fame can soon be consigned to oblivion after falling from power.

Our Sunday ended with a trip to the nearby ice cream parlor that became a nightly favorite. It's always nice to chill out after a hot day's work.

*

Each day started with group prayer, and our photographer took a striking picture of our hands joined in a team pile, with a great variety of textures and skin color showing the medley of our mix.

Lunch brought rice, beans, and fried chicken that tasted greasy and delicious. For dessert we devoured fresh mangos that'd been carefully cleaned and prepared for us. Small boys entertained us by scrambling up the mango trees that had grown about thirty-feet high with a circumference that could shade half a basketball court.

"Don't walk under the trees," a local warned. "It could be dangerous if one of the mangos fell."

The young men on our trip liked to eat the fresh mangos so much that we ended up calling them "mango boys" (or sometimes "stinky boys" as they got hot and smelly while working on construction of the upper story of the building). Hoards of flies frequented our clinic, and the group's young men caught them in their hands, throwing the flies against the pavement to stun them. The boys used dental floss to tie them up, providing entertainment for us at lunch, while engaging the local children's interest as well. Not many flies survived the ordeal.

Dominican Republic

A ten-year-old team member presented stuffed animals and toothbrushes to child patients

In the afternoon, a close and deafening crack of thunder pulled us to the window in a flash. Dark, formidable blankets of clouds covered the sky, and within moments, sheets of torrential rain deluged the area. A cement slab on one side of the building attracted a group of children who gleefully spun in the rain, sliding on the cement with their bare feet. One burly young man, soaked to the skin, dragged children wildly around on a large, black garbage bag. The kids splashed and hydroplaned gleefully. On the grass they flailed in the muck and sludge, with many little bodies floundering and groping in a slimy dog pile.

I chuckled. "Look at the dark arms and legs wrestling with American white arms and legs! It's nice to see that hilarity and fun disregard racial barriers!"

*

For a break after two intense clinic days, we bussed four hours to Santo Domingo, the first European city founded in the Western Hemisphere. The capital of D.R. claiming over two million people, it is the best example of

Spanish colonial architecture from the early 1500s. The city, battered historically by earthquakes, hurricanes, and desperate pirates, has undergone restoration to much of its former glory. Enclosed with old city walls, a hundred city blocks hold over 300 buildings of historic importance. Castles, palaces, and mansions have been turned into restaurants, boutiques, hotels, galleries, and eclectic museums that connect through shady courtyards and cobbled alleys.

"Overall, Dominicans seem to be an outgoing, gregarious race," we acknowledged.

Nita agreed. "They live their lives outdoors on the street or in the fields. The warm, tropical climate encourages sunny dispositions, and the residents eagerly strike up conversations over thimblefuls of strong, black, sweet coffee or a glass of the local Presidente beer. Developed in the 1920s, engaging meringue music is named after the dessert made from whipped egg whites and sugar, as the accompanying dance reminds one of an eggbeater in action."

DOMINICAN REPUBLIC
Some patients posed for us.

Street musical entertainment seemed to be everywhere, including the seafront promenade. Close to the harbor, a massive, concrete structure reigns, constructed as a monument and tomb claiming to hold Christopher Columbus's body, although Spanish Europeans are convinced that Columbus's bones reside in Seville, Spain. As his body was moved several times after his death, the tomb in Santo Domingo might conceivably also hold part of his remains. The tomb structure looks to be nine stories high from the blocks on its face, with only one row of windows on the first floor.

Configured as a crucifix, the building has lights on the top that project a shining cross into the dark sky, a spectacular sight on a cloudy night. Designed to be a lighthouse beacon for ships and planes, it never reached completion. The beams of light thrown up from the two arms were designed as a metaphor for Columbus's supposed endeavor to bring Christianity to illuminate the Americas. "That became a sad joke, however, as Columbus never gained respect or popularity." Nita explained. "Columbus brought cruelty, abuse of power, and many destructive patterns to the island. Due to disease and mistreatment, the indigenous Taino population effectively became extinct, only fifty years after the arrival of the first European colonists."

> "Meringue music is named after the dessert made from whipped egg whites and sugar, as the accompanying dance reminds one of an eggbeater in action."

The monument now holds a chapel and some exhibitions from different countries. Construction lasted over fifty years, resulting in shanty settlements surrounding the building site. During the middle years of the project, over 2,000 families were evicted, each family receiving a paltry sum of fifty dollars for their homes. It adversely affected over 100,000 people during the construction. Because of this controversy, the king and queen of Spain declined an invitation to attend the 1992 celebration of its completion, and the pope withdrew his acceptance to open the building officially. Two days before the scheduled ceremonies, the president's sister inspected the building and hours later she died, inspiring further belief that a curse hovered over the area. President Balaguer was held responsible for the whole enterprise and avoided the ceremony while he mourned his sister.

The Columbus family's old house was fortified and constructed without nails by the first viceroy, Diego Colon (Columbus's firstborn son) from 1510-14. It served as the seat of the Spanish Crown in the New World and four generations of the Colon family lived there until leaving for Spain in 1577. Ignored since Drake's pirates sacked it in 1586, the house restoration began in 1957. It currently contains the intriguing Viceregal Museum, which charges visitors a one-dollar admittance fee.

A short distance away stood the first cathedral founded in the New World. Diego laid the first stone in 1510, and the building was completed in 1540. Drake's motley crew took anything of value in the original interior decoration and also destroyed the bell tower, which remains exposed. A statue of Christopher Columbus (Cristobal Colon) stands in Parque Colon, with an adoring Taino native woman at his feet, a symbol now considered rather politically incorrect. The history there seems riddled by controversy, blunders, and failures. We philosophized that errors aren't all bad, since Columbus discovered America by mistake.

Bob joked, "Columbus is the guy—except for the Natives, Vikings, Egyptians, and possibly space aliens—who discovered America!"

> The history there seems riddled by controversy, blunders, and failures.

Wrought-iron balconies bloomed with bougainvillea, and weathered facades and ornate statuettes from days gone by smoldered tawny in the sunlight. We lingered in a small plaza of chic shops and jewelry stores. The larimar stone, a beautiful, shimmering aqua gem unique to this area, provided a delicate cross for my collection.

After sampling dishes at a lovely Italian restaurant (the break from beans and rice was welcomed), we soaked in the glowing rural countryside as we drove back to Santiago in the late afternoon.

*

The next morning we headed four hours to the northernmost corner of D.R., next to Haiti. Arriving around noon, we set up our dental clinic in a children's project building still under construction. The inside walls were see-through two by fours. With only enough power to run one dental unit, Nita arranged for a generator that provided electricity to run the other five units and sterilization. Less than a year earlier, the building had been a brothel, but was now in the possession of our Christian organization, whose goal to rescue young people from victimization contrasted with remarkable irony!

The rudimentary bathrooms had toilet seats, but no outside doors. The first day we propped unmanageably large plywood pieces against the restroom doorframes, but finally locals brought shower curtains. They were often blown by the wind at the most inopportune times. After literally being caught with our pants down, we learned to take someone with us to stand guard.

DOMINICAN REPUBLIC
Clinic held in a former brothel, now a child development center.

"This is unbearably hot," we all complained the first afternoon as we treated patients through steamy glasses and rivers of sweat flowing down our faces. It reminded us of why we'd been hesitant to travel this time of year. Although we preferred to come during spring break in March, we had to wait for summer vacation since we had students on our team. Early June seemed bad enough, and we vowed never to come in July or August.

Life didn't improve when we reached our hotel, which definitely reflected a minus-star rating. With the toilet completely full of human waste nauseating stench emanated from our room when we entered. It took several visits to the front desk to resolve the issue, and we became slightly amused while witnessing the workers heatedly arguing over who must attend to us.

One of our team members lifted her napkin at dinner, and a huge spider ran across the table toward her, causing a shriek that brought hilarity and a diversion from our fatigue.

The air-conditioning didn't work, and the rooms seemed small when lit only by the bare light bulb hanging from the ceiling's center.

"It's good for our newbies to experience this for two days," I told Bob, "since the hotel in Santiago almost seemed too fine for a mission trip. After all, one should sacrifice a little!"

Our interpreter, a tall, handsome, and charming retired school teacher, resembled the American actor Morgan Freeman. He helped immensely with the children, especially one group of kids who seemed terrified. One after another, they came to the dental chair and dissolved into tears with extreme anxiety, so much that we turned almost all of them away as their agitation made it impossible to treat them.

Finally, we met the project director, who brought a mouthful of troubles. Her acute fear explained why so many of her underlings responded with trepidation. But we gently worked with her, removing her rotten front teeth pain free. Bob built her a lovely bridge of false teeth. She smiled in delight.

Bob instructed our translator, "Tell her to re-educate her children about dentistry. Hopefully, the children will have the opportunity to receive dental work next time."

A year later, we convinced our local church to form a partnership with these projects. Our desire is to take another team to treat the frightened young ones.

*

After work that afternoon, we drove a mile to the Haiti border. Although an expansive, ten-foot, solid wood gate blocked the dirt road entrance, commerce had not ceased. People passed bags of food over the portal, and money exchanged hands. Standing on a bridge over a small river, we saw many, some with bags of produce on their heads, fording the waist-high water, traversing between the two countries without inspection.

Another rain squall occurred as we departed the bus by our hotel. Everyone loved playing in the rain, and our teen boys ran and slid on the cement walks around the hotel. Imitating them, a little D.R. boy fell very hard, upsetting us all as he hobbled away.

Our German exchange student, Allyson, seemed enamored with the inches of standing rain. Impulsively, she lay down in front of the bus, trying to make a "rain angel." But as she rashly dropped to the street, my scream of warning was drowned out as a motorcycle flew by at a fast clip, narrowly missing Allyson's head. Yikes! We still shiver at the near disaster.

"Is there a beach nearby that we can visit?" Bob asked the national director on our last clinic day.

We'd stopped working early so we could drive back to Santiago to catch our plane the next day.

"I know of one," the driver replied. "It's just a few miles off the road home. You'll be amazed by its beauty!"

We parked high above a stunning panoramic vista. A huge expanse of unoccupied sand led to blue swells as far as the eye could see. A trail dropped down a half mile to the water's edge.

DOMICAN REPUBLIC
We experienced a heavenly beach.

One of the dentists ran ahead. From our position above, we saw him pulling off his clothes, thinking he was out of view. He stripped down to what we later razzed him about as his "whitey-tighties" and dove in. Except for our German exchange student, who changed into a teeny-tiny bikini she had packed in her bag, we all ran and splashed in our scrubs into the warmest, cleanest water we've ever experienced. Several who were recently back from Hawaii claimed the superiority of this D.R. beach. Like children in a wonderland, we ran and played in wild abandon. We ended up dubbing it "Our Slice-of-Heaven" beach. Thrilled that the excellent trip was complete, we considered it all over but the shouting.

*

Back home from our trip for a week, we soaked in the success, until we got a call from the mission coordinator at church. It seems that Allyson told her sponsor parents that she'd snuck out with several of the young men on the team the last night in Santiago, against the knowledge of all parents and adults. This surrogate mom was upset, even to the point of telling the mission coordinator at church that maybe we were incapable leaders (although we'd not gone under the auspices of the church). That truly shattered our happy bubble. *What to do?*

We'd believed all the young people involved were older than eighteen, but found out in hindsight that Allyson was only seventeen, although graduated from high school. Too late we understood we probably should not have taken responsibility for her on the trip. We decided to deal with the perpetrators at the group reunion and picture-exchange potluck scheduled in several weeks. We found a time between the meal and the dessert to pull the young people into a side room.

"We heard about your escapade on the last night in D.R. We just want you to learn to do what's right because you see the light, not just to avoid the heat of being caught. You're all old enough to know what the correct action should have been, even if you thought you'd get away with it." We looked glumly at them as their gazes fell.

"We did sneak out to several night clubs," Michael, our pre-medical student, admitted, while Jared, our knife-wielding renegade, examined his shoes.

"Did you think of the danger, especially for Allyson as a young, under-age, German Fraulein?" We tried to keep it light since no evil had resulted.

Michael and Jared eyed each other sheepishly. "We kinda see the spot we put you in."

Since they seemed very contrite, we didn't belabor the point, hoping an important lesson had been learned. The mission department leader at church told us later that Jared called to apologize and to ask that they not blame our leadership.

Fifteen of the new people traveled with us on later missions along with our old faithful friends, Dr. Frank and Shelly. Despite the youth incident that surfaced after we came home, we knew learning curves had been stretched significantly in this adventure together. We certainly gained more confidence in leading a large dental team, something still quite new to us.

Would we score on our next mission involving a final attempt by the orthodontist father of four to interest a daughter in dentistry?

URUGUAY

Ranching Outreach
on a Balmy Christmas Holiday

* * *

THE ORTHODONTIST, WHOSE WIFE AND TWO DAUGHTERS had accompanied us to Guatemala several years previously, was ready to try again to steer yet another daughter toward dentistry. With dentists in the family, dating back to the Civil War, the daughter would be a seventh-generation dentist.

His wife had never visited her missionary sister, brother-in-law, and their two children in Uruguay, who'd always desired that a dental team come to help them.

A third sister from Oregon was a dental hygienist and wanted to join, bringing along her husband. They hoped we could help by bringing our equipment. The only time for all to be free from work and school emerged as the week between Christmas and New Year's Day. We plotted to go, savoring the idea that it would be summer in Uruguay, the opposite season from the blustery winter in Colorado.

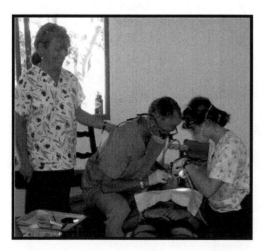

Uruguay

Sixth-generational dental family exposes daughter to dentistry, hoping for seventh-generation interest.

148

Complications seem to appear before any trip, just to remind us that we can't hide from tactics of the enemy of our souls. It's become a usual occurrence to expect adversity. Right after we purchased the tickets, we found that the three sisters' father had taken to his deathbed. They congregated at his home in Denver. Even the sister from Uruguay flew in. We decided on the "wait-and-see" approach, not cancelling our trip. Miraculously, his health improved right before the holidays, allowing us to proceed.

"Tell us about Uruguay," we asked the missionary sister at a meeting at the orthodontist's home.

"It's a tiny nation, wedged between Argentina and Brazil, made up of the descendants of Italian and Spanish immigrants who arrived in the late 1800s. Black and mixed-race minorities descend from former slaves, and Brazilian immigrants also comprise a significant group. Spain won possession in the early 1700s from the Portuguese, the first Europeans to settle the region. Uruguay considers itself a pioneer of social reform and still reflects the richness of colonial life contrasted with rural frontier life not far from elegant beach resorts. Its nickname is the 'Switzerland of South America,' due to its size, its democratic tradition, and its dependence on upscale business. The country covers territory about the size of Oklahoma, and more than half of its 3.5 million people live in the capital, Montevideo. The countryside is home to cattle, sheep, rice, and fruit production, which is our livelihood."

"We have to hear the story of how you got there," we beseeched, definitely intrigued.

"My husband, Derek, is the visionary of the ministry," the sister said. "Our beautiful farm in rural Uruguay is about an hour from Montevideo. We give local orphanage children a place to learn about the God of the Bible, as well as to enjoy His creation with outdoor recreation, gardening, swimming, and animals. We provide a Christian camp experience for children and youth and supply food for local ministries through our produce and livestock. We open our ranch for retreats and refreshment for pastors and leaders." Her spirited enthusiasm and stories sold us on the mission.

*

When we arrived in Uruguay, the customs officials wanted to charge an import tax on our equipment or to require a deposit equal its price, thus guaranteeing it would not be sold. Due to communication problems, Bob was taken to another part of the airport to speak to a top official who learned we had come to help the disadvantaged children of her country. The official insisted she wanted to help but felt powerless to bend the rules and demanded a large sum of money.

"But it's not new equipment," Bob explained again, having tried to assert that repeatedly. "We use it in many countries. We are not going to sell it."

"*Sí! Bueno!*" The official at last understood it was used equipment and immediately signed the papers that allowed us to pass through customs without any problems or expense.

Upon arrival, the heavenly ranch stunned us. "How did you find this paradise?" Now we wanted the whole story.

Upon arrival, the heavenly ranch stunned us.

The missionary sister elaborated, "Derek grew up in Arkansas, where he farmed professionally for thirteen years. He moved to Colorado in 1986 and became an elder and associate pastor of a church in Breckenridge, where I attended. Several significant spiritual dreams occurred where God spoke to him about meeting the needs of hungry, hurting people. The church administration offered him a six-month paid sabbatical to seek God."

"That seems incredibly generous of the church staff," we agreed.

"Yes! In 2006, Derek took an investigative trip to Uruguay," his wife continued. "He found a country largely unreached by the Gospel of Christ, with many abandoned youth ripe for faith. A vision began to form of a place where the 'fatherless' could experience restoration and could be exposed to the love of God, hopefully passing it to others in their own country and beyond. A farm setting seemed the perfect location, as Uruguay is an agriculturally based country that matched Derek's background."

While visiting an inner-city Montevideo church, Derek met the pastor's wife, who'd written in one of their newsletters that their dream was to have a farm where homeless young men could go for restoration and discipleship. So the next year Derek took his family to Uruguay once again to see if they could find a farm to fit their needs. All the places they saw had little accommodations, requiring substantial building and upgrading to make them livable. Construction in Uruguay is exorbitant and heavily taxed.

"A few mornings later," Derek explained, "God spoke in a whisper to my spirit and said, 'I have a farm for you.' That day the real-estate agent came by with a picture of the most beautiful farm I'd ever seen. It had just gone on the market and seemed too good to be true. We immediately visited and saw the pictures didn't do it justice. God's glory remained evident in the beauty and peacefulness of the 140 acres. The well-conditioned buildings met all our

150

needs, even adding the luxuries of a swimming pool and a soccer field with goals. But the price at $350,000 was $200,000 above what we could afford. We asked God to protect and to provide for it. After writing a newsletter sharing about the property, many generous people donated. During three weeks, other offers presented for the property, but it became ours for $320,000, including the furnishings and farm equipment we'd requested. We didn't think we'd given the best offer, but the Lord worked it out."

Within two months, Derek's family moved to Uruguay. Through all the chaotic changes, they held on to the verse from Proverbs 23:10: "Do not move an ancient boundary stone, or encroach on the fields of the fatherless; for their defender is strong. He will take up their case against you." The ranch became debt-free through donors shortly thereafter, and they have been making improvements on the land and the buildings as other monetary gifts are given.

Because Uruguay is characterized by humanism—those without a belief in God—for over 100 years, it is the most secular state in South America. Founded with the intent of having a society free from religion, Uruguay became one of dysfunction. Uruguay holds the second highest suicide rate in South America, with hundreds of young children abandoned in Uruguay every year. With legal prostitution, many children are born to unwed women or have parents in unresolved conflict, often sending children to the state orphanage system or out onto the streets. Uruguay prohibits adoption of children out of the country, and in-country adoptions are few due to governmental red tape.

> Founded with the intent of having a society free from religion, Uruguay became one of dysfunction.

Derek's family came to serve in this tumultuous system. They began assisting an orphanage that cares for abandoned or orphaned children, as well as elderly people whose families are either unable or unwilling to care for them. This organization, approximately twenty-five minutes from the farm, is not an institution but literally a family where the children call the couple who heads the ministry "Mama" and "Papa." Started by a German mother who arrived in 1966, it is now led by her son. Many young people have grown up in the home and now live healthy, devoted lives because of the love, the care, and the discipleship they received there.

Derek's family also uses the farm to work closely with the inner-city church in Montevideo, whose congregation consists of businessmen, homeless youth, sweet old ladies, and transvestites.

As Derek brought in children and staff from these various connections for us to work on dentally, we thoroughly enjoyed the clinic held in the reconstructed barn, a nearly completed building used for youth meetings, food preparation and preservation, butchering, and housing needs. Large windows, concrete floors, and electricity made a great setting for the clinic. At a group's arrival, we started with games, inspirational talks, and cavity-prevention briefings, followed by dental work.

Our translator intrigued us, as he'd learned his flawless English through his job as a hunting guide for foreign tourists. He'd experienced several long-term, live-in relationships with women, although his party lifestyle did not seem to satisfy. Derek befriended him as he witnessed the loneliness and the search for truth evident in the guide's life.

"My job is stressful," the guide told us. "I deal with foreign tourists who came to Uruguay to hunt birds and boar. They are often disrespectful and wild, especially concerning the ecological condition. I want to protect my

country." We exchanged meaningful talks about religion, and it became obvious that he respected Derek.

We also held a dental clinic for neighborhood orphans on a fifteen-by-ten foot porch of a local house. Although we played bumper-bodies all day, we reached out to many young orphans nearby.

*

Our work came to an end as New Year's Day approached, and on New Year's Eve we enjoyed going to a church party for the youth of the church. One girl celebrated her fifteenth birthday. The elaborate celebration was similar to a "sweet sixteen" party in America. Fireworks illuminated the darkness as the clock struck midnight.

The missionary's son asked his pet dog, "So, what do you think the New Year will be like?"

The dog barked in excitement, "Ruff, ruff."

We all laughed when it did sound like the animal had said, "Rough."

Derek quickly toasted, "If that's true, may your troubles only last as long as your New Year's resolutions!"

Since we didn't see dental patients on the New Year's holiday, we decided as a team to paint the outside of Derek's big barn, which had grayed with peeling patches. Since no one felt as comfortable as Bob with the spray gun, we spent hours in the hot sun blowing paint on the building while the others worked on window trims. "The couple who sprays together stays together," we joked.

URUGUAY

We painted the barn after we used it for a dental clinic.

Some also weeded the enormous garden. The camaraderie of accomplishment brought joy as we worked together. We all relished a swim in the lovely pool to cool off from the sweltering day, and later we rode horses in the warm sun along the expansive plain. The enjoyment was multiplied after we heard that Colorado was frozen in the midst of a huge snowstorm.

Derek, who also had a culinary degree, treated us to fresh, backyard produce and delectable meat from his own cattle. One night his ranch-hand butchered a sheep and cooked it over an open fire. Fresh corn-on-the-cob straight from the garden adorned our New Year's meal.

Each night we sat at long tables by the pool and listened to the dusk's music provided in a chorus: birds in soprano, crickets in alto, the sheep's tenor crying, and the cattle lowing. Erratic yellow beams from an army of fireflies glittered in a nightly light show, or as the children remarked, "The bugs are carrying flashlights." Drenched in moonlight, the nightly scene produced perfect peace.

*

On the Sunday morning before we left, Derek led us in a service demonstrating his theological gifts. I kept the notes, as it spoke to me of how God can rewrite on our hearts, changing thoughts of fear and devilish lies that often plague us for years. It's fascinating to note that the phrase "Don't be afraid" is quoted in the Bible 365 times, one for each day of the year. Derek stressed how Jesus died for our sins and how we can be free from fear and condemnation by accepting God's love into our lives. So often we get it all backwards when we feel criticized by others or pass sentence on others. We must learn to be witnesses for good, not judges or executioners of others.

The week ended with heartfelt hugs and presentations of amethyst stones from their property. We contributed to their ministry, as they refused to accept any payment for room and board. Updated emails detail their work and their continued success.

Our next trip two months later would bring sharp contrast to the idyllic scene we left as we flew over the teal ocean toward home. Haiti would undeniably become the hardest assignment we've had.

HAITI

Troubled, Corrupt, and Sad

* * *

HAITI EVOKES HAUNTING IMAGES OF AGONY. We were deeply shaken by a land crippled by successive swigs of sadness. Since our child-sponsorship group hosts projects in northern Haiti and since we had stood at the border just nine months before while in Dominican Republic, we decided February weather might work best. We arrived thirteen months after the horrendous earthquake that had left over 1,500,000 people homeless and destitute. Everyone claimed this tragedy exemplified the worst catastrophe on the island in 200 years.

Known as the poorest nation in the western hemisphere, Haiti is a place where widespread malnutrition accompanies the lack of access to clean drinking water. Even on its best day, Haiti persists as a public-health disaster, but at that present time, the spread of cholera threatened. No Haitian city has a public sewage system, and nearly 200,000 people live with HIV or AIDS. Only half of Haitian children are vaccinated against basic diseases like diphtheria and measles.

Ten years prior we'd attended a humanitarian conference identifying the most medically challenged nations. A speaker had described Haiti. "Poverty is their greatest asset! Drawing support and handouts from other countries is their most prosperous resource." Corruptocrats forge a land hindered by exploitation and unscrupulousness, creating a hustling, hard-scrabble existence for most of its citizenry.

Hurricanes in 2005 and in 2008 displaced hundreds of thousands of people, but relative calm preceded the 2009 massive quake. The earth shrugged and Haiti once again collapsed. Most Haitians know nothing beyond a society constructed on a precipice above the abyss. Attempting to overcome slavery, the country was born in poverty, struggle, and faltering faith.

"Haiti is synonymous with corruption," noted Nita, our beloved child-sponsorship administrator who accompanied us in what we'd thought of as a bold threesome. "The United Nations is here in force, but the real help comes from the non-governmental organizations (NGOs) from every corner of the planet. There are 10,000 NGOs working in Haiti, the highest number per capita in the world, except for India."

"Haiti seems to be an unlucky, star-crossed country," Bob said. He had visited in 1994 with the U.S. Army as the commander of dentists from Ft. Bragg, North Carolina. At that time he'd provided a dental clinic in support of a mobile hospital for peace-keeping operations.

"Haiti seems to be an unlucky, star-crossed country."

Nita explained, "Although there are other French Caribbean islands, none of them have Haiti's unique Creole character. It is a distinctive mix of West African religious and cultural influences. The blend of voodoo and other peculiar religious traditions causes an evil backdrop. A devilish influence is almost palpable, and morality mirrors it. Anything goes for survival. The children either learn aggressive behaviors, like shoving, pushing, and slapping to cope or slide into defeat and hopelessness—like dead-eyed zombies."

"I've studied the history," Bob said. "Haiti suffers constantly from local misrule, foreign intervention, and economic exploitation. Look at this guidebook." He pointed to the historical timeline. "Occupied by American forces from 1915 to 1934. Then life became worse from 1957-86 when Francois Duvalier and his son Jean-Claude, known as Papa Doc and Baby Doc, controlled the country. The corruption and the repression under their regime crippled the nation, leading to wide-scale emigration among its educated classes. In 1994 America intervened. In fact, some of the soldiers I commanded came on planes, ready to attack. When former President Jimmy Carter and others brokered a peace, they turned those planes around mid-air. I remember it vividly."

"So it averted a military intervention. How interesting," Nita commented. "I don't remember that."

"Then the American military ousted the government of Jean-Bertrand Aristide, the charismatic priest who'd been elected president in 1990. After a decade of political disorder, they forced Aristide—in his second term as president—into exile in 2004. Since then the United Nations peacekeeping force has been in place, the latest in a long series of outside forces that have attempted to establish peace and a measure of security, a seeming impossibility."

"Wow, that's really cool we're now coming to help these people. It's an interesting contrast, since I remember the tensions when you came in 1994 representing the military. You'd be at meetings on the Army post for hours in the evenings." I gazed at Bob with admiration. "Seems like a full circle."

"The earthquake in 2010 really brought world attention again," Bob explained. "They say the death toll of 2,230,000 was not so much due to the earthquake's strength but because of Haiti's shoddy buildings and poor infrastructure. The bad construction caused most of the fatalities. Just think, the quake in the San Francisco Bay Area came close to the same magnitude as Haiti's, yet only approximately sixty people died."

> The death toll of 2,230,000 was not so much due to the earthquake's strength but because of Haiti's shoddy buildings.

Nita nodded. "There were less than 400,000 orphans in Haiti before the earthquake—still a gigantic number—but now it's close to a million."

We flew into Santiago, Dominican Republic (D.R.) again, planning to meet some locals we'd known before, and riding by van with Nita over the border we'd visited the previous year.

On the porch of the D.R. project director's house, we spent a morning performing dentistry, and taking care of children and adults who'd been in pain. Tired from our trip, we still couldn't resist an invitation from the local mission director, Antonio, to take us on a tour of Santiago. Forty-year-old Antonio, who'd broken with a past of poverty and dysfunctional family dynamics, now works for the child-sponsorship organization after marrying a lovely young woman who is working on a psychology degree. Their chubby, curly-headed, baby boy entertained us at lunch.

We visited the local, modern cultural museum that shone in comparison with the dingy and dirty Egyptian museum we'd recently seen. Next door we entered a cigar factory and remembered the fellow traveler, an American, who worked in cigar importation, a popular export product from D.R.

The area around Santiago produces quality tobacco leaves, owing to the ideal combination of substantial sunshine, rich soil, and temperate mountain air. The workers rolled all cigars by hand. We watched as each cigar took about ninety dexterous movements to produce through the blend of a variety of leaves, each flavor appealing to the tongue's different taste zones. Five months of growth and three months of drying precedes the aging process of *seven years*. We received instruction on how to hold a cigar and on how to smoke one—savor for at least three hours to finish it, as one's saliva would ruin it if extinguished for later use.

The Dominican Republic is a pleasing country, where many American tourists travel for luxurious vacations, destination weddings, or honeymoons.

It's difficult to understand why its pleasures contrast so sharply with Haitian hardships on the other half of the island.

As we drove the four hours toward Haiti the next day, we enjoyed the unexpected presence of Colin (the child-sponsorship executive who had recruited us in the beginning by taking us to Honduras) and pastors who came to investigate donation and service possibilities for their church in Arkansas.

We felt sorry for the church staff when another volunteer who thought his previous trips abroad made him an expert on developing countries insisted on accompanying them. This self-appointed ring leader had the personality of a chain saw, spewing cutting opinions and biting, unfounded warnings. We've met superior-acting people elsewhere, and we're always saddened when narrow minds are hooked to wide mouths.

This man's joy-sucking, dictatorial, and know-it-all pronouncements of doom concerning the food kept the big boys munching on granola bars from home until their supply ran out. We admired the bravery and the generosity of the church staff, who had brought suitcases of clothes to the orphans and the project children. Although they came with great intentions, they were overwhelmed by the untenable orphanage devastation.

> We're always saddened
> when narrow minds are hooked to wide mouths.

The prolonged wait to cross the border brought poor, begging children and disabled young people to our van windows repeatedly. Expecting bribes, we saw our bus driver negotiating with some unofficial riff raff behind large vehicles. To cross the bridge into Haiti more expeditiously the next day, Antonio asked for our passports the night before. We figured he could organize some of the paperwork beforehand, but giving up our passports made us all uncomfortable. No one likes to be without a passport in a foreign country, although we always keep copies in our luggage and on our bodies.

Along the border, groups of somber-faced people sat on benches or walked by with dazed, blank looks. Many young men milled around, their eyes shifting about as if looking for weaknesses to be exploited. We felt our white skin gleamed like light bulbs against a dark background.

After creeping over potholes in a line of old vehicles, we rolled down rutted, narrow, sandy roads, our van barely clearing through the littered streets. Congested with pedestrians, bikes, and stray animals, the neighborhoods held naked or partially clothed black children as adults hung around small shacks, preparing food, sitting aimlessly, or talking with friends.

All that seemed missing was a sign, *Welcome to the Nightmare.*

Haitians heat food with wood and charcoal as the cheapest energy sources, since the people are too poor to purchase gas, propane, or electricity. Most trees and shrubs have been cut down for fuel or building materials. Without adequate foliage to cool this rock of an island, the tropical moisture rises and does not return as precipitation to bathe the island properly. This once-upon-a-time island paradise has become an ecological disaster due to almost total deforestation. From the air one can follow the border between Haiti and D.R. by the lack of trees in Haiti.

After reaching the school, we set up our portable clinic in classrooms upstairs. Wire mesh covered the sides of the buildings that opened to the air above waist level. Partially completed buildings surrounded the school. The rooms held broken desks and rough-hewn tables on cracked, dirty cement floors. Filthy bathrooms held unflushable toilets in drastic disrepair, all without doors. Manual flushing could be managed with a scoop made of an old bleach bottle that floated in a large plastic tub of brackish water.

We assembled our dental clinic quickly, and the Arkansas church staff videotaped as they seemed impressed with our portable equipment and the organized operation.

Each group of patients started with a lesson from our flip chart on expectations for their dental visit, stressing preventative health and tooth-brushing.

The first children from the nearby orphanage came in appallingly listless and apathetic with hangdog expressions. Several weeks prior, the medical team for our sponsorship organization had visited. They had placed several of the children on intravenous liquids immediately, as their precarious health indicated dehydration and malnutrition.

The orphans appeared hopelessly thin, sick, and barely responsive, with an emotional numbness we've never encountered. As we attempted conversation, they avoided our gaze and responded slightly and softly with lips scarcely moving. At other times they stared meekly at us. I tried to sing with them, again without acknowledgement.

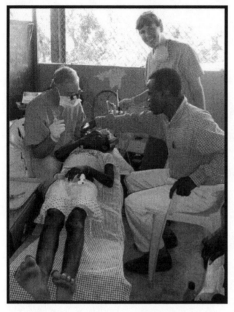

Later, as project children entered with their leaders, we were relieved to see them neat and clean in their uniforms, with responsive reactions more characteristic of children. It was a starkly opposite experience to work on the two different groups of little ones, and we soon saw why the orphans revealed such passivity.

The local Haitian pastor of the church doubled as the orphanage director, and it surprised us that he never visited the dental clinic. His wife, cold and distant, supposedly also helped with the orphans. She rarely smiled and seemed uninvolved with the children and uncommunicative with us. We noticed her rotund figure (obesity is an unusual thing in this area of scant food sources) and her nice outfits, which she changed several times a day. The Arkansas team that toured the orphanage shortly after our arrival returned, extremely distraught and horrified at what they'd seen.

Since we'd arrived around noon, we treated only a few patients as the men from Arkansas strongly requested lunch. The four large men obviously enjoyed food. We drove to the only "safe" restaurant for foreigners in the area and found it hidden behind tall, cement walls with the door guarded by a hefty hombre wielding a rifle. Catering to foreign visitors (the only ones who could afford the fifteen-dollar meal), the restaurant's dozen tables never seemed full. The clean atmosphere, accented with pretty pots of plants randomly spread about, still seemed subdued and dark behind thick walls.

During the next three days, we ate lunch and dinner there. With no apparent menus, we ate what they brought us: chicken, rice, beans, and American-canned vegetables. Although the monotony of the menu rankled after three days, we found the meals edible and without harmful side effects.

Owned by an exotically beautiful, well-educated, Haitian woman who'd lived many years in America, the restaurant seemed a potentially positive business venture for the region. There certainly wasn't any competitive market along the fine dining line in northern Haiti. Although she lived a comfortable life in Dominican Republic much of the time, the restaurant owner had political and family connections to one of the candidates for president of Haiti in the election scheduled just weeks away. We read later that her relative didn't win the election, a relief to many as rumors suggested the relative planned to install voodoo as the country's religion, if she were elected president.

The staff from Arkansas ate little at lunch, still cowed by the comments of the rabid ring leader, who begged Nita to let them go back to D.R. before nightfall, as the hotel seemed sketchy and scary to him. By then we'd realized he was fluent in three languages—English, sarcasm, and negativity. We felt the lodging was doable and had committed to stay for three nights. Unfortunately for the church staff, it had become impossible to leave, as they would miss the lengthy border process that closed in the afternoon.

> By then we'd realized he was fluent in three languages—
> English, sarcasm, and negativity.

When we saw the Arkansas team at breakfast the next morning, they'd barely slept and had been up for several hours, packed and ready to leave at the first opportunity.

Although we'd been tired after the tough dentistry of our first day, we slept adequately after we'd cleaned up. It took a manager to help us figure out how to adjust the water in our shower, as it stayed either scalding hot or freezing cold. The hotel breakfast carried some resemblance to scrambled eggs. It had supposedly been cooked safely for visitors, but the Arkansas four refused to eat. They almost had a meltdown when they realized they would have to drive four hours to Santiago to find a safe restaurant. The driver who came back for us reported that several of the fellows had *two* steaks—each the size of a dinner plate—when they made it back to the nice hotel in D.R.

With just the two of us working on the children, the clinic remained calm and productive. It had been over three years and twelve trips since we'd traveled without other team members.

We acquired a soft-spoken pastor named Jeremiah, who translated for us. His gentle and spiritual nature blessed us, although he struggled to stay engaged in the dentistry. He seemed thin, fragile, and weak, with an air of resignation and surrender to life's hardships. Pushing age thirty, he'd planned to marry until the earthquake hit Port-au-Prince, wiping out his house and causing economic calamity that forced the postponement of his marriage. His fianceé lost her job after a serious sickness—another reason their wedding had to wait.

Since Jeremiah suffered with broken-down lower teeth, Bob made him a partial that pleased him. Jeremiah made it clear he hadn't asked for the assistance, as he wanted to make sure we knew he wouldn't take advantage of us, as so many in the country did of foreigners. Jeremiah's humble attitude endeared him to us. It broke our hearts to think of the hard path he'd had, and we wondered if life would ever get better for him.

After finishing the clinic one afternoon, we asked for a tour of the orphanage, a request we were almost sorry for afterwards. A horrific place, we wept over this shell of an abode. The roofless structure consisted of a dirt courtyard enclosed by cement walls, with a few slabs that served as room partitions. Filthy, misshapen mattresses hung over the partitions. Without functional toilets, we heard the courtyard often became covered in human excrement, which explained the piles we saw against the walls outside the gate. The ten-foot-square kitchen had one large pot, which sat on a shabby counter, with no other dishes in sight.

HAITI
The sad, dysfunctional orphanage we visited.

One room held two large baskets piled with soiled, well-used clothes for the twenty children who resided there. The compound boasted only one bed, which belonged to the children's caretaker. She was a sullen, teenage girl who barely passed for sixteen. Other adult chaperones didn't appear to live on-site, although the pastor and his wife declared some involvement (grabbing the majority of donations for themselves, we surmised). The atmosphere appeared wrong and suspicious.

Upon questioning, several children hesitantly admitted to Nita that they only received a bowl of rice to eat and a cup of coffee to drink on most days. Nita checked for receipts for the sponsor money that had been sent, and she found no evidence of record keeping or accounting procedures. The Dominicans who comprised the child-sponsorship staff had been responsible to cover the administration of these projects, but it'd become obvious that they, like most nationals across the border from Haiti, carried prejudice against the Haitians. The entire business smacked of fraud.

"When I went to shake the 'pastor's' hand, I almost wondered if I should count my fingers," Bob admitted. "What a shyster he seems to be."

Street-savvy teenage boys who were not part of the orphanage hung out in the courtyard. They slouched about, a threat on all levels to the younger boys and budding girls. Without supervision, we only could imagine the possible abuses sustained by the younger children.

The entire business smacked of fraud.

Captivated by one adorable three-year-old boy with dark and soulful, puppy eyes, Nita told me she couldn't bear to leave him behind. He'd recently been placed at the orphanage after being found wandering alone close to the border. Speculating on his parents' frenzied escape attempts, we envisioned how Joseph had been dropped in their hurry and panic as they fled. The team took turns rocking him gently in age-old comforting motions as he slept, and we kept him with us at the restaurant. The proud expression he displayed as he reigned in the high chair resembled that of a blissful child prince.

"You know, the hunger for love is harder to relieve than the hunger for food," Nita murmured as we all watched Joseph.

We wanted to scoop up the boy and bring him to America, growing sad as reality set in. We hugged him lingeringly as we left the orphanage.

In the bus on our way to Santiago, we idly wondered if we couldn't have hidden him in the back. At each of the five inspection points through Haiti and Dominican Republic, the guards waved us through without checking out the bus. "Joseph, Joseph," we'd laughingly call out softly after each stop, "you can come out now!"

We only wished we would have had the nerve to grab him, but

prosecutions and imprisonment punished church groups who had come after the quake to "rescue" children by taking them to America. The ramifications made it all so complicated.

Nita decided to pass out the clothes the Arkansas church had brought to the children at the orphanage and the projects, rather than giving anything to adults who might sell the items elsewhere. Dressing each child carefully in their new outfits took most of one afternoon, but the children adored Nita's doting and their new duds.

As we sat at our final breakfast at the Haitian hotel before we headed back to D.R., we asked Nita if she knew where we could find a plate or a souvenir to add to our mission collection at home. An NGO worker from Germany overheard from the next table and told us of a convent nearby that helped indigent street people produce art work to support themselves.

When heading toward the border later that morning, we stopped at the Catholic center and met the wonderful nun who ran the place. She'd labored in Haiti for years but originally had hailed from Ecuador, like Nita. They hit it off immediately. Within moments, the nun pulled Nita into the back room, filling her ears with many disturbing stories about the viperous "pastor" who ran the church and the orphanage. The nun was convinced the pastor's regime persisted as a raunchy piece of work.

"He is bad to the bone." The nun's eyes glinted hard and bitter. "He's reprehensibly corrupt, fleecing many ministries out of support money, hurting the children with physical and sexual exploitation, and other sordid offenses." She'd been attempting to expose this "pastor" for some time, but he'd hired a crooked lawyer who helped with false paperwork and carried a gun as a threat if he couldn't scare others into silence. Sickened by the appalling abuses our hearts already suspected, we were thankful our innocuous request for a souvenir had led to this valuable connection.

We left the country that day with resolute ideas for action.

Two weeks later our sponsoring organization sent their strong arms to remove the sponsored children from the sleazy control of this evil pastor. Our administrators gathered local witnesses to the corruption.

We left the country that day with resolute ideas for action.

But in the end, the Haitians refused to testify against the pastor, undoubtedly fearing for their lives. They couldn't leave like the Americans would after completing the business. The pastor lost the financial support, which was then given to an honest and caring project director. Sadly, the

164

orphanage remained controlled by the corrupt pastor and could not be taken from him. Our group warned other NGOs about his manipulation of orphans for personal gain, which is not an uncommon occurrence in Haiti.

The Catholic diocese relocated the Ecuadorian nun to another country due to threats against her life by the pastor. She'd given her best to bring justice to that area, and we only hope and pray that the innocent victims will be unharmed until fair and compassionate country leaders can address corruption. The Arkansas four had planned to help the orphanage and stayed involved by switching their funding to building a school with another branch of the child-sponsorship organization.

The pastor had been involved with a slave-selling business, but he lost out when his political party was defeated in the elections. Everything we saw pointed to what we'd often heard about Haiti—that it had a generational curse due to broken covenants, defilements, bloodshed, immorality, idolatry, and many other sins.

> The pastor had been involved with a slave-selling business.

Our sweet pastor and translator, Jeremiah, described voodoo ceremonies that involve music, dancing, trances, and spirit possession. Some groups sponsor human sacrifice and bring curses on others, causing spells in attempts to invoke death or illness on their enemies. Voodoo promotes superstitions, witchcraft, and contact with supernatural dark powers. Jeremiah verified that these foul practices engage wide cross sections of the population in search of cures for all manner of ills. Marketplace stalls and shops sold varied religious paraphernalia, testifying to the country's fascination with spiritual and supernatural forces.

Several young, dedicated Haitians encouraged us with their commitment, and Pastor Jeremiah stunned us often with his mature spiritual perceptions. One day, as Nita talked about serving God in a forsaken place like Haiti, she asked, "Do you think you'd be willing to give your life for the cause of Christ?"

Immediately and without hesitation, Pastor Jeremiah blurted, "I would die for my faith."

We had barely processed the question. Yet Pastor Jeremiah had definitely developed dogged hope, thinking through what God's followers have to be ready to do on any given day in Haiti. We recalled the words of the author Robert Louis Stevenson who wrote, "Life is not always a matter of holding good cards, but sometimes of playing a poor hand well."

The devoted Christians in Haiti can offer mere drops of sweet water in a deep well of despair. But we thought, *It sure is worth something!* Our prayers stand firm with them as our hearts stay forever changed.

*

When we returned to D.R. to catch our plane the next morning, we checked on the projects by the baseball field where we'd worked when we had our large team there nine months before. Along with some work colleagues, Nita sponsors a family that involves a poor mother who'd been forced into child prostitution in Haiti.

This mother became involved with a man who promised her a good life if she'd follow him to D.R. He treated her poorly and became an alcoholic, abandoning her often. He'd come occasionally to live with her for short intervals, each time leaving her pregnant and alone. She produced five children, but without citizenship in D.R., difficulties defined life for her and the little ones. When she started to attend church and heard of Nita's child-sponsorship organization, the Haitian woman became a Christian and started working in food preparation for the project. Gradually, her own children became part of the project.

Since this poor mother had nursed a toothache for some time, Bob unpacked some necessary instruments. Not happy that it involved removing tough wisdom teeth without any follow-up, Bob ably accomplished the extractions and left her with a stash of pain pills. She experienced no complications Nita later told us, and the mother sent her great appreciation for the resolution of her pain.

Recently Nita had built a new little home for the Haitian woman's family, and that last night we walked through the quiet neighborhood, enjoying Nita's satisfaction at these six lives so touched by Christian generosity.

"Look at the fun that kid is having rolling the old bicycle tire rim with a stick," Bob said.

"I love that about kids in these countries," Nita agreed. "Once I gave a kid a stick of gum, and he used the wrapper for a toy for hours!"

*

When we returned from our trip and told Shari, our oldest daughter, about the dysfunctional orphanage, at first we were surprised to see huge tears well up in her eyes. But then, knowing her, it was completely understandable.

Shari had perceived immediately the horrific situation of those little victims, as she is enamored with children. As a small child, she enjoyed her dolls, which were very real to her as charges and needy beings. Shari, the consummate mother, was totally distressed by the thought of the poor, mistreated orphans. She and her husband have a cute family of four little children under the age of seven, and they now sponsor a child from there, a sweet "brother" from the island.

Our next trip included the best of everything and, yet, the most marring event we'd ever faced!

KENYA

Four-wheeling to the Tribal Bush

* * *

CARING AND CONFIDENCE FILLED THE ROOM as the sixteen-member team assembled on a bitterly cold, Colorado afternoon. A foray to warm Africa seemed just the ticket as Kenya beckoned, a popular destination for humanitarian adherents and safari aficionados. Each person seemed dedicated to mission work and exuded experience, accompanied with willing and conscientious spirits. We've learned, however, that the "perfect trip" is a mirage, and that we must be ready to face any calamity that may come after the highs of a trip. This journey proved no exception.

Nita and her child-sponsorship group thought us hardy enough to take on the African "bush," which included outlying areas with age-old tribes still practicing life as they had for generations. We found it all quite intriguing, mysterious, and somewhat frightening. We'd been told many clan members had never seen a white person before!

Bob clutched a patient list that showed we'd see eighty to 100 children each day, as a Kenyan dentist had "screened" the hundreds of children represented by the child-sponsorship projects. The pages of names identified those with the greatest dental needs, allowing us to concentrate on treatment so we'd not waste time and energy transporting and examining patients who didn't require or want work.

Our trip across the world went like clockwork, other than having every bag we'd packed opened and checked before we left Colorado Springs, something that had never occurred at that small airport before. We passed through Dallas and London on our way to Nairobi, Kenya, walking off one plane and right onto the next without difficulty.

Along the way we held interesting conversations with other groups going to Kenya. One Atlanta-based church group of six was headed to their second trip to West Kenya to build water wells, costing about $13,000 each. They expected a journey of over eight hours to reach the mud huts (without showers) that they would occupy for five days.

Their leader, Carol, a well-groomed, classy, former flight attendant, had two daughters who "would never consider" volunteering for an austere mission. She and her construction husband contributed $10,000 for the well, and the other $3,000 had been raised by their church. We talked about "finishing well" (no pun intended) and how we demonstrated to the next generation some priorities, including clean water, required in the world. Carol admitted that her husband hadn't joined her this time because they were building a new "mountain" home. We wondered about our own "needs" versus "wants," especially after seeing the tribal people living in small mud huts barely the size of a large American bathroom.

Three pastors from North Carolina were preparing for a large crusade of music and Christian speaking that they would present the following year in Nairobi. Their vision struck a refreshing note.

> We wondered about our own "needs" versus "wants," especially after seeing the tribal people living in small mud huts barely the size of a large American bathroom.

I talked to a nonreligious young financier from London, who said, "While bored in my cubicle one day, I clicked on vacation sites and impulsively booked an eleven-day safari trip that will include a stay with a primitive tribe in Kenya and a flight to Cape Town, South Africa. It seemed to be just what I needed to get out of my routine."

"So you just came by yourself?" I asked.

"Precisely, it's a first," he replied with a tint of sadness. "Usually I come with a girlfriend or family member, but everyone's schedule is full these days."

I felt his loneliness and lack of fulfillment throughout the conversation and tried to talk about spiritual focus, without reaction from him. In contrast, our team seemed united and purposeful.

*

Exhausted upon arrival in dark Nairobi, the capital of Kenya, we breezed through customs with no attention paid to us. We'd been told that we might have trouble getting all our dental equipment into the country, but we came with a crowd and mingled through without incident. It took some serious effort to pile all thirty, fifty-pound bags holding our six-chair dental clinic on the top of a bus that had come for us. The vehicles were driven on the opposite side of the road—British-style.

Commenting on the bus driver's erratic driving, it didn't surprise us the next day when we heard he had run into another vehicle on his way to pick us up that morning, bashing in the nose of the bus and lacerating his face. The accident drew attention to his alcohol-laced breath, and our African guide acknowledged he'd smelled a similar concoction on him the night before.

We all breathed a prayer of thanks when we realized what we had escaped. Our local guides shook their heads, saying the driver would certainly lose his job and face severe consequences over driving while intoxicated. Several times during the trip we discussed with locals the persisting problems associated with moonshine brewed in various locales.

That first night we traveled through the dark over fast-paced roads until we reached the "H.E.A.R.T. Lodge" (Health Education and African Resource Team), which provided a refuge for foreigners reaching out to others in the area. The lovely meal of rice, chicken, and fresh fruit pleased all. In Kenya, tea reigns more popular than coffee, due to the country's past as a British colony. We enjoyed spacious rooms with African-themed décor. A large basin collected the shower water, and signs advised us to leave the used water for the workers to recycle for their mopping and for watering plants. A drought of several months continued.

> In Kenya, tea reigns more popular than coffee,
> due to the country's past as a British colony.

At breakfast I talked with one of our guides, who said his adolescent boys attended a boarding school, the preferred method of British-influenced education. He claimed that over 70 percent of young Kenyans attended these high schools. When he left, I struck up a conversation with an American professor who'd come to the area on a Fulbright scholarship to study educational practices.

"Nonsense," the professor said. "There is no way that many students go to boarding school. We've found that less than 10 percent can afford high school in this area. Most are forced to help with the family herding business."

That proved an amazing difference in statistics and fascinated us that the local guide tried to portray his country in the best light. We have found great variation when people quote statistics, as it often depends on their orientation.

Other foreigners in the breakfast room spoke of their work in women's rights, AIDS, and sexuality issues. They commented on the difficulty in communication with Swahili as the main language, and with around forty other tribal languages and dialects in use. Once again they addressed the tragedy of female circumcision that pervaded in the area.

As we drove through Nairobi, we saw huge, stork-like birds with nests in many trees. The downtown seemed developed, including a large soccer stadium.

When we stopped for the five-dollars-per-gallon gas for the bus, one team member snapped a picture of policemen standing nearby, as she thought them striking in their uniforms. They noted it immediately and demanded that she delete the picture or they would confiscate the camera. We'd been aware in most countries that it is inappropriate to take pictures of government officials, military personnel, or state buildings, but we'd forgotten to address that this trip. Luckily, they showed leniency toward her.

On the edge of town gigantic cement factories poured out supplies for the many roads under current construction. But it wasn't long before the highway turned to gravel on our two-hour drive to Kajiado, a town of 11,000 citizens, where we would be staying while we worked the projects associated with our child-sponsorship ministry. Our agency employed thirty Kenyan employees for the eighteen projects in the country that served over 3,000 children. The children represented differing heritages and religious beliefs, including many with Muslim background. Christians have become a minority in Kenya, as Muslim beliefs have spread due to the surrounding countries of Somalia and Sudan. Animism also infiltrates religions in Africa.

> Christians have become a minority in Kenya, as Muslim beliefs have spread due to the surrounding countries of Somalia and Sudan.

Animism, often called "folk religion," defines spirituality that sees the physical world as interwoven with sacred forces. Events are thought to have spiritual causes. The personal spirit-beings of animism often have power over various aspects of nature and can be influenced by sacrifices or manipulated by a person's will. The spiritual forces and instruments of magic can be used for either good or evil purposes and offer the power to cope with immediate, everyday needs.

In many hunter-gatherer cultures, the human being often holds equal standing with animals, plants, and natural forces. Therefore, it is morally imperative to treat these agents with respect. Ritual is considered essential for survival, as it wins the favor of the spirits of one's source of food, shelter, and fertility as it wards off malevolent entities. Not only here in Kenya would we see versions of animism, but also we had found it prevalent in Mongolia, Madagascar, other parts of Africa, and Haiti.

Nita, proud of the child-sponsorship organization, elaborated, "More direct support is given to each child in our projects, unlike many humanitarian groups who have layers of administrative costs. The parents at first didn't understand what the projects tried to do for each child, since most of the projects were in the bush, where change and new ideas come slowly. It's taken at least three years for the local leaders to gain the respect and the support of the families, and some initially said the projects were 'of the devil.' "

"It's amazing it's progressed to the point where the parents allow their children to be brought to us for dentistry, never having met us," said Bob, as each day over 100 children arrived with minimal chaperones. They often came about thirty at a time, standing packed tight in the back of a small, rusty pickup truck. This safety snafu worried us, as we're so used to having each child harnessed into a car seat. As parents, we all commented on the faith these families placed in us, and we determined to give them our best.

A week prior to our coming, the Kenya church we'd be attending informed Bob that they'd like him to speak on the Sunday morning after we'd arrived. In preparation, he took a power-point projector and a laptop computer, which did work following a few tense moments manipulating the electrical system. Someone searched for a large white sheet for the wall.

Bob had no idea who would translate for him, but he was assured by the national Kenyan ministry leaders that it would be best if one of the locals translated, as they wished to empower the national people whenever they could. A young man did a fair job of translating, and it excited many parishioners to see "pictures" in church, something revolutionary to them.

Kenya

A packed church where Bob spoke

Projecting joyful energy, the congregation numbered around 200, mostly women and children. Although people didn't generally work on Sunday, the men herded cattle—the main livelihood of the area. Driving out, we'd seen groups of over thirty cattle with tall, slender men draped in bright red capes designed with traditional plaid or striped patterns. The men's hair remained long, while many of the tribal women sported shaved heads. With few cars on the roads, most people walked on the sides, with occasional donkey carts plodding along.

"I guess everywhere is within walking distance," one of our new team members noted. "We get in our cars for even short trips, while these people undoubtedly walk for days."

Children did not expect to interact often with their fathers. In church they sat with their mothers on the side opposite from any men. The children offered their foreheads to be touched by acknowledging adults. I patted them on the heads until corrected by our leaders that we should just place our hands on the child's forehead with one gentle motion.

Sometimes Kenyan adults shook hands with some hesitancy or the men clasped hands in a "soul-brother" style. We often repeated the two words of greeting we'd learned: *"Jambo"* or *"Salama"* in answer to their welcome: *"Karibu."* We learn a few words in each language we encounter.

> "We get in our cars for even short trips, while these people undoubtedly walk for days."

The All Nations Gospel Church rocked with ear-splitting electronic music and drums, and performers danced nimbly as they sang. Clapping and gyrating as they demonstrated gymnastic-type moves, some performed full-body flips. Enthralled with the exceptional and ecstatic talent, we were invigorated by observing their pleasure and passion in praise of God. Though we arrived late due to the accident of our original bus, chairs at the front of the church were reserved for us.

Young children crept up to sit in our laps and to stroke our skin and hair, so different from theirs. Since most Kenyans have no hair on their arms, they showed fascination with our men's arms, especially with our large, red-haired, freckled team member. They looked wonderingly at our white skin, as it seemed very unusual to them. One girl looked questioningly at our white leader, who quipped, "I guess God forgot to bake us. We don't look done, do we?!"

Two hours at the church service included Bob's sermon, elaborate music numbers by a variety of performers, and long announcements and prayers. Our leaders finally whispered that we must leave for lunch and to check into our rooms, since the church service would continue for hours longer.

One girl looked questioningly at our white leader, who quipped, "I guess God forgot to bake us. We don't look done, do we?!"

Our home for the week was a small, gated conference center run by the local Catholic diocese. Reportedly a new wing had recently been constructed, and we laughed to see workers hurriedly completing our rooms as we arrived. We became the first occupants, and staff gestured to fresh paint and wet floors as we hauled our suitcases from the bus.

The rooms held two twin beds with mosquito nets to discourage insects carrying malaria. Small built-in closets, a round table, a straight-backed chair, and two pairs of flip-flop sandals completed the dorm-like room.

Positioned next to the outside door was a tiny bathroom with a toilet, shower stall, and a sink. The room was so cramped that one could almost reach each of the four walls by standing in the middle. The bathrooms flooded with standing water most of the time, explaining the sandals. It took several sessions to learn how to use the hot water, which involved a switch that turned on coils to heat the water as it spurted out of the shower head. The fuses easily blew.

*

On the first morning the team all got up around 6:00 a.m. We tried to access electricity at the same time, and the power went out completely. Everyone showered in cold water and dressed in the darkness. We knew we'd brought an exceptional team when no one complained about the inconvenience.

We've often taken our own pillows but didn't think we had the space this time. However, we'd never needed them so much as here. Rectangular blocks of stiff styrofoam served as pillows. I stuffed the bedspreads in the pillowcases each night, but it was far from satisfactory.

Jet lag often grips us on long trips overseas. Now, nine hours ahead of our home time zone, it'd take a week to adjust to sleeping at the right time in Africa. Then we'd be heading home, where it takes another week to regulate. One's body is seriously out of sync for the entire trip and for the week following the return. Many travelers try to compensate by taking sleeping pills, and we've accepted this as one of the irritations of short-term missions.

On the way to the hotel, we heard news of an explosive bombing in Nairobi just an hour after we'd left. Early reports questioned a terrorist attack. Several days passed before investigations identified it as an accidental gas storage tank eruption, but officials restricted passage out of the city until checks had been completed. We might've been trapped there if we hadn't left when we did. Since the incident wasn't reported in America, we were glad our families hadn't worried about our safety.

After the Sunday meal of chicken, rice, cooked greens, and watermelon in the dining hall of the conference center, we visited homes belonging to project families. Driving around the sparsely populated countryside, we saw mud and dung-covered shacks so typical of the herdsman tribes.

We pulled off the dirt road where a diminutive, sun-baked, leathery-skinned man greeted us. His ears resembled those we'd noticed on men all day. Pierced and grotesquely stretched over years, the lobes became stringy pieces of flesh. The distended rope of skin drooped so low that the lobes had to be looped around the top of the ear so they wouldn't flap into the men's faces as they moved. Most tribal men wore their hair long and braided as it fell around their marked faces, and distinctive circular brands on their cheeks had been burned with white hot wire when they were children.

Bob asked one warrior if he remembered the rite, and the warrior replied, "I remember it well as I'd just reached my seventh year. It hurt a lot, but we Maasai are tough!"

> Distinctive circular brands on their cheeks had been burned with white hot wire when they were children.

Draped in red capes, most men brandished a decorative rod. These clubs seemed threatening until we noted it reflected the typical male behavior of the area. Most held a spear-like weapon—a *rungu*—traditionally used in warfare and hunting. About twenty inches long, the rungu has a heavy knob or ball at the end. At important tribal gatherings, the designated speaker holds a special one. They are common tourist souvenirs, and Bob and the male teammates all received one from the Maasai men we served. When we heard they sometimes beat them on the ground, Dr. Jerome, an avid golfer, said, "Now we have something in common. When I beat on the ground with blood-curdling screams, you can bet I'm playing golf."

"So you say those magic words to patients needing fillings, 'You have a hole in one!' " one of the dentists joked with Dr. Jerome, as we all chuckled.

The little man whose hut we first visited had lost his wife three years previously. Her death left five children, including three young teen boys who lived with this father in a midget-sized, two-room hut, where each room measured about eight feet square. The girls lived with an aunt, since they'd be unprotected when the men and the boys herded goats.

A narrow cot showed where the father slept, and the three boys shared a twin-sized bed that seemed hardly large enough to hold them. A miniature, homemade wooden chair and a low, three-foot-square table were the only pieces of furniture. The kitchen held three stones on the floor, where a pot could be heated for preparing their meager meals. What did they eat? The only visible food was a scanty bit of rice in a bag. They probably butchered some meat now and then from their herd, as goat meat was prevalent. The drought-induced, dried-up garden seemed as pitiful as the frail family, who looked stringy, skinny, and shriveled in their poor existence. The confined and dark shack leaned thirty feet from what might have been the outhouse, although no one cared to investigate.

> What did they eat?
> The only visible food was a scanty bit of rice in a bag.

"Just think of the lavish digs of our town compared to this neighborhood. It's a world of difference," I noted sadly.

"I know. We often comment how American homes have gotten progressively larger and taller over the years, with so much unused space. Our residences are more than comfortable, but sometimes it's rare for families to be in them," Bob reflected.

Our second tour showed similarly small, unlit, enclosed shelters, which are preserved on the outside with a mixture of mud and cow dung. The women hard packed the "goo" into a meshed framework of twigs, which made up the walls and the ceiling of these primitive structures. These families, considered "squatters," didn't possess land of their own. Three people at a time could fit in each restrictive room of their little dwellings, sitting knees to elbows, and ducking to enter. It always took several minutes for one's eyes to adjust to the interior darkness.

An undersized outbuilding they called the kitchen was no larger than a nook in a tiny apartment in America. The outbuilding contained a fire pit with two miniscule windows. It seemed ironic that they constructed such cramped rooms, since we admired the women as tall, statuesque beauties. The wives, striking in colorful wrapped fabrics draped around their model-like bodies, had necks and limbs adorned with multiple, bright, hand-made bead necklaces. Their shaved hair accented their voluminous eyes, and they seemed exotically attractive with their sculpted features and soft smiles. The earlobes of most women had been stretched with sticks and had dangling loops of skin with beads and colorful earrings woven into the holes. Sandals made from tires brought jokes about how the treaded bottoms must be good for at least 60,000 miles.

The life span of the Kenyans, reportedly between fifty to sixty years, could be explained by their healthy lifestyles of almost continual walking, clean air, and weight control, although their diet seemed unbalanced. One of the enormous challenges in Kenya is clean water, and many women and children traipsed far to find water sources. They must bring enough to hydrate themselves, a limited garden, and a few chickens.

The third house we visited on the outskirts of town resembled a tin shed divided into two rooms, each about nine feet square. Residing with her blind, fragile grandmother, a thirteen-year-old girl kept a wee kitten that fit in the palm of her hand. Although many of us were smitten by the kitten, we'd been warned not to touch strange animals. "I'll give it a CAT scan from here," someone joked.

The third house we visited on the outskirts of town resembled a tin shed divided into two rooms, each about nine feet square.

The two subsisted on the girl's monthly support—less than thirty dollars—received from American sponsors. The girl's mother had died the previous year, probably of AIDS, although it wasn't clearly stated and no one wanted to pry. The girl, shy and bright, prepared the food and managed the home. As we stood out front waiting for everyone to tour the barren home and garden, young, ragged children gathered with the facsimile of a soccer ball. It'd been mended and wrapped in worn materials, and we kicked it around with the joyful children.

One cute boy pointed to us repeatedly while waving his arms like a bird. We asked the English-speaking social worker about him and she said, "Oh, he wants to fly home with you." We wished we *could* scoop him up to take with us, our frequent desire in developing countries.

Although providing for school, the government charges tuition and additional costs too steep for many families to afford. The social worker spoke of people who also needed food due to the recent drought. We pictured years of drought, since it would take some time to feel a food-shortage pinch in

America. When we asked the duration of the drought, they replied, "Three months."

I felt incredibly sad. "It makes me realize how hand-to-mouth they live," I told Bob.

"I know, I know," he replied. "The seriousness of these people is getting to me, too. I know this is hitting everyone a bit hard. Maybe tomorrow we'll feel better as we get a chance to help."

"Hey, we're four-wheeling in a bus," I said, and that made us laugh.

But when it became almost two jarring hours down winding, rut-beset, dirt roads through the "bush" to our first clinic, we transposed our tune.

We felt like insignificant bugs in the expansive ranges that defined African savannah landscape. The tall, slender Maasai tribal men tended herds of thin goats or cows. At one point we crept over a narrow bridge that seemed hardly wide or strong enough to bear our bus. Later, we vacated the bus as it crawled over immense holes with just inches to spare, as our weight wouldn't have allowed the bus to proceed.

The flower-sprinkled meadows bloomed with white morning glories in the shadow of huge termite hills. Bob balanced on a hill while I snapped his picture. Several herds of zebras delighted us. We wouldn't want to be out at night due to leopards and other roving lions and hyenas, but we enjoyed the small animals, including a turtle the size of a big pot. We infrequently passed small huts and often saw a collection of yellow jugs on the roadsides where a "milkman" came to collect the milk to be sold around the region.

Accompanying us were two local, darkly handsome men who administrated the projects and spoke excellent English. One we nicknamed "Sidney Poitier," since he looked hauntingly like the celebrated actor. Nita, our lighter-skinned administrator from Ecuador, laughingly called herself their "slave," although she was actually the boss from our Christian organization at home.

The Maasai tribal people had surprisingly strong teeth due in part to the naturally occurring fluoride in the water. Fluoride, an essential building block for the formation of teeth, significantly decreases the incidence of decay. Many communities in America add fluoride to municipal water supplies when the natural water lacks this critical element. Too much fluoride causes *fluorosis*—a whitish-brown discoloration of the enamel—and can cause the enamel to have surface defects.

The Maasai diet, consisting of more milk than sugar, combined with the natural fluoride, gave these children fewer problems with decay than in many countries. Due to the screening, we treated the worst cases, with most

178

children needing extractions and fillings. However, we have seen greater need in other places.

In a highly unusual tradition, all members of the Masaai tribe removed the two lower, middle incisors as a mark of beauty and the clan's identification rite. Parents restrained each two-year-old child and extracted the two lower "milk teeth"—as baby teeth were called—by nail or knife without anesthesia. They repeated the removal of the two lower permanent incisor teeth when they came in at six to eight years of age. This brutal and painful procedure came with the expectation that the children *would* tolerate it, as this tribe valued "toughness."

KENYA

Our team poses with Maasai tribal patients.

It looked odd when everyone smiled without their lower, central incisors. One social worker asked if we could give her false teeth to fill in that gap, as she felt it a heathen practice. We didn't intervene in a foreign cultural system, and she ate fine without the teeth. When we asked about their opportunities for orthodontic treatment, we received blank looks as no one understood or had seen anyone with braces.

Our clinic with six dentists was held in a tent that had a tarp roof and two walls. Within forty minutes (an all-time record due to our experienced team), the clinic was completely functional, including all dental chairs and units operational, the generators roaring under Bob's hands, sterilization ready

to cook, and my instruction completed to the first group of children on what they could expect during treatment. We'd also given a lesson on oral hygiene, brushing, and basic nutrition.

Translators for each station were assigned, and we'd greeted all with warm handshakes to the adults and an acknowledging touch to the top of each child's head. The clinic percolated smoothly.

One little girl cried and carried on about her dental procedure at one point, which is a rare happening in our clinics as we attempt to keep patient emotions from escalating to that extent.

When this emotional upheaval erupted—and before Bob could intervene in the situation—another pre-teen Maasi girl stood outside shaking her head and tut-tutting in Swahili about the cowardly girl. The translator told me she mocked, "If she can't get a tooth out, how is she ever going to handle the circumcision?"

With sadness, we once again encountered the local practice of female circumcision, considered a rite of passage in much of Kenya, where 80 percent of the females undergo the procedure. Our Kenyan hosts explained that in their Christian worldview it's actually considered a devilish ploy to undermine the beauty of marital intimacy.

With our Kenyan child-sponsorship administrators we carried on a frank discussion of the cultural ideas associated with sexuality, understanding that there are two aspects to physical intimacy: 1. Procreation and 2. The loving union of man and woman as one. In developing countries where multiple wives are accepted (as was the norm here), the sexual act is often limited to procreation and is the male's prerogative. In western countries, the focus is on enjoyment for both the male and the female, since procreation is easily blocked with contraception.

We drove past a circumcision rescue compound that is funded by a church from our home state. Since the procedure is perpetrated on young girls, however, it would constitute a major lifestyle change by taking them from their family and culture.

*

The team spent two days in the bush, taking the long ride back to our compound each evening. One of the dentists proved to be the most dedicated Catholic we've ever seen, and we admired his devotion. Each morning he rose early to run to the church two blocks away for mass. I grabbed him some breakfast so he could be back in time to hop on the bus and devour his meal, reading his catechism on the way. He became friends with the local Catholics and priest, and we all joined him at Mass on our free day, while he joined us for our daily group devotionals and prayers. Many of us appreciated his strong love for God.

"Who wants to ride an ostrich?" Bob asked as we headed to an ostrich farm on our day off.

KENYA
There's nothing like riding an ostrich.

It materialized as a lovely resort on a huge acreage, owned by a wealthy Kenyan politician. Our local guides admitted that 80 percent of the wealth of the country stayed in the hands of 1 percent of the people. The ostrich resort held a deluxe hotel, luxurious garden, swimming pool, and nice restaurant. Each male ostrich claimed three to four females while living an average of thirty to forty years. The ostriches were definitely "aesthetically challenged." One of our teammates also discovered the bird's aggressiveness when one of the males pecked him with swift ferocity over the fence.

Our guide explained, "The ostriches have a small brain with poor problem-solving skills. They lay two to three eggs a season but can be fooled into producing more if the original eggs are snatched by a sneaky person who gathers them as someone else distracts the ostriches. Females then lay up to forty eggs from June to December. The gray females sit on the eggs in the dusty-colored grass during the day, and the black males sit on the eggs at night, disguised in the darkness."

The leather-like ostrich skin is also crafted for wallets, belts, and tanned skins. The feathers stuff pillows, and each feather sells for a dollar. The young ostriches are butchered for meat at the optimal age of eight months. I liked the ostrich burgers, although Bob thought them gristly.

I liked the ostrich burgers, although Bob thought them gristly.

Over lunch we chatted with our Kenyan friends, discussing their earlier visit to Colorado to be trained as leaders at the child-sponsorship organization. They commented on the orderliness and the structure in America, especially in the cities, saying it contrasted starkly with the chaotic culture of Africa. Surprised at how empty America looked to them, they had learned that people stayed inside either at home, work, or in their cars, not out walking and roaming the streets as is seen in developing countries. They thought the bathrooms strange, especially when the water came on automatically after they'd searched everywhere for the faucet handles. One laughed that the soap "spit" at him from the automatic dispensers.

Our last clinic location took us to a town, where we set up in a church. Keeping a translator engaged at each dental chair proved to be a big challenge there. The interpreters constantly wandered around, changed places, or used their cell phones. We learned to say *"toonyo"* for "bite" and *"tabolo"* for "open" for ourselves. The young, attractive locals gave us an amazing sendoff, complete with singing, dancing, and gifts of beaded jewelry for the women and beaded sticks for the men—to control their women, they were told. Two of the families on our team sponsored children in this area and met the little ones and their clans. What a touching scene as they hugged and gave gifts to their "Kenya" kids.

"Whoa, I'm trying to think how to pack this," Bob said on the last clinic day.

He had 26,000 items valued at about $100,000 that he'd brought for this six-chair clinic. From previous trips, I realized that the most dangerous emotional time is while Bob is focused on efficiently and safely packing the clinic items in fifty-pound bags for the plane trip home. The curious national people and the Americans want to help organize. One team member coined the phrase, "This is Dr. Bob time," meaning, "Everyone else scram." My job is to nudge people away without hurting feelings.

After packing, we enjoyed free time. Awed by a safari at Amboseli National Park for a day, we saw countless gazelles, impalas, elephants, and zebras. We viewed a few waterbucks, wildebeest, and a lion and a hyena against the backdrop of the snow-capped Mt. Kilimanjaro. We ate a sumptuous dinner at a restaurant, The Carnivore, where waiters roved with gigantic skewers of delectably grilled meat that included (along with the usual beef, chicken, and pork) livers, gizzards, ox balls, turkey, ox heart, camel, crocodile, and ostrich meatballs. Due to its "all-you-can-eat" style of service, we needed "Draino" for our arteries afterwards.

The market in Nairobi did not disappoint, although it included the usual aggressive salespeople found in developing countries. With our large team, we vied for luggage space to bring items home. We bought blanket fabric that the Maasai tribe wore for clothing and wooden bowls shaped like the continent of Africa with delicately carved safari animals around the rim. I bought a wooden Kenyan cross necklace and a lovely plaque to commemorate our visit.

We had experienced a genuinely primitive Africa, where humans and animals share the boundless wilderness in centuries-old tradition. We'd viewed the contrasts between modern city life and the unspoiled "bush," where the tribes still lived in harmony with nature as their ancestors taught.

We had experienced a genuinely primitive Africa, where humans and animals share the boundless wilderness in centuries-old tradition.

It'd been a perfect trip, and we thrilled to our team's satisfaction and fulfillment. We glowed about the trip for several weeks, giving reports to all who asked about "our best trip ever."

*

A month later, we received a call from Nita, the child-sponsorship administrator who had accompanied us. Several weeks after we left the tribal area in the "bush," there'd been a night attack at the routinely guarded project center. Word had spread that we'd been there, and the assumption that valuables had been left for the children of the project precipitated the robbery. Raiders stole a computer, audio-visual equipment, and medicines donated by the American medical team who had come months before. We hadn't left anything, but the thieves assumed we had. It horrified us that during the robbery the guard had been killed!

We were crushed beyond words. Nothing about what we do seemed worth the precious life of a national person. We shed tears and agonized deeply over the tragedy. After corresponding with the national leaders of our organization, we paid for the lost equipment and provided monetary support to the widows, as the guard had two wives and five children. We saw no gain in sharing this tragic, evil event with the rest of the team.

As time passes, we may find ways to express it, but we will always grapple with the loss. We briefly entertained the thought of going to only very established countries, but that would defeat our purpose of reaching the poorest people. Much intentional condemnation could easily come from the enemy of our souls, so we fight against that within ourselves. We call upon God to help us, and He gives us His peace.

Upon his return, Bob was nonchalantly reading a Colorado Dental Society newsletter and found that he had been chosen for the 2011 Colorado Dental Association Volunteer of the Year Award. We laughed to think he'd been volunteering when they had announced the award.

At the request of our child-sponsorship organization, we looked forward enthusiastically to joining their medical team to see if combined teams would work. We would find Bangladesh to be a challenging and rewarding experience rolled into one fast trip.

BANGLADESH

Merging with Medical
in an Impoverished Delta

* * *

SEVERAL COUNTRIES WE'VE VISITED have bordered on the "fourth" world category—those lumped unfortunately as "places of almost no hope." Haiti still haunts us with its needs. Now we approached Bangladesh, one of the poorest countries anywhere. Bordered on three sides with the northeast section of India, Bangladesh was called "East Pakistan" until a bloody, nine-month civil war in 1971 brought its independence, at the steep price of the deaths of millions of its citizens (accurate numbers were not possible due to the overwhelming chaos).

Visitors can hear the sighs and feel the sorrows of humankind in Bangladesh. Its 165 million people pack the often flooded, low-lying plains with lives bearing the challenges of survival, poverty, strife, and recurring disasters. One of the local missionaries described the numbers: "If one could visualize a line from New Orleans to Canada, and think of all the people west of that line—to include Alaska, Hawaii, and Canada—and then imagine that population in a state the size of Arkansas, that would be the position Bangladesh sustains." With only forty people per square mile in Colorado, people have room to roam. What a contrast with the 2,500 people per square mile Bangladesh endures.

With its river sources in the Himalayas, this country has the largest delta in the world. Most of the inhabitants farm or fish for a living. At least a fourth of the people have no safe drinking water, and over 50 percent are without acceptable sanitation.

The literacy rate lingers around 25 percent; they're often counted as literate if they can sign their name. Most people finish only a few years of primary education. The average life expectancy holds at around age sixty, with over half the population under the age of twenty-five. Fortunately, alcoholism and drug addiction are not significant problems since Bangladesh is poor and 89 percent Muslim, with 9 percent professing Hinduism. Only a third of a percent (.3%) are Christian, mostly of Catholic persuasion.

Our child-sponsorship organization wanted us to merge with the medical team that has worked voluntarily around the world on project children for seven years. We'd become curious about the medical team as well, having heard impressive descriptions of their doctor in charge and his devoted team.

Dr. Brown, a motivated crusader in his sixties, is blessed with a fortyish registered nurse, Jeannette, who runs the organizational details for the team. We'd also heard of their vibrant Chaplain Doug, who accompanies them on each trip. We wanted to experience their operation and found we thrived with the combination.

As one of the more strenuous trips we've taken, Bangladesh held many similarities to India, a country we insisted we wanted to visit only once. Throughout the ten days, we grinned at each other several times, saying, "Here we are again!"

> Bangladesh held many similarities to India,
> a country we insisted we wanted to visit only once.

The usual Asian dress of brightly colored saris on the women, and the lunge—a tight skirt-like garment worn by the men—brought back images of India. In both places, many people remain barefoot. Our team wore black polo shirts and navy blue scrubs, as the leadership desired our team to match for easier identification. That seemed laughable as our height, along with skin and hair color, made us easy standouts among the short, dark, black-haired nationals. However, we'd been thankful for the matching shirts in Denver. When she saw our logo, one sweet lady approached us to describe the child she sponsors through our agency.

It also helped as we approached the ticket counter.

"I'm sorry that I'm going to have to charge you for your second bag," the agent at the ticket counter said as she checked us in. "Why are you goin' to Bangladesh?" she asked Bob.

I waited a few paces behind Bob, praying for the nice woman's heart to be softened.

"We're going to help little children who have never seen a dentist, and these bags contain a full, portable dental clinic."

"Lookee that!" she squealed as the four bags each weighed exactly fifty pounds on the scale. Bob prides himself on redistributing contents until each suitcase weighs as close to the limit as he can get them. "Looks like you sure know what you're doin'. Who pays for all'n this?"

"Well, to tell you the truth, we do," Bob answered. "We travel about four times a year and have provided dental care in over thirty countries now."

I watched as the check-in lady's face melted into folds of dimples and smiles. "I'm just goin' tuh waive these fees this time for yuh."

We were on our way in minutes, thankful that our logo-imprinted shirts advertised our mission and knowing that once again our prayers were answered. Fees also were waived on the way back because of our retired military status. We believe prayer saved us $400 in luggage charges for our four checked bags,

When we reached Chicago, we met all twenty-one members of our team for the first time. Although volunteers hailed from the Phoenix area, participants also called South Dakota, Las Vegas, Chicago, and Colorado Springs home. The team included four medical doctors, Bob as the dentist, seven nurses (counting me), a physician assistant student, and seven non-medical people who helped with the clinics in various capacities (weighing and measuring children, entering data into the computer, filling pharmacy orders, and teaching preventative classes, including the tooth-brushing technique lessons). We settled into the huge plane in Chicago to fly to Abu Dhabi in the United Arab Emirates for our connection to Dhaka, the capital of Bangladesh.

The ride stayed uneventful until we closed in on our destination after over fourteen hours in the air.

"We did not anticipate the strong headwind we've experienced," the pilot announced over the intercom. "Since we're running low on fuel, we'll make an unplanned stop in Kuwait, only taking an hour or slightly more. We'll keep everyone on the plane."

The ride stayed uneventful until we closed in on our destination after over fourteen hours in the air.

Groans erupted. By now the packed plane smelled like armpits and old socks. We never relish long flights and like to say that airplanes are like diets—wonderful for someone else to go on! When asked about our plane reservations, we wish we could say, "Of course we have 'reservations about flying,' but we'll go anyway!"

We jabbered to everyone and found a sweet, young Bangladeshi-Muslim woman, Aisha, headed our same direction. She'd traveled from Denver, where she lived with relatives and worked in the high-tech industry. Her husband by an arranged marriage had remained in Bangladesh, and she'd traversed between the countries for several years to see him on her breaks. Like us, Aisha worried about the connections into Bangladesh, as there was little time to spare for the transfer.

We indeed missed our connecting flight. The officials at the ticket counter suggested if we flew to Karachi, Pakistan, we could possibly find a flight to Bangladesh. Aisha glued herself to our team, and now there were all the black shirts and her hot pink shirt.

*

When we arrived at the Pakistan airport, Aisha surprised us by purchasing ten dollars' worth of goodies for the team to share and helped us converse with the guards. Taken into our own airport "holding" lounge—since we didn't have visas or permission to be in Karachi—we were edgy and wondered at our imprisonment. Now we worried about our four checked bags that were full of dental equipment. I reached into my minimalist fourteen pounds of clothes that we'd been allowed for the carry-on luggage and gave Aisha my extra black shirt with our mission logo. This kindness brought a radiant smile as Aisha donned the T-shirt with an instant bonding to our group.

We at last caught our flight into Bangladesh (after a nine-hour wait in the Pakistan airport, where they'd fed us scrambled eggs and toast twice). Over the years we've been amused with flight attendants' attempts at humor. One woman announced when the plane's doors closed that she'd found a wallet. When the plane quieted immediately, she laughed and said, "Now that I have your attention, we'll go over the safety regulations."

On the Pakistani plane we giggled as the flight attendant struggled with English, as we're sure we amuse others when attempting to speak a foreign language. The flight attendant announced, "Welcome to Pakistani Airlines, the 'worst' (she meant 'first') airline in the business." Later, she warned, "Watch as the contents in the overhead bins may enjoy ('injure') you as you open them after flight." We wondered what she might come up with next.

> The flight attendant announced, "Welcome to Pakistani Airlines, the 'worst' (she meant 'first') airline in the business."

Bob laughed. "Just once we'd like to hear an attendant say at the end of the flight, 'Thanks for flying with us today. The next time you get the insane urge to go blasting through the friendly skies in a pressurized metal tube, we hope you'll think of us!' "

"Hey, I'm not afraid of flying," I retorted. "I'm just afraid of crashing."

Bob quipped, "I'm not afraid of dying. I just don't want to be there when it happens!"

We chatted and talked with Aisha about her life and shared our faith and the Bible's message. She willingly accepted my New Testament and deposited it in her pocket. As we parted after arriving at the airport in Bangladesh, we blew kisses to Aisha as she departed with her husband.

Our airport changes caused the team boxes of medications to become lost, but we had our dental equipment. The rest of the team remained visibly upset about their lost supplies. How could they see the children without their medications at the first clinic, scheduled barely twelve hours from that moment? We'd arrived a half day later than planned and were at least six hours from the first clinic site.

Dr. Brown stayed in Dhaka to trace the medicines. He joined us the second day, proudly toting the boxes. Misconstrued as cargo since they'd been packed in cardboard boxes, the many look-alike cartons were finally traced to a storage area in an outbuilding at the airport.

After leaving the airport, we registered at a nice hotel (one of the few in Dhaka, a city of sixteen million people) to refresh following the forty hours since we'd left our homes in America. Hot showers, four hours of sleep, and a scrumptious breakfast buffet revived us.

Soon we were on the road to our first clinic. Packed into vans with national staff people and translators, the traffic—like India—was unbelievably hectic and scary. Horns blared constantly as the vans careened around rickshaws, pedestrians, odd-shaped carts, scooters, and Bangladeshi buses packed with bodies overflowing into the aisles, with people and animals even riding on top. It was a disaster waiting to happen as we blazed along, clearing oncoming traffic with inches to spare.

> The traffic—like India—
> was unbelievably hectic and scary.

Although we'd learned not to watch when we'd been in India, unseasoned team members cringed and melted in fear and trembled at the chaos. The van driver even dodged stacks of snails drying on the roads, as the snails were harvested as food for the prawns cultivated in that area. For hours we were jerked every which way due to the surging traffic. We'd heard that Bangladesh has a very high accident rate, which seemed substantiated as we passed several accidents where buses had run off the road.

We spent two hours crossing the Ganges River by ferry, a crowded, nasty, functional boat with the worst "hole-in-the-floor" bathrooms we've ever experienced. Some of the women literally held their noses while entering the putrid, slimy, phone booth-sized toilet. On board we met two handsome, chatty white men, one from Australia and the other from England. They flew often to the country for jobs concerning energy resources. We ran into them the next several nights at the main restaurant in Kulna that catered to foreigners, as only two restaurants were considered safe for foreigners in the town of 500,000 citizens.

Agriculture employs 80 percent of the workers but can't produce sufficient food for the large population due to outdated tools and methods. Sometimes we saw men pulling the plows because their poverty prevented them from owning oxen. Man power is cheap in such an overcrowded country.

> Sometimes we saw men pulling the plows because their poverty prevented them from owning oxen.

We viewed frequent, vast rice paddies in vibrant green shades. Farmers harvest three crops of rice during most years, and Bangladesh ranks among the leading rice-growing countries. Jute production, the main export crop, ranks first in the world. The jute plant fibers are made into string, rope, or burlap, and often woven into cloth. The dark, fertile soil also produces wheat, sugar cane, tea, and tobacco. Brick-making endeavors visible in many places sported large chimneys that fired the bricks.

The villages consisted of huts on built-up mounds of dirt, with footpaths of piled earth marking the boundaries between properties. Without these efforts to raise the level by building up the ground (sometimes bolstered by brick underpinnings), the land would be swampland in the dry season and an endless body of water during the monsoons. Brick homes were rare. Rural dwellings, often on stilts to protect from varying water levels, are made of bamboo, with one or two rooms and no electricity or plumbing. Often the only way to cross the water to the small shanties is to traverse foot bridges that are one or two bamboo branches wide, somewhat like balancing a thick tightrope. Luckily, we weren't asked to try that, although Dr. Brown had attempted it on a previous visit and fell, injuring his leg so severely that he'd returned to America early.

Bangladesh has a gift of rivers and tributaries with over 300 bodies of water crisscrossing the country. The outflow is the third highest in the world, after the Amazon and the Congo areas. Many of the lakes we passed housed gigantic net contraptions for fishing. Access to our first village clinic required crossing a river by skiff. Strong young backs carried and placed our four dental bags on our boat, the first time we'd been rowed to a clinic.

Upon arrival we ate a plate of rice, spicy chicken, and highly seasoned fish, and were instructed to keep the fork and the spoon that our sponsoring agency had purchased for us. None of the villages would have enough extra silverware to feed our group of over twenty. The locals ate with their right fingers, squishing up the rice and the meat toppings into little balls, and then stuffing them into their mouths. Since left hands are used to wipe bottoms with water in the absence of toilet paper, they are considered unclean.

We set up in the chapel next to open windows that provided light, but we lost the illumination as the opening stayed shadowed by round, brown faces and curious, beautiful eyes. In the clinic our workers weighed and measured the children, took blood pressures, and tested for diabetes, worms, skin diseases, and other maladies. One girl had an extremely swollen face due to a tooth abscess. An extraction and antibiotics relieved that serious problem.

We met our lovely translator for the week. Deva was an adorable sixteen-year-old with a musical, lilting voice. She'd lived in a Christian orphanage for most of her life, sponsored by a couple from New York through the organization we represented. Deva told us she'd rarely been outside the walls of the orphanages, and this was the first time she'd traveled beyond Dhaka.

She earned the privilege of coming to help us by being first in her class and speaking English well.

"My mother had an arranged marriage at the age of nine, giving birth to my older sister at age fifteen," Deva told us. "My birth came two years later, followed soon by a brother. My parents divorced." When I asked gently what brought that about, Deva hesitated and replied, "A man came to work in our home, gave medicine to my mother—who was very cute—and she divorced my father and went to live with the man." The sisters were abandoned to the orphanage, and the son stayed with their father, who remarried.

"I am close only to my sister, who recently married in an arranged nuptial. I don't like my sister's husband and rarely visit," Deva commented. Impressed by how many arranged marriages still occurred in this culture, Bob and I were taken aback several times when locals asked if we had a "love marriage" versus an "arranged marriage." We smiled and assured that it was definitely the former.

> Bob and I were taken aback several times when locals asked if we had a "love marriage" versus an "arranged marriage."

*

One night later in the week, Deva invited me to the hotel room she shared with four other translators. Deva had borrowed someone's laptop, pulling up music videos that showed her and other orphan girls dancing to contemporary Christian songs. She had created choreography that showed breathtaking beauty and skill. Deva stayed front and center in the videos and looked as spectacular as any dancing contestant on American television.

Each day our lovely translator arrived quietly to the clinic in her stunning outfits of bright colors and beaded tops she'd made herself. Sometimes she wore them over stylish jeans. Her lengthy, dark cloud of hair always appeared meticulously groomed. Toward the end of the week Deva called us "Grandpa and Grandma."

A Christian center with clean rooms became our guesthouse for the week but had chilly shower water. The breakfasts, adequate but boringly the same for the five days, included scrambled eggs, white toast with jelly, bananas, and coffee or tea. One morning Bob requested juice, and the next (and only) morning, little mango juice boxes were at each place.

Each day, we boarded our vans and drove at least two hours to varied remote villages to set up yet another medical and dental clinic. It seemed like a drop in the bucket out of the forty projects and 6,000 sponsored children our agency supported in the country. With over 69,000 villages and towns in Bangladesh, we could hardly comprehend the need.

Dr. Brown analyzed the children's diet and planned to consult his nutrition specialists in America. Then he would send recommendations to the project staff on how to improve the children's dietary intake. It might only take adding a daily egg to avoid malnutrition. Reportedly, almost half of the youth in Bangladesh remain malnourished, so we hope the country staff for our organization can make inroads for change through the team's interventions. It's sad to think the children often develop mental deficiencies due to inadequate diets.

*

We set up the second day's clinic in a small project area where it rained periodically, something not unusual since the country receives over 100 inches of precipitation each year. Monsoons, coined a "mixed blessing," occur in June, July, and August. Unpredictable and whimsical, the season of heavy rains brings a dark side of flash flooding and drownings, as people survive by living on their roofs for days until the water subsides.

Our dental clinic was in a corner of a tiny church, with irritating issues of inadequate electricity and poor patient flow. Our chaplain hovered, praying over us and helping in every way possible. We adored Chaplain Doug as an amazing, no-nonsense, man of God, who carried a rich vein of inner crazy from the beginning. He sustained a humorous, positive outlook throughout the trip, with a special affinity for enthusiastic and energetic retorts. We

called him our go-to guy for everything large and small, and he always appeared just as we needed him.

He so enjoyed diagnosing dental priorities that Bob called him over at one point. "Hey, Chaplain, here's a tooth you can pull!"

"Get outta here! Really, you'd let me?" Excitement and instant heat flushed his jovial face.

193

"Permission granted. I'll stand right over you and guide your hand." The simple extraction occurred easily, and the chaplain posed proudly with his trophy, a bloody tooth clutched in the jaws of the forceps, and with the biggest smile we'd ever seen. It wasn't long before he'd posted the picture on Facebook, and stored the tooth in a baggie to take home to show his four children and wife.

No one wanted to eat the lunch provided at this village. Instead of the straight chicken, fish, and rice provided at the first clinic site, this project contrived an elaborate, spicy, curried casserole of mixed curiosities that burned so hot it brought sheer torture when swallowed. Mystery meat and unusual flavors did not go well with our group, and the locals' feelings were hurt when little food was consumed. Since the national staff sent word ahead to the next clinic sites to keep food simple and recognizable, the labors for the meals were greatly appreciated.

*

Early on the second morning, the national sponsorship staff—who all kept cell phones in this seemingly primitive land—received a call from the first village we'd served. Several of the patients who'd experienced difficult extractions complained of pain and bleeding, and the Muslim community was plainly upset. They demanded that the dentist return, and we wondered if this was a ruse to get more treatment.

By phone we reassured that these normal symptoms needed only a little more time and healing, and we never heard from them again. Although we always talk to each patient individually and leave pain pills, we realized that maybe that didn't suffice. Processing this event as something not occurring previously, we realized it wouldn't be hard to leave simple, written, post-operative instructions in English so that someone could certainly be found to translate. We determined to give the local project directors extra pain medication to dispense as needed. We often learn ways to make things better and always hope to leave the best impression after each visit.

We'd been highly inspired by Dr. Brown's morning talks, where he provided tidbits of medical facts: what the malnutrition score meant on each child's chart, how to recognize skin diseases, and physical assessment tools. Dr. Brown also emphasized his theme of servanthood, humility, and compassion toward the less fortunate.

Tears often filled his eyes as he relayed stories of people who'd been reached in the past with the faith, care, and love the medical teams provide.

One desperate mother approached him with her sick child and asked, "Will you help him live?" We discussed the importance of not only saving a life medically but also of helping these children possess a life *worth living*.

One desperate mother approached him with her sick child and asked, "Will you help him live?"

Dr. Brown, a brilliant doctor for many years, compiled a résumé of seventy pages detailing his many published books, articles, and outstanding accomplishments through his pediatric medical practice and teaching expertise. As the son of an American diplomat, he'd grown up in Somalia with his father after his parents' divorce when he was young. Raised in the Jewish religion with an excellent secular education that complemented his brilliant intellectual abilities, he spoke of feeling like a "god in a white coat" as he deliberated about life-and-death medical scenarios.

He'd married a lovely nurse somewhat later in life, and they'd produced two boys, one born with mental and developmental challenges. With all his knowledge and abilities, he still could not cure his son or find peace in his life. Dr. Brown pursued huge humanitarian efforts by running extensive refugee endeavors, instituting hospitals and medical facilities around the world. His soul remained empty, however. He attended a Christian retreat, where he gave himself to God. When asked for his résumé now, he's replaced his telephone book-sized résumé with one small sentence: "I am a servant of the living God."

Dr. Brown seemed a bit larger than life in more ways than one. With concern that Dr. Brown's own health needed addressing, Bob asked him about his hefty, barrel-chested physique.

"My wife says I'm just nicely upholstered." Dr. Brown chuckled. He remained a shoe-in for Captain Kangaroo, especially in how he cared for children.

Although the leadership wanted the inspirational Chaplain Doug to have devotionals each night, everyone revealed weariness after our strenuous days and ongoing jet lag. An attractive newlywed couple of nurses provided wonderful music, since the handsome husband was a classical guitarist and the striking wife, his best fan. We met together as a team for several nights, with everyone struggling to prop their eyes open.

*

Our third village impressed us with cleanliness and organization. After handing us lovely roses, the children indicated honored seating for us on colorful plastic chairs. The young people provided a sweet program of singing and appeared well disciplined and adorably respectful.

Beautiful clinic areas, partitioned off with striking fabric dividers, were complete with mismatched, wooden furniture. A generator provided enough electricity to run the dental operating unit, and Bob appreciated the chance to do a nice filling on the project director's beautiful daughter. Bob also fixed the front teeth of a young man who had black holes between his incisors. In conversation, we discovered he'd received awards for his superior conduct in the Bengalese Army. We'll never know the impact of his newfound confidence in his appearance.

Dr. Brown always seemed to show up to observe our big dental cases. His encouragement and wish to add dental care to his medical teams made us feel warmed and accepted.

The van we'd ridden in for three days broke down, so we transferred to the lead vehicle, a Jeep that had no air conditioning but boasted great shocks compared to the van. We decided to stay with that vehicle, even after our repaired van returned, and we enjoyed the fresh air that blew through the vehicle as our driver flew down the road. We wondered if he'd ever heard of NASCAR, as he certainly drove like a wannabe race car driver. He used his horn incessantly, which actually did seem to be a necessary safety feature as he warned others on the road that he was blasting through.

> We wondered if he'd ever heard of NASCAR,
> as he certainly drove like a wannabe race car driver.

At breakfast I graciously announced Bob's fifty-ninth birthday. He grinned in delight when everyone sang to him. As we rode to the clinic, one of the national young men also sang a slightly off-key solo of the Bangladesh birthday song. One of the team ladies had secretly asked the restaurant if we could have a cake and candles at dinner, which wasn't an easy request. Runners had been sent out around town to surprise Bob with a small, square, nicely decorated cake with one huge candle on top. The whole restaurant sang to him, and the manager presented an amazing bouquet of beautiful flowers to Bob, who paraded around the restaurant like Miss America. What a memorable birthday!

The only drawback to the night was the spicy food. We truly couldn't touch it as it burned our lips unmercifully. That night we chatted with an

American who had lived in Bangladesh for thirty years, and he suggested we order chicken cutlets and fries. We did that for the remaining dinners and had food close to the chicken nuggets we enjoy at home. It's important to appreciate the local fare but not if it can't be swallowed.

*

At our fourth day clinic, Bob almost lost some fingers, a catastrophe that would definitely be disastrous for a dentist. The day started wonderfully with the children lined along the walkway into the remote village. They showered us with homemade confetti of flowers, leaves, and bright bits of colored paper. We were so covered that bits fell off as we undressed that night in the hotel.

> Children showered us with homemade confetti of flowers, leaves, and bright bits of colored paper.

This children's project exuded poverty, with one rusty, antiquated water pump and a nasty outhouse, both of which drained into the fetid water surrounding the village. As the local residents had not seen Americans before, the village people came and gawked at us for minutes at close range.

The diminutive local pastor read a Bible passage and praised God for our presence. He delivered a cute little sermonette slowly in broken English. He begged at the end, "If you see anything good in what we do here, then praise God. If you see anything bad, please forgive us."

Since our translators' van broke down on the way, we didn't know if they'd even arrive. Thinking the pastor could speak some English, we asked him to help translate. But we soon found out that his talk in the morning must have been carefully prepared, as we couldn't communicate with him at all in the dental clinic. Also, the generator didn't give us enough electricity to even turn on the sterilizing pressure pot.

The pastor sent for someone from the nearby village, who eventually came and, by changing the fuel filter, coaxed the generator into running briefly. The pressure pot never worked correctly that day, and one batch melted plastic instruments that stuck to the pot temporarily. We carried all of the afternoon instruments back to the hotel to sterilize in our room.

It became a short afternoon of work as the crowd registered restlessness in the small project area. People surrounded the roped-off area and seemed angry that we didn't have time to treat adults or others not involved with the sponsored children. The tension became tangible.

Since Dr. Brown lives in Phoenix, he developed the code *Phoenix Suns,* which we all were instructed to recognize as a sign to vacate the area if violence should break out. That concern certainly seemed to be justified at this place. When Dr. Brown circulated mid-afternoon, he announced that we would pack up early, as soon as we'd seen the children we came to assess. We would not treat anyone else, as that could fuel a riot since all the adults desired access to care. We'd been shocked to hear that Bangladesh has only one doctor for every 4,000 people.

The tension became tangible.

As the afternoon sweltered, Bob laughed. "Look! It's so hot that condensation has obscured the face of my watch."

Ceiling fans spun like sideways karate chops in the tiny church. With short ceilings, we could barely stand without the risk of decapitation. Our translator showed up late and advised Bob to be careful with the oscillation above, as her relative had lost several fingers to a fan. Although Bob kept reminding himself, he stretched his arms up once between patients, and the fans whacked his fingers so hard that the skin severed with instant bleeding. Luckily, Bob had his gloves on, but they were sliced into shreds. He vowed not to connect with the fans again, but on the way out, as he lifted his arms to put on his backpack, his hands were thoroughly thwacked once more.

"I turned into quite the injury magnet today." Bob shook his head.

He carefully treated his hands with antibiotics and wrappings the following day, as it's not prudent to have cuts when dealing with others' fluids. He could move his bruised and wounded fingers well enough the next day to perform the needed dentistry at the last village.

Months later, as the last black nail bed grew out, Bob reflected, "I've looked at these wounds many times, thankful that God saved my hands."

Our extrication from that village—the first time we'd ever felt threatened by an angry mob—seemed tenuous, although Dr. Brown's teams said they'd experienced pressure before. An incensed man shouted words we couldn't understand in Bob's face. Heads and hands poked through our open Jeep window as we waited for the other vans to load.

*

Our fifth and final clinic seemed to be at the end of the world. We descended from highways to two-lane roads to a dirt path—until the vans could progress no farther. Then we walked for a half mile through tiny settlements. Some young men placed our bags of equipment on tall tricycle carts. Even the pastor of the area didn't have the money to own a bicycle himself.

BANGLADESH
Transporting the dental clinic on a bikecart.

We planned to work for only several hours, as it became the smallest project we'd seen. We set a board on sawhorses to hold our dental supplies and sterilization pot, but we never had electricity. At the end of the morning Bob bumped the edge of the table, which caused it to capsize, making a shot-like bang that startled the whole compound.

"Everything's okay, nobody's hurt!" The voice of our Chaplain Doug rang out, as once again he became the first one on the scene of any crisis. "So, how does a dentist break a table?" he said later, smirking.

"Don't know, but I can tell you've been waiting for this one," Bob replied.

"Acci…dentally," Chaplain Doug quipped and sprinted out as Bob threw a cotton ball his direction.

Our dental clinic windows looked over a green lagoon, pretty and still but obviously putrid. As we left the village, we saw children swimming and bathing in the murkish water. Dr. Brown presented water filters for each village we visited, and it reminded us of the Bible verse from Matthew 10:42: "And if anyone gives even a cup of cold water to one of these little ones because he is my disciple, I tell you the truth, he will certainly not lose his reward."

Dr. Brown's water filtration system had a micro-filter that screened out bacteria, viruses, protozoa, worms, and other unhealthy particles, turning contaminated water into safe drinking water. A team member took a five-gallon bucket and drilled a hole about three inches from the bottom where a hose with the attached filter connected. When water filled the bucket, the sediment settled to the bottom of the bucket. Gravity-fed clean water came from the hose.

To demonstrate the effectiveness of the filtered water, the team members placed dirt in the bucket of water and either Dr. Brown or Chaplain Doug then drank the filtered water. It made an impressive presentation, and the villagers didn't realize that the drink sampler then secretly took antibiotics. Although the water was much cleaner, a foreigner could still get sick.

The girls of the village wore dresses the Phoenix church ladies had created out of pillowcases. The opening was the hem; and the top had been cut open for the children's head. Tie straps were sewed on. Colorful and attractive flower-decked hats had been coordinated for the girls' heads. I resolved that this lovely sewing idea could be passed on to my church quilting group at home.

> The girls of the village wore dresses the Phoenix church ladies had created out of pillowcases.

As we hiked down the path to the vans, we came upon a man weaving a large jute screen and a woman running what looked like a giant pestle that she operated with her leg to smash rice into rice flour. The strenuous and time-consuming pursuits made us feel that we were experiencing a "living museum" of primitive times, but this remained their unfortunate reality.

As we reached the village where our vans had been parked, the streets teemed with so many people that we could hardly navigate through the crowds. Most were Muslim, but one young man came up to Bob and yelled loudly in English, "I am Christian," he pronounced forcefully. "But we in Bangladesh are not happy at all! We have too many people. But we are trying to serve God." His angst and emotion made us feel deeply for the individuals of this trying country.

Although we left early, we heard it was at least an eight-hour drive back to the capital of Dhaka, and it was much longer. Multiple van breakdowns, including flat tires, non-functioning brakes (yikes!) and problems with our driver's horn occurred. When the driver stopped at a shop for parts, Bob jumped out to fix the shorted electrical connection caused by the rain we had just driven through. We passed near a famous mangrove forest in southern Bangladesh, but we decided there was no time for a live encounter with the famous Royal Bengal tigers found there.

When trying to depart the ferry, one van's key broke off in the ignition. Our Jeep attempted to pull it, resulting in the strong smell of burned rubber and serious skidding. Luggage and bodies were once again transferred and redistributed, while the leased van and the driver were left for the rental company to handle.

It had started raining, the first time we'd been cool in this country. We'd planned the trip during the country's winter season, but temperatures still ranged within the 80s with 100 percent humidity. In the overwhelming darkness, we wondered how our driver signaled others without his horn, as it had stopped working again. Lights on vehicles didn't seem mandatory and were rarely used.

"All I can think about is to make peace with God," I whispered to Bob as time dragged on with the treacherous, trying traffic. We couldn't believe the driver's concentration as he drove for hours in the densely dark and challenging conditions.

> Lights on vehicles didn't seem mandatory
> and were rarely used.

We spent twelve hours on the road returning to Dhaka, and Deva transferred to our Jeep after the van they rode in broke down. Bob moved to the front seat as we'd lost some of our local staff to locations along the way.

I, alone in the back seat with Deva, kept moving closer to the door as Deva inched toward me. The two of us sang songs and talked endlessly. I tried to think of everything I could possibly talk about, sighing when Bob snickered as I asked Deva about her favorite color. Finally, I—a normal American desiring at least a foot of personal space—was pressed against the door. Deva stuck like Velcro and eventually fell asleep with her head on my shoulder.

Finally, we all just closed our eyes, but the squalling horns, frantic swing of the wipers, and jostling ride would often jolt our eyes open. It was shocking to see the surrounding, huge trucks within inches of all four sides of our Jeep. The rain continued to fall in sheets, resembling a car wash.

After the gridlock of Dhaka's barely moving traffic, we finally reached the nice hotel we'd stayed in upon our arrival. Deva presented us with jewelry, a loving letter, and tight hugs when we parted. We gave her some hair clips and jewelry. The hotel was a sight for terribly sore eyes. Everyone stumbled from the vans and wordlessly headed to their rooms for their first hot shower in a week.

No one, except Bob, wanted to discuss the plans for the next day. We deeply desired to spend our one partially free day touring the historical museum in the city. But the rest of the group planned to shop and to get henna designs temporarily tattooed on various parts of their bodies.

*

The next morning Bob arranged a van to take several of us to the museum, which turned out to be fantastically full of cultural treasures from all centuries, even those with B.C. dates. Rooms devoted to the political struggles of the nation saddened us as we saw atrocities waged against this poor mass of humanity.

One team member, a petite, attractive nurse on her first trip to a Muslim country, tagged along with us to the museum. About halfway through the tour she edged over next to me. "I keep getting these flirtatious looks from men, and it's making me quite uncomfortable."

"Maybe you don't realize this, but in male-dominated societies like Muslim or some Latino cultures, you have to be careful where you put your eyes," I advised. "One difficulty we have as Americans is our desire to make eye contact with those around us. We like to smile and to connect. Bob and I grew up in small towns where everyone offered friendship. We have to be careful of customs in other places. I especially watch my eye contact with men, as it can be easily misconstrued. If you meet their eyes here and smile, they probably think you are a prostitute making a pass at them."

She edged over next to me. "I keep getting these flirtatious looks from men, and it's making me quite uncomfortable."

"Oh, my!" Our nurse friend looked shocked. "I hadn't put that together at all. Thanks for letting me know."

"Another thought along this line is something we encounter, especially in the Middle East," I continued. "Many cultures believe that the 'evil eye' is a look that causes injury or bad luck for the person at whom it is directed for reasons of envy or dislike. In most cultures, the primary victims are thought to be babies and young children, because they are so often praised and commented upon by strangers or by childless women."

"Oh, no, I love to coo over little children," our nurse friend cried. "Does that mean I can't do that, either?"

"You have to be aware that it might be inappropriate in many places. I'm the same way, though," I said. "I like to notice and to acknowledge little ones, as that's what I do as a teacher in America. But I take care in other cultures not to overdo that."

Talismans—disks or balls consisting of concentric blue and white circles—represent an evil eye and supposedly ward off the curse. Often found on the prows of Mediterranean boats and elsewhere, talismans purportedly bend the malicious gaze back to the sorcerer. We found that Islam believers feel that God is the only one who can protect against the evil eye, as no object or symbol can. Traditionally, many Muslims say *"Masha' Allah"* (God has willed it) and also *"Tabarakallah"* (Blessings to God) to ward off the evil eye when receiving a compliment.

We thoroughly relished the museum before meeting up with the shoppers. Driving back through the congested streets of Dhaka, we encountered a huge elephant on a side street.

We learned that Dhaka is projected to be the second largest city in the world in 2015. Even now it holds the record for the highest lead content in the air of any city, attested to by our burning eyes. In our taxi van we discussed whether it would be better to be poor in the city or in the country here. We couldn't decide, as it seemed like endless hardship in either case.

> Driving back through the congested streets of Dhaka,
> we encountered a huge elephant on a side street.

Most people in Bangladesh make less than one dollar each day, with 30 to 40 percent of the population living below the poverty line. It is shocking to note that our yearly poverty line in America (income below $20,000 a year) is *100 times the average yearly income there*, which is around 200 dollars. As a Muslim in a male-dominated society, a woman without a husband is destitute. If a man's wife dies and he is left with children, he cannot both work (the work day is ten to fourteen hours) and watch and provide for the children.

We saw cases where the babies were given away or starved because the father or the mother couldn't meet their needs. This is truly a country of "have nots" and those of us with "haves" could not comprehend the truly empty "nothing" that these people deal with.

Most Americans rarely wonder when their next meal will materialize, or find themselves impoverished with resources completely absent. With the safety nets and the credit possibilities in our country, struggling people have places to turn. I recall several instances where I felt poor, but I was never without options.

Once while in nursing school, I decided to see how long I could go without calling home for food money. Since attending college for almost four years without a break, I borrowed from my parents under the condition I'd repay them with my nursing wages after graduation. But, while in school, I stayed dependent on their loans. I ate my food until all that remained was a half jar of peanut butter and a little bread. My roommate noticed and asked, "Diane, are you okay with money?"

I sighed. "All right. I guess I should call my parents. I just wanted to see what it felt like to run out of food."

Within a day I'd received a check for food, but I often remember that bereft feeling of having little to eat. I recalled that feeling when we visited Madagascar, where it was routine to leave a little jam in the jar for the poor who combed the garbage areas.

I often remember that bereft feeling of having little to eat.

We'd gone into debt after having two children while Bob studied in dental school, even though Bob worked two part-time jobs. I cut corners on everything, including not shopping for a warm coat as winters in Oregon rarely got extremely cold. I remember shivering as we walked into church on an unusually brisk day.

An usher turned to Bob. "Buy that gal a coat, would ya?"

I also decided not to purchase static sheets for the dryer, as that seemed superfluous to me. When my dress stuck to my legs with static cling one Sunday at church, an older, well-meaning woman pulled me to the side to advise, "Maybe you don't realize, but you can buy dryer sheets to keep that static cling out of your clothes." Those comments stung and still make us wonder what we say without thinking to people of fewer resources.

Another time in dental school when we felt quite poor, my older sister got a first generation microwave, as they'd just been invented in the early 1980s. Bob, wanting to provide for me, spent money meant for other priority purposes to buy me one too. He loved to surprise and to provide functional luxuries for me. I thought it very sweet of him. However, the needs of many around the world are vastly more serious than these little examples of perceived need that we experience.

The tragedy of children as victims in these developing countries is almost incomprehensible. Millions of youngsters work in Bangladesh by begging, planting rice, scouring for scraps of paper for fuel, and working as household laborers. Many children labor in the garment industry. Activists in America rail against sweatshops, and it is truly a horrific problem, although the families often have no options. The sweatshop may be the only opportunity for survival.

Without the factory pay, they can't eat. Do we have the right to shut down the factories? Are activists willing to pay more for their clothes or to give money for food or schools for the families? Do they provide funds to replace the meager salaries those children bring home to help support their families? It's tragic that these children work in terrible conditions with poor pay. But it's also a vicious cycle that must be addressed in the human family.

> Do we have the right to shut down the factories?
> Are activists willing to pay more for their clothes
> or to give money for food or schools for the families?

No one seemed too enamored with the henna (a reddish temporary tattoo) they'd sat for hours to have applied. Chaplain Doug tried to scrub his off, as the Scripture verse from Philippians had come out poorly with the country, Philippines, written as the verse reference. It'd seemed like fun body art, but it didn't hold a candle to our colorful American tattoos.

The previous night, after our horrendous trip back to the hotel, I'd painstakingly ironed our clothes for the sightseeing days, as well as for our airplane ride home. Although desperately exhausted, I waited while Bob took a long shower, as I knew things wouldn't settle down until he did. I'm a wrinkle-free addict, and it pleased me to have all the clothes ready so I could enjoy the last day in Bangladesh. The room, a two-area suite, allowed me to arrange carefully the ironed clothes on the couches and the chairs in the living area we didn't use anyway.

After our sightseeing, though, we returned to our groomed room, where some helpful maid had folded all the ironed clothes, causing more extensive wrinkles than had resulted in my careful folding in our suitcases all week. Of course, I felt compelled to re-iron!

We visited a local craft shop, where we purchased dolls, little Asian mermaids that represented the watery land we'd just visited. Bob had begun finding simple dolls in each country we visited to start a collection for the women he works with. Some of the team bought the pearls that were cultivated there, and we received metal, painted rickshaw models as thank-you gifts from the national staff. At dinner, Dr. Brown presented everyone with nice certificates and lapel pins. We enjoyed a farewell dinner of chicken shish-kabobs.

We slept for three hours in the hotel, leaving at 2:00 a. m. for the airport. We appreciated the long and uneventful flight back, although neither of us found a seat that had a little movie screen that worked. Some of the team watched three to four movies on the flight to Chicago, but we vacillated between reading and sleeping, restlessly ready to be home.

By comparison, our next adventure seemed easy and fun as we planned a trip to Honduras the last week of December. We'd enjoyed traveling to Uruguay between Christmas and New Year's the previous year as heading south seemed the perfect antidote for those weary of winter. We wanted to keep up that schedule, as Bob's dental office closes each year for the holidays. The Honduran dentist, Dulcia, and her husband, Colin—the vice president of our child-sponsorship organization—wanted to return to Honduras, especially so Dulcia could be with her family for the holidays. We saw all of our family, too, before we left at midnight on Christmas night. Sunny weather called to us after snowstorms hit late fall in Colorado, and we rejoiced that our dear traveling partners, Dr. Frank and Shelly, agreed to go, as well. We were in our zone, with trips planned for the next several years.

But that December, a surprise of gigantic proportions awaited us in four words that changed our lives forever: "Diane, you have cancer."

HONDURAS

Gangs, Corrupt Police, and "Flabulous Food"

* * *

WE WERE COMPLETELY OFF GUARD BY THE NEWS that I had breast cancer. The possibility had been nowhere on our radar! Without family history of the disease and no known risk factors we were aware of, I received a clean report on my yearly mammogram in November. When I found a lump in my armpit in December, merely a month later, I registered denial. After a visit to the doctor and a whirlwind of exams, referrals, ultrasounds, and a biopsy, two days before Christmas and our trip to Honduras, we received the unbelievable diagnosis of metastatic, Stage II cancer.

"You might as well go on your trip," our wonderful Christian surgeon told us the day we heard the results. "Most of the clinics and the tests can't be accessed until you return after the New Year anyway."

It had been a miracle and a blessing to find this doctor. His wife was Bob's patient in his dental chair one day when I was to undergo a biopsy. In small talk, Bob discovered the woman's husband ranked the premier specialist for breast cancer at the Army hospital. Bob rushed to the phone and caught me just a step away from the doors of the hospital, where cell-phone reception stops.

"Ask for Peters," Bob said breathlessly. We believe the angels allowed those connections, both with the surgeon's wife and the cell-phone timing. As Squire Rushnell says, "Each of us is born with a built-in GPS, God's Positioning System, a sophisticated navigational package that divinely aligns us with people and events and keeps us from losing our way."

So off we went to Honduras.

*

Since our flight left at midnight, we headed out on Christmas evening for the airport. We found a corner in the airport to stretch out and to get an hour's sleep before we boarded. Dr. Frank and Shelly arrived, distressed to have severe head colds that'd lasted over ten days. We worried that we might catch their colds, as they coughed strenuously—but with precautions—the entire trip, often in an enclosed van with us. I couldn't afford to return sick as I was scheduled to start treatment the day I returned. But God protected me from contracting a cold or any respiratory ailment.

We'd decided not to burden the two other couples with the unfortunate news of my cancer, since a holiday atmosphere permeated the air.

*

The first plane was overly hot and the second freezing cold, but we arrived at Honduras's capital city airport at Tegucigalpa at one in the afternoon. We drove through the narrow streets to the project center and church, where we set up the dental clinic. Blessed with a beautiful and clean hotel—even nicer than ones we usually stay at in America—the food was gourmet and safe. A lovely swimming pool graced the grounds, but the water stayed cold.

The clinics went impeccably, with temperatures very pleasant and balmy even into the late afternoons. Bob set up next to Dulcia, who needed reassurance and instruction with tougher dental cases. Dulcia's sister, Jacinta, translated. She'd assisted us on our first mission trip to Honduras two years previously and now seemed even more settled and mature at age twenty-six. Her fiancé, the country director for all the projects for children, kept close and charming as we treated the neediest children from each of the twelve projects.

We wished to see everyone, but three dentists could not treat over 1,200 children in a week. One leader told us that up to 60 percent of the children from each project needed dental attention.

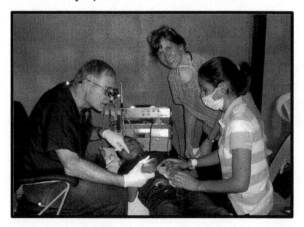

Honduras

Treating American-sponsored children

"It's all just a blur," I confided to Bob. "I'm trying to engage, but the 'white noise' of this cancer issue just rattles around in my head all day."

I embraced the daily distractions of working on children at the dental clinic, but as long, sleepless nights in the strange hotels hovered, I tried to get a grip on the future so full of unknowns. We talked privately of the four trips we'd already planned for the New Year, knowing they'd not be possible for us considering the treatment ahead.

> As long, sleepless nights in the strange hotels hovered,
> I tried to get a grip on the future so full of unknowns.

We'd been informed before we left that the doctors projected a nine-month course of treatment, including chemotherapy, a mastectomy, and possible radiation and reconstruction surgery. It all seemed totally overwhelming, and we'd been unable to get much information at that point. We still didn't know how far the cancer had spread in my body or how responsive the tumor would be to chemotherapy treatments. Waiting caused anxiety and stress, but we tried to put it out of our minds. I kept Scripture verses in my pocket to reassure me that God stayed in control.

Both of us kept thinking about the missions we couldn't participate in the coming year. I held tickets for Dominican Republic (D.R.) in January, as our church planned to begin a long-term relationship with churches and projects in Dajabon, a city on the northern border of D.R., within a stone's throw from Haiti. We'd been instrumental in helping activate that through our place on the mission committee at church. Bob could not go because a year prior we'd booked a trip to the Philippines for four days after I'd return from D.R. Bob still debated going on the Philippines trip without me since tickets had been purchased previously.

We also planned to travel to the Congo in Africa with a team in May, but we knew that was out for both of us since it was the projected time for my surgery. We still remained hopeful that we could keep the trip to Nepal the next October.

The busy clinic days flew by, and we worked on adults, pastors, and their families, and project directors in addition to children with dental problems. I kept busy sterilizing the instruments for the three dentists and also helped assist Bob as needed. The best thing about the trip included all the kisses and hugs we received, reminding us once again of how we love the Latino cultures. We also agreed that we adored Latino food.

One night we visited Dulcia's home for a lovely, traditional Hispanic feast prepared by her mother and cousins, including homemade tamales, beans, tostados, cheese tortillas, and many other treats to include cake and special drinks. "This is one of those countries we go home knowing the food has been 'flabulous,' " we agreed, and laughed.

I'd sewed an apron for Dulcia's mother, who loved it and wore it the rest of the night. We gave gifts to the family for helping us with our clinics. Jacinta especially liked the little gold Bible on a chain that had the Lord's Prayer printed in miniscule writing with dainty pages that turned. Dulcia's mother kept hugging us and even escorted us back to our hotel, while Dulcia said her mother rarely left her home.

We'd driven into the family courtyard in our dark-windowed van and didn't get out until the tall gates were securely locked behind us. We understood how unsafe it was for a local person to be seen with white people, who were always assumed to be rich. If seen with connections, the locals would be blackmailed for a "war tax," a monthly fee a person paid to gang members to retain their own safety. If not paid, threats of death or destruction to property would ensue.

> We understood how unsafe it was for a local person to be seen with white people, who were always assumed to be rich.

They told us of one man who died when shot after leaving church. He'd tried to drop out of his gang and they'd killed him, with his pregnant wife still inside the church. It remained very dangerous to go out at night, and we kept the windows rolled up in vehicles at all times, as gang members would reach in with weapons and try to steal the cars.

In Honduras, frequent kidnappings for ransom occur when local criminals think they can succeed. The police staff exists in a system of corruption itself and can easily be bought off. The project administrator, Jacinta's fiancé, told us he stayed off Facebook, afraid that someone would find he networked with Americans and blackmail him over that.

Another night we dined at a traditional restaurant and had skewers of shish-kabobbed meat and fish and dips for chips that came heated in ceramic pots that glowed on the table. The happy, roving band of musicians played Latino music that set feet to dancing and eyes to shining. The flamboyant tunes beautifully soared in the timeless, melodious harmonies of Spanish guitars, trumpets, and accordion.

*

With the clinics finished, we spent several days on a Caribbean island for a break after the mission. Colin drove us in a rented van, and, once again, we flinched at the dangerous passing and insane driving experienced in developing countries. We propelled for four hours through the lush countryside of Honduras to a ferry on the northern coast of Honduras.

After an hour's ride to Roaton Island, we arrived in the dark at a decent hotel. Although famished, we felt too exhausted to eat at one of the many nice restaurants on the tourist strip. Now with almost a week's inability to sleep, I begged Bob to bring some food to the room. He traipsed downstairs to find pizza.

After he left, I started sobbing. When he returned, he found me bawling like he'd never seen in our marriage.

"This is the first time I've been able to let down since my cancer diagnosis," I managed to tell him. "I'm so angry and upset and haven't been sleeping, and..."

"Okay," Bob soothed tentatively, clearly unsure what he should say. "You've held up so well. I've been amazed at your fortitude."

> "This is the first time I've been able to let down since my cancer diagnosis...."

"It seems all you think about is the trips we're going to miss and how you feel obligated to go to the Philippines even if I can't accompany you. This is all making me crazy." My feelings at last bubbled up, cracking the thin coating of my composure. Suddenly my sobs again ruptured the night. "And I don't even know how sick I am...and if I'm going to die...and if I'll get to see my grandkids grow up..."

"Sweetie..." Bob instantly dove to my side. "I've been thinking about us going alone on those mission trips, and I've decided we just shouldn't—ever, never. We do these together. We are mission buddies, and we have to do this joined always, or we don't do it! We've gotten so close. I kind of like not always knowing where I end and you begin. I want to be there for you every minute with the cancer, too. If one of us has something, the other has it, too. We are one."

I slowly stopped crying as Bob paced the floor. "Okay, it's a deal—always together," I finally vowed as I wolfed down half of the cold pizza.

The next morning we strolled up and down the beautiful beach, the sun golden and warm on our backs and bare legs. The world seemed peaceful, as the tourist strip woke up slowly. When the bands played loudly until 2:00 a.m., both of us had struggled with sleep. We found the diver's shop and decided to take a snorkeling trip late in the morning. Dr. Frank and Shelly planned to scuba dive, and we saw them off on their boat. We laughed into the wind as our boat skimmed over the waves to the snorkeling site. We saw schools of blue and yellow fish, stunning coral, and feathery underwater vegetation, all while swallowing a large amount of salty water.

"This is some way to spend New Year's Eve." We grinned at each other. Last year we'd been in Uruguay on the ranch and loved that memory, as well.

"Hopefully you'll be well next year and we can plan another warm trip between Christmas and New Year's," Bob encouraged. "This is getting addicting."

That afternoon we shopped, enjoyed ambling on the beach in different directions, and in our room watched a movie about a man who, under a spell, could see the inner beauty of women rather than their outward appearance. It resonated with us as I faced the body-changing surgery.

Bob fell asleep (of course, I couldn't), and I awakened him at 11:30 p.m. to ask if he wanted to watch the New Year's fireworks. We'd located a picturesque, little white Baptist chapel on the strip and walked down to see if there was a service. Noticing the chapel packed with everyone in dressy Sunday clothes, we decided not to go in. But we stood on the porch and prayed quietly through our thoughts, wondering what the next year would bring for us with the medical challenges ahead.

One young woman stood with us a minute. "The Bible says 'Come as you are.' I'd go in, but I've already had two drinks and don't think I should," she told us.

> We stood on the porch and prayed quietly through our thoughts, wondering what the next year would bring for us with the medical challenges ahead.

Right before midnight we heard the pastor start the final prayer. We noticed a large, beautifully dressed, older woman rise and come out.

"I'm leavin' before all the kissin' starts." She smirked. "I just don't like all that."

Soon spectacular fireworks shot off over the bay, and we slept fitfully as the music raged until 3:00 a.m.

*

"Let's go to church this morning," I said.

I'd stayed awake most of the night and watched the sun rise on the first day of January, a Sunday morning. Since we couldn't locate a visible sign, we'd asked before in various shops what time church started and had received five different times in answer to our inquiry. So we took our books and sat near the church around 9:00 a.m. Finally, a few stragglers entered around ten.

At 11:00 a.m. we entered as Dr. Frank and Shelly arrived. With members showing friendliness and a welcome spirit, the church service started with traditional old hymns and a sermon of platitudes yelled out by an exuberant and animated pastor. Conducted in English, strangely it brought exactly what I yearned for in the strong gospel message of God's control over our lives in the coming year.

As our last night arrived before flying home and I still couldn't sleep, I read some books on cancer that I'd downloaded on my electronic reader. They scared me to death.

*

The next morning we rode the ferry back to the mainland and watched the sunrise over the still water. Colin drove erratically like everyone else for the three hours to the small airport to board our flight to Miami. Often he passed with barely enough room, forcing oncoming vehicles to move to their shoulder lanes. Uneasy, I decided to quietly buckle my seat belt.

Colin must have noticed. "Do you think I'm driving too fast?" he asked.

"More like, I think you're flying too low!" I commented.

A few minutes later we approached people walking along the side of the road as we wedged between a big truck on our right and an oncoming van while Colin attempted to pass. We bumped the big truck, which retaliated by tearing off the side mirror and sending large scratches along the side of our rented van.

We just kept going, since to stop, with white people aboard, could be disastrous. Hondurans would probably assume we had money and would push for our arrest. The van's windows were darkly tinted so no one could look in, although we saw the raging face of the truck driver. It turned into a $400 repair bill when Colin returned the van.

"I have to tell you something," I informed Dr. Frank and Shelly as we sat over dinner in Miami waiting for our flight to Colorado. "I didn't want to spoil our trip, but five hours after we get home, I'll be at the hospital for a surgical insertion of a port to begin chemotherapy for breast cancer."

Their jaws dropped, and tears immediately welled in Shelly's eyes.

From that point forward we had many people who petitioned God on our behalf. I loved it when people stopped what they were doing and immediately prayed for me—including one friend who pulled her grocery cart over in the dairy aisle to pray aloud when I told her of the diagnosis. We'd had mission trips planned to Dominican Republic, Philippines, and Congo during the months that now required my treatment. Bob equipped the teams and sent them out.

We were greatly saddened not to be a part of them, but thankful to God for their reported successes.

Little did we know what God had in mind for our time "in the meanwhile."

COLORADO

Time in the Cocoon

* * *

THROUGH THE SEVEN MONTHS OF CHEMOTHERAPY, surgery, and recovery time, I became not only a cancer survivor but also a "cancer thriver" in the end. Naturally, we encountered intermittent, tough times. I lost my hair after the first drug dose and battled brain fog, nausea, distorted taste buds, watering eyes, mouth sores, numb toes, loss of nails, sporadic insomnia, and frequent fatigue. Due to my low immunity, I avoided groups of people, as I could become extremely ill if I contracted infections.

The isolation gave me the time and the motivation to take our mission trip notes and chronicle our travels. The writing took me to happy places through remembering enjoyable occurrences and inspiring events. Writing became a therapeutic and productive process.

Bob, wanting to be helpful, signed me up for two writer's conferences. One was a few miles from home and had a secular focus, highlighting classes on fictional and fantasy stories. Although the weekend occurred when I was at a better place in my chemotherapy treatments (which happened about every third week), I didn't receive much help from the lectures or visits with several editors. They had little interest in a spiritual, nonfiction, lengthy book. They barely glanced at the summary or writing samples I provided.

The second conference featured Christian writing of all genres, including some editors looking for nonfiction manuscripts. Unfortunately, I had just received my last chemotherapy treatment after four months of an intensive regimen, and the cumulative effects were overpowering me. Bob went along as support but did not register for the conference held in a beautiful setting in the Colorado mountains.

I felt miserable while attending two days of classes, but we received a little encouragement for our book topic. A panel of editors interested us on the day before the conference was to end. One editor, Ramona, stood out in her helpful and knowledgeable comments, and her last name happened to be my maiden name.

As I left for my last class, Bob found himself near Ramona and ventured, "I just have to tell you that my wife and I were impressed by your ideas and outstanding suggestions. Thanks so much! Also, it's fun that your last name matches my wife's maiden name." He turned to leave.

"So, why are you here?" asked Ramona.

"My wife and I have collaborated on a book about how God has worked in our lives and our mission trips. We didn't make an appointment to pitch our book to you because we saw you were looking for fictional material."

"Tell me something more about your book," Ramona persisted.

"It's about our travels to the poorest regions of the world using dentistry to spread the Good News."

She paused. "That sounds intriguing. Would you walk with me and tell me more? I'm going to a class I'm supposed to teach in several minutes."

"We are hoping to encourage others to use their gifts, espouse Christian truths, and bring significance to their lives by helping the less fortunate. We have amazing adventures in thirty different countries and want to tell our story."

"Hmm..." She appeared thoughtful. "Do you have something from your book that I could peruse?"

"Sure!" Bob handed her the first several pages and practically held his breath as she glanced over them.

"I like this writing style!" Ramona looked encouragingly at Bob. As they moved towards the door, she smiled. "I'd like it if you'd come to the back of the class and download your entire book on my computer."

Bob gulped but did as she asked. When he reported his actions to me that evening, I barely smiled through my fatigue and discomfort. "That's nice, but I think we need to go home soon. I'm just not feeling well."

"Well, let's try to get a good night's sleep since it's already dark, and we'll see how you feel tomorrow. Why don't you go take a warm bath?" Bob put his arms around me and kissed me on the top of me head. "Remember our saying, 'Never underestimate the power of tomorrow'?"

We didn't know how true that'd be.

> "Never underestimate the power of tomorrow."

I didn't feel much better the following morning but agreed to go to the last session of the conference. Another panel featured the same lovely editor, Ramona. When introducing herself, she looked up to where we sat and said, "We're thinking of starting a nonfiction line in our publishing house."

Following the meeting, she headed right for us. "Bob and Diane Meyer!" She called us by name. "I was up late reading your manuscript and you engaged me far into the night. I grew up in a home with high regard for missionary endeavors, and two parents who were very involved in Christian ministry. You've brought tears to my eyes in some places. Let's keep in touch."

We were thrilled, but her encouraging words faded from our memories as weeks passed. I had my operation with a slow recovery of several months. Although I wished to edit the book once more, I was too weak to write. Five months went by, and I slowly regained my strength. After several months, I pulled out the manuscript and finished it. Thinking we might self-publish the book, we gave it to a local editor, who provided excellent suggestions and ideas for improvement. I had several meetings with her.

A few hours before I was to meet with the local editor for the last part of the book, we received an email from Ramona:

> I have not forgotten you two, nor your wonderful book! We've been launching two online bookstores this summer so apologies for the delay. After careful consideration, we'd love to publish TWO books out of your material. The stories are so intriguing! I'll be sending a contract today for TWO volumes.

We were ecstatic and knew without a doubt that God had intervened by allowing the chance meeting with Ramona. In God's timing we'd heard from her—any earlier and we wouldn't have been ready. If she'd written right after the conference, I would have been too sick to respond. It seemed like this positive outcome might give some credence and reason for my illness. As humans, we always hope there is a purpose for our suffering. It is often hard to see how God is working during our trials and crises. We completely credit God with any favorable results.

We've discovered the comparison of a serious medical diagnosis or an apparent catastrophe to the transformation of a caterpillar into a butterfly. As caterpillars crawling along in life, we sometimes come to stopping places due to threatening tragedies. To cope, we may need to spin a cocoon around a combination of our body, soul, or emotions. Inside this safe sack, we hibernate, while God works on our essence, changing us more into His likeness.

As caterpillars crawling along in life, we sometimes come to stopping places due to threatening tragedies.

After a period of dormancy and healing, the cocoon bursts open. A new and beautiful creation emerges as a glistening and liberated butterfly. The wondrous transformation has occurred in the cocoon. To our amazement, we have new freedom and opportunity! We receive a fresh perspective, uncontainable joy, and restored confidence. As a caterpillar, we viewed the cocoon as life threatening. As a butterfly, we view the cocoon as life giving.

After a period of dormancy and healing,
the cocoon bursts open.

We used the time of my imprisonment in the cocoon as a time to write our story, which has become the TRUTH, TEETH, AND TRAVEL series and to prepare for the future we trust God holds in His hands. I have been declared cancer free, and we can now go forth with renewed delight to experience God's continued work in our lives.

Currently, we have plans for missions to Nepal, Cambodia, Mozambique, Swaziland, Dominican Republic, Uganda, and Ethiopia. With God's strength and providence, we hope for more tales of TRUTH, TEETH, AND TRAVEL.

Heartwarming, adventurous journeys into fascinating, exotic cultures

Dr. Bob and Diane Meyer

Plunge into true-life, pulse-racing tales
of adventures around the globe.

Dr. Bob Meyer, ex-Army commander and dentist, and his wife, Diane, a nurse and educator, decided to go on a quest—to support faith-based organizations through their gift of dentistry and satisfy their own passion for travel by making a difference in the world, one life at a time.

Capture the spirit of joyful service that triumphs over cultural, political, and socio-economic barriers as you experience African adventures, Latino flair, post-Soviet ploys, and Asian allure amidst exploits on small planes, jeeps, rickshaws, and yaks.

Who knew that combining truth, teeth, and travel could be so tantalizing and rewarding?

www.oaktara.com

TRUTH TEETH & TRAVEL vol 3

Heartwarming, adventurous journeys into fascinating, exotic cultures

Dr. Bob and Diane Meyer

Have you ever ridden an elephant?
Flown over Mount Everest on your birthday?
Feasted on goat, rat, fried bugs, fermented fish, and frog shish-kabobs?

Plunge into true-life, pulse-racing tales
of adventures around the globe.

Come with us on our next journeys, including a trek to an orphanage in Nepal and the mountain villages next to Tibet, to Swaziland, the only country ruled by a true king with unlimited powers, to Uganda, "the pearl of Africa," and other fascinating countries.

Capture the spirit of joyful service that triumphs over cultural, political, and socio-economic barriers as you experience our work with the survivors of Pol Pot's killing fields and the Khmer Rouge in Cambodia and learn how we saved a life on a back country road in Uganda.

Always around the corner is another chance for us to spread God's love while experiencing travel adventures, all under the guise of dentistry!

BONUS FEATURE:
Amazing, inspirational adventures from other missionary dentists!

www.oaktara.com

Acknowledgments

Our story is as accurate as possible, and we wish to depict truthfully our lives and ministry. However, in order to protect the privacy of the many dedicated individuals and organizations who helped make our journeys possible, we intentionally left out or changed all names, except for our immediate family.

Without the support and the encouragement of our family, friends, and associates, our outreach ministry would not have evolved and improved. Thank you for your love and prayers.

Foremost, we thank our faithful prayer warriors. We send forth heartfelt appreciation to the compassionate dentists, hygienists, assistants, sterilizers, physicians, nurses, administrators, interpreters, missionaries, workers, drivers, cooks, and supporters who have given of their time, talents, and resources. Often you have stepped out of your comfort zone to carry Christ's love and dentistry to the poorest regions of the world. You are forever in our hearts, and God knows your names. May your lives be blessed as you have made the world a better place and have furthered His Kingdom.

We thank these organizations for contributing in so many ways to our dental ministry outreach: Academy of General Dentistry, American Dental Association, Aseptico International, Bell International, Body of Christ Ministries, Bridgeview Community Church, Casa Hogar, Centurions, Christian Dental Society, Colorado Dental Association, Colorado Airlift Outreach International, Colorado Mission of Mercy, Colorado Springs Dental Society, Dobbin Dental Practice, Evangelical Mission Hospital, Fellowship of the Rockies Church, Fields of the Fatherless, First Nazarene Church of Colorado Springs, First Presbyterian Church of Colorado Springs, GC America Incorporated, Global Action, Habitat for Humanity, Hands of Hope, Happy Horizons Children's Ranch, Heralding Christ Jesus Blessings, Henry Schein Incorporated, Kids in Need of Dentistry, Luke Commission, Medical Assistance Programs International, Medical Mercy, Mexican Medical Ministries, Mission of Mercy, Mission to the World, Navigators International, Nazarene Compassionate Ministries, New Hope International, Project CURE, Raleigh Fitkin Memorial Hospital, Resource Exchange International, Septodont International, Ultradent Incorporated, United States Army, Whispering Eagles Ministry, and World Dental Relief.

A special thanks to OakTara Publishers and their cofounder and editorial director, Ramona Tucker, along with our editor, Sharyn Markus, for their encouragement and support.

About the Authors

Dr. Robert D. Meyer, DMD, MAGD
and Diane K. Meyer, RN, MST

For 16 years, DR. BOB AND DIANE MEYER have led 35 short-term, portable dental missions in 30 developing countries, while working with 15 Christian organizations. They are passionate about providing dental care, education, and encouragement to others at home and overseas. Dr. (Colonel) Bob completed a 30-year career in the Army, works as a dentist in a comprehensive dental office, and is the president of the Christian Dental Society. Diane's experience as a registered nurse, a certified teacher, and a dental assistant complements their mutual desire to serve those people God places in their path.

Bob earned a Bachelor of Science degree at the United States Military Academy at West Point and a Doctor of Dental Medicine (DMD) degree at the University of Oregon Dental School. He completed a two-year, post-doctoral residency in comprehensive dentistry at Fort Knox, Kentucky, and the Command and General Staff College at Fort Leavenworth, Kansas.

As commander of the world's only airborne dental unit, Bob's responsibilities included training, equipping, and deploying portable dental teams in support of Army military missions, which advanced his expertise and confidence to pursue dental missionary work. Bob directed the Army's Advanced Education in General Dentistry Residency program, where he prepared young dentists to function independently and competently, often in austere settings. Bob conducted the first Tri-Service Dental Symposium on Field Dental Equipment. He continues to advise on standardization, design, testing, and fielding of new portable dental equipment.

Diane received a Bachelor of Science in Nursing degree at the University of Oregon Health Sciences Center and a Master of Science in Teaching degree at the State University of New York.

Diane has worked intermittently as a registered nurse and an elementary school educator while fielding the primary responsibility of raising three children and homemaking at 12 Army locations. Desiring to participate in missionary work as a small child, Diane is now using her nursing, teaching, and parenting experience in the dental mission field.

Bob's publication and research produced a wide variety of articles written in many dental journals to include the *American Dental Association, General Dentistry, Journal of Prosthetic Dentistry, Journal of Endodontics, Compendium of Continuing Education in Dentistry, AGD Impact,* and the *U. S. Army Medical Journal.* Bob published manuals on the *Expert Field Medical Badge* as well as *Standard Operational Procedural* manuals for clinical, field, and garrison dental operations, infection control, and dental company operations. He authored a *General Dentistry Residency* program handbook. Bob and Diane collaborated on articles found in Christian Dental Society publications, World Dental Relief newsletters, a teacher activities publication, and several women's magazine articles.

Bob and Diane have been featured speakers on portable humanitarian and missionary dentistry in numerous venues on five continents to include: Global Missions Conference, Christian Dental Society conference and meetings, Rocky Mountain Dental Convention, Colorado Springs Dental Society, Voice of Truth, Mission of Mercy, elderly support gatherings, and many other small groups. They have educated and contributed in churches for 40 years as teachers, deacons, and members of various boards and committees. Bob and Diane are on YouTube presenting "How we do short-term portable dental missions" and "Why we do short-term dental missions."

They have received the Colorado Dental Association Volunteer of the Year Award, the Christian Dental Society Outstanding Missionary Service Award, American Dental Association Certificates of Recognition for Meritorious Service, Mission of Mercy Certificates, Kids in Need of Dentistry Participation Certificates, and Military Outstanding Volunteer service awards.

Happily married for 34 years, Dr. Bob and Diane Meyer adore their three children and their spouses, and six grandchildren. Relaxation times include family get-togethers, hiking, reading, crafting, music, and sports.

www.oaktara.com